MAKING POLITICS WORK FOR DEVELOPMENT

Policy Research Report

MAKING POLITICS WORK FOR DEVELOPMENT

HARNESSING TRANSPARENCY AND CITIZEN ENGAGEMENT

Policy Research Report

WORLD BANK GROUP

Contents

Figures

Tables

Foreword

The challenge of economic development goes beyond economics. Social norms and customs matter, as do politics and political institutions. The transparency, efficiency, and inclusiveness of governments have a large impact on economic outcomes; and citizen participation is also an important determinant of the policies that are chosen and, as a result, the path that an economy takes. Further, in today's participative world, citizens exert influence not just by queuing at voting booths but by taking to the streets, using modern communication technology, and engaging the media.

This major report is part of the World Bank Group's effort at recognizing that to do good economics we need to go beyond economics. It draws on the best research on the interface between politics and economics, and focuses in particular on the role of transparency and citizen engagement.

The report is aimed at serving our clients and the development community with a technical knowledge product on politics, to learn from mounting research on the economic consequences of these forces of political engagement and transparency. Synthesizing available research, the report draws lessons about the political behavior of citizens, public officials, and leaders, and how they respond to transparency across a variety of institutional contexts. Policy makers can use this knowledge to shape public sector governance in ways that are suited to their institutional contexts. For example, national leaders are concerned about monitoring and managing local-level public officials, who are often on the front lines of service delivery, and about generating local revenues to support local government. National leaders across the political spectrum are considering how best to use citizen engagement and transparency to solve this "last-mile" problem, including through well-managed local elections.

The analysis in this report points to ideas for relaxing political constraints to pursuing technically sound policies, as opposed to choosing "second-best" solutions that are available when these constraints are taken as given. Rather than lowering expectations when politics is a problem, technical experts and policy makers can use a better understanding of political incentives and behavior to improve outcomes.

A lesson for us at the World Bank also comes out of this research. We can do more, through relatively small changes in what we are already doing, to leverage our technical strengths in generating credible data and evidence, and to work with our clients to diminish political constraints to achieving development goals. We can provide more targeted, specific, reliable, and impartial information that will help citizens to work with their leaders to build effective public sector institutions that are capable of tackling public good problems. To do this we have to overcome the fear of talking about politics, and confront it as part of the challenge of development. That is what we are doing through this report.

Kaushik Basu
Senior Vice President and Chief Economist
The World Bank

Acknowledgments

This Policy Research Report was prepared by the Development Economics Research Group of the World Bank by a team led by Stuti Khemani. The other authors of the report were Ernesto Dal Bó, Claudio Ferraz, Frederico Finan, Corinne Stephenson, Adesinaola Odugbemi, Dikshya Thapa, and Scott Abrahams. Valuable contributions were made by Jimena Luna and Sahr Kpundeh.

The work was carried out under the supervision of Asli Demirgüç-Kunt, Director of the Development Research Group, and Kaushik Basu, Senior Vice President and Chief Economist of the World Bank. Aart Kraay, Senior Adviser at the Development Research Group, provided invaluable feedback during the whole process.

We are grateful to a number of people for comments and discussions that contributed to the report. We would especially like to thank our discussants at review workshops for helping us with their critical feedback: Pedro Alba, Shantayanan Devarajan, Philip Keefer, Luis-Felipe Lopez-Calva, Jeff Thindwa, and Yongmei Zhou. Many others inside and outside the World Bank provided valuable comments. Despite efforts to be comprehensive, the team apologizes for any oversights and expresses gratitude to all who contributed their thoughts. We thank Maria Amelina, James Anderson, Abhijit Banerjee, Kathleen Beegle, Hana Brixi, Miriam Bruhn, Tiago Carneiro Peixoto, Rob Chase, Punam Chuhan-Pole, Andrew Dabalen, Jishnu Das, Uwe Deichmann, Avinash Dixit, Quy-Toan Do, Frank Fariello, Jonathan Fox, Adrian Fozzard, Marine Gassier, Varun Gauri, Garance Genicot, John Giles, Maria Gonzalez de Asis, Helene Grandvoinnet, James Habyarimana, Zahid Hasnain, Guenter Heidenhoff, Johannes Hoogeveen, Melissa Johns, Leora Klapper, Steve Knack, Sarwar Lateef, Victoria Lemieux, Benedicte Leroy de la Briere, Varja Lipovsek,

Maria Soledad Martinez Peria, Yasuhiko Matsuda, Neil McCulloch, Deepak Mishra, Ezequiel Molina, Nachiket Mor, Ameet Morjaria, Ekim Muyan, Roger Myerson, Irfan Nooruddin, Benjamin Olken, Owen Ozier, Rohini Pande, Lant Pritchett, Gael Raballand, Rakesh Rajani, Anand Rajaram, Rita Ramalho, Francesca Recanatini, Bob Rijkers, Dan Rogger, David Rosenblatt, Audrey Sacks, Valentina Saltane, Roby Senderowitsch, Gil Shapira, Emmanuel Skoufias, Stefanie Teggemann, Joel Turkewitz, Adam Wagstaff, Deborah Wetzel, and Michael Woolcock. We are also grateful for a wide range of comments from participants during the review of this report and from the presentation of its working drafts at seminars and workshops.

The World Bank's Publishing and Knowledge Division coordinated the report design, typesetting, printing, and dissemination. Special thanks to Patricia Katayama, Aziz Gökdemir, Rumit Pancholi, and Andrés Meneses. The report was edited by Sherrie Brown and Dina Towbin. The team is very grateful to Ryan Hahn, Na (Sheela) Cao, Philip Hay, and Vamsee Kanchi for their guidance and support on communications. Finally, we are indebted to Tourya Tourougui, Imran Hafiz, and Swati Raychaudhuri for exceptional administrative support throughout the process of preparing this report.

About the Team

Stuti Khemani is a senior economist in the Development Research Group of the World Bank. She joined through the Young Professionals Program after obtaining a PhD in economics from the Massachusetts Institute of Technology. Her areas of research are the political economy of public policy choices and institutional reforms for development. Her work has been published in leading economics and political science journals, such as the *American Economic Journal, Journal of Development Economics*, and *American Political Science Review*. Her research and advisory work spans a diverse range of countries, including Benin, China, India, Nigeria, the Philippines, Tanzania, and Uganda.

Ernesto Dal Bó is the Phillips Girgich Professor of Business at the Haas School of Business and Professor of Political Science at the Travers Department of Political Science at the University of California, Berkeley. He is co-director of the Berkeley Center for Economics and Politics (BCEP), director of the Institutions and Governance Initiative at the Center for Effective Global Action (CEGA) in Berkeley, a research affiliate at the International Growth Center (IGC), and a faculty research associate at the National Bureau of Economics Research (NBER). Over the past decade, he has published extensive research on institutions and the political, economic, and behavioral factors that affect state capabilities and governance.

Claudio Ferraz is the Itaú-Unibanco Associate Professor of Development Economics at the Pontifical Catholic University of Rio de Janeiro (PUC-Rio). He is a research affiliate of BREAD, JPAL, EGAP, and IGC. He has been a visiting professor at MIT, Stanford University, London School of Economics, Universitat Pompeu-Fabra, and the Einaudi Institute of

Economics and Finance. His research focuses on the intersection among development economics, political economy, and public economics and has been published in leading academic journals. He has been awarded the Global Development Network Medal for Research on Development; the Haralambos Simeonidis Award for the best paper published by a Brazilian economist (twice); and the Mario Henrique Simonsen Memorial Lecture by the Latin American Econometric Society. Claudio is associate editor of the *Journal of Development Economics* and the *Latin American Economic Review*, and co-director of the LACEA Political Economy Network.

Frederico Finan is associate professor of development economics and political economy at the University of California, Berkeley. He received his PhD in agriculture and resource economics from UC-Berkeley in 2006. His affiliations include a variety of international organizations such as the Abdul Lateef Jameel Poverty Action Lab, Centre of Evaluation for Global Action, National Bureau of Economic Research, and the Bureau for Research and Economic Analysis of Development (BREAD). He has centered his academic research on economic development and political economy.

Corinne Stephenson is a research analyst at the International Monetary Fund. She previously worked in the Development Economics Research Group of the World Bank and at the United Nations World Food Programme in Dakar, Senegal, on a Princeton in Africa Fellowship. She has an MA in social sciences from the University of Chicago and a BA cum laude from the Department of Politics at Princeton University.

Sina Odugbemi is a senior communications officer (Policy) in the Operations Communication Unit, External and Corporate Relations Vice-Presidency of the World Bank Group. He works on anticipatory reputation risk management and advises on governance initiatives. In addition, he is the editor of the blog, *People, Spaces, Deliberation*. Between 2006 and 2011, he was program head of the Communication for Governance and Accountability Program (CommGAP). He has over 25 years of experience in journalism, law, and development communication. Before he joined the World Bank in 2006, he spent seven years in the United Kingdom's development ministry, DFID. His last position was program manager and adviser, information and communication for development. Sina holds a bachelor's degree in English (1980) and law (1986) from the University of Ibadan, a master's degree in legal and political philosophy (1999) from University College London, and a PhD in laws (2009) also from University College London on the subject, *Public Opinion and Direct Accountability between Elections: A Study of the Constitutional Theories of Jeremy Bentham and A.V. Dicey.* Sina's publications include a novel entitled *The Chief's Grand-daughter* (Spectrum Books, 1986) and three coedited volumes: *With the Support of Multitudes: Using Strategic Communication to Fight Poverty through PRSPs* (2005); *Governance Reform under Real-World Conditions: Citizens, Stakeholders, and Voice* (2008); and *Accountability through Public Opinion: From Inertia to Public Action* (2010).

Dikshya Thapa is a sociologist currently working at the Water and Sanitation Program (WSP) within the Water Practice at the World Bank. Her current work focuses on governance and political economy diagnostics in water and sanitation delivery. Previously, she worked within the Social Development Unit in the Europe and Central Asia Region of the World Bank on social inclusion of the Roma population, and Poverty and Social Impact Analyses (PSIAs) in Central Asia. She has previously carried out research on gender and labor markets and the social impact of trade and economic liberalization policies. Her current research examines the relationship among community-driven development, nongovernmental organizations, and state capacity in fragile states. Dikshya holds a PhD in sociology from Brown University, an MSc in gender and development from the Gender Institute at the London School of Economics, and a BA in economics from Lancaster University, U.K.

Scott Abrahams has consulted on economic research with the World Bank and Inter-American Development Bank and taught at the Johns Hopkins University School of Advanced International Studies, where he also received his MA. He is currently completing a PhD in economics at Duke University.

Abbreviations

ACAs	anticorruption agencies
CDD	community-driven development program
CSOs	civil society organizations
EITI	Extractive Industries Transparency Initiative
FOI	freedom of information
FOIA	Freedom of Information Act
GCB	Global Corruption Barometer
HUMC	Health Users Management Committee
ICTs	information and communications technologies
KPU	Indonesian Election Commission
MGNREGA	Mahatma Gandhi National Rural Employment Guarantee Act
NGOs	nongovernmental organizations
OBI	Open Budget Index
OECD	Organisation for Economic Co-operation and Development
PPP	purchasing power parity
QOG	Quality of Government
RGI	Resource Governance Index
RTI	Right to Information Act
VECs	village education committees
WDR	*World Development Report*

Overview

Too often, government leaders fail to adopt and implement policies that they know are necessary for sustained economic development. They are encumbered by **adverse political incentives**, which prevent them from selecting good policies, and they run the risk of losing office should they try to do the right thing. Even when technically sound policies are selected by leaders, implementation can run into **perverse behavioral norms** among public officials and citizens, who seek to extract private benefits from the public sector. Such behavior might be supported by widespread beliefs that corruption is the norm.[1] Even countries with low corruption and strong institutions experience problems of political incentives and behavior that prevent the public sector from solving shared problems. Ideological polarization among citizens and capture by special interests can lead to policy gridlock and the failure of the state to provide public goods, even in advanced economies.[2] Even educated citizens can hold ideological beliefs about the role of public policy that lead them to deny technical evidence contrary to these beliefs.[3]

Harnessing citizen engagement and transparency to address government failures

This report is about addressing government failures, such as the ones described in box O.1, by making politics work for development rather than against it. It draws on research about how political markets function in determining which citizens become leaders and what incentives they have for using their powers when in government. It distills lessons for how a variety of policy actors—from sovereign governments to international development partners and civil society organizations—can harness political markets to serve the goals of economic development.

Two forces—citizen engagement and transparency—are shaping how political markets function across and within countries. The report brings together dispersed strands of research and forges connections between them to gain an understanding of their implications. Research shows how citizen engagement and transparency in the political process shape incentives and behavioral norms in the public sector, with profound consequences for economic development. These lessons yield implications for policy actors who want to build effective public sector institutions that can deliver the public goods and services needed for development.

Box 0.1 Examples of adverse political incentives and perverse behavioral norms in the public sector

- The Treasury Secretary of a country in Africa prepares a budget that allocates a substantial share of spending to increase the salaries of public school teachers. But these teachers are known to be absent frequently and exert little effort at teaching even when present.[a] The secretary is well aware of the problem from his department's gathering of forensic evidence in the field, as well as from a body of international research (Chaudhury et al. 2006; World Bank 2004). Yet political forces in the country prevent the secretary from taking up technically sound policy recommendations to address absenteeism. These forces range from the power of organized teachers unions to popular demand from citizens at large for jobs in the public sector. The secretary poses the following questions: *Can research help reform leaders understand why politics yields such inefficient outcomes, not just in education but*

across the board? What can leaders do through the power of their office, even when encumbered by political constraints, to change things? Will budget transparency help, as is being advocated, especially for countries where the public coffers are swelling with natural resource wealth but where politics is an impediment to spending that money wisely?

- Bureaucrats leading India's National Rural Health Mission identified absenteeism by frontline public health workers as a significant problem.[b] The bureaucrats responded with a technological innovation to enforce attendance: a biometric monitoring system to digitally capture the thumbprint of each staff member at the start and end of the working day. Researchers invited to evaluate the impact of this initiative found a significant increase in the attendance and improvements in health outcomes. However, the results suggested that

(continued)

Box 0.1   continued

other forms of malfeasance, such as the diversion of patients to private practice and reductions in benefits to which patients are entitled, may have been substituted for absenteeism. Furthermore, the researchers encountered low motivation for taking up the policy and implementing it effectively. The researchers noted that locally elected politicians, whom they thought would have better incentives than the bureaucrats to monitor the provision of health services (because the politicians could be voted out of office if services were not provided), did not think absenteeism or service delivery were problems. Similar questions arise from this example: *Why are there weak incentives and motivation in the public sector to take up and effectively implement sound technical solutions to delivery problems? How can information and mobilization campaigns to engage "ordinary" citizens, who hold no public office, help solve the delivery problem when powerful technocrats and political leaders are not solving it?*

• Establishing and building the capacity of anti-corruption agencies raises similarly difficult questions. Instituting anticorruption agencies and building their capacity often fail to make a dent in corruption in the absence of political incentives to reduce corruption (Maor 2004; Meagher 2005). These agencies can even be deliberately designed to be ineffective or can face political resistance when trying to fulfill their mandate. *How can policy actors complement investments in building state capacity with investments in strengthening incentives and behavioral norms among public officials to use that capacity to deliver public goods?*

• Widespread corruption and poor quality of public services can diminish the legitimacy of the state in the eyes of citizens, who respond with disrespect for state institutions, with disregard for the law, and even with violent conflict (World Bank 2011). Citizens can take other actions that, although not as tragic as violent conflict, can nevertheless contribute to problems in the public sector, such as throwing garbage in the streets or stealing electricity from public utilities. Citizens can regard theft from the public sector as "legitimate" when they believe that others, including powerful leaders, are stealing from the state. *How do changes in citizens' behavior come about? What role can transparency play?*

a. This example is drawn from an actual conversation between the Treasury Secretary and one of the authors of this report.

b. This example is drawn from Dhaliwal and Hanna (2014) and pertains to the state of Karnataka in India.

Growing space for political engagement

A global shift in political institutions is providing space for greater citizen engagement in the political process—or political engagement. **Political engagement is defined as the participation of citizens in selecting and sanctioning the leaders who wield power in government, including by entering themselves as contenders for leadership**. The dramatic spread of elections at national and at local levels, even within countries with authoritarian national political institutions, has created unprecedented opportunities for citizens to influence governance. Citizens are engaging in the political process as individual voters and as contenders for political office.[4]

Figure O.1 Global shift toward democratic institutions for political engagement, 1980–2013

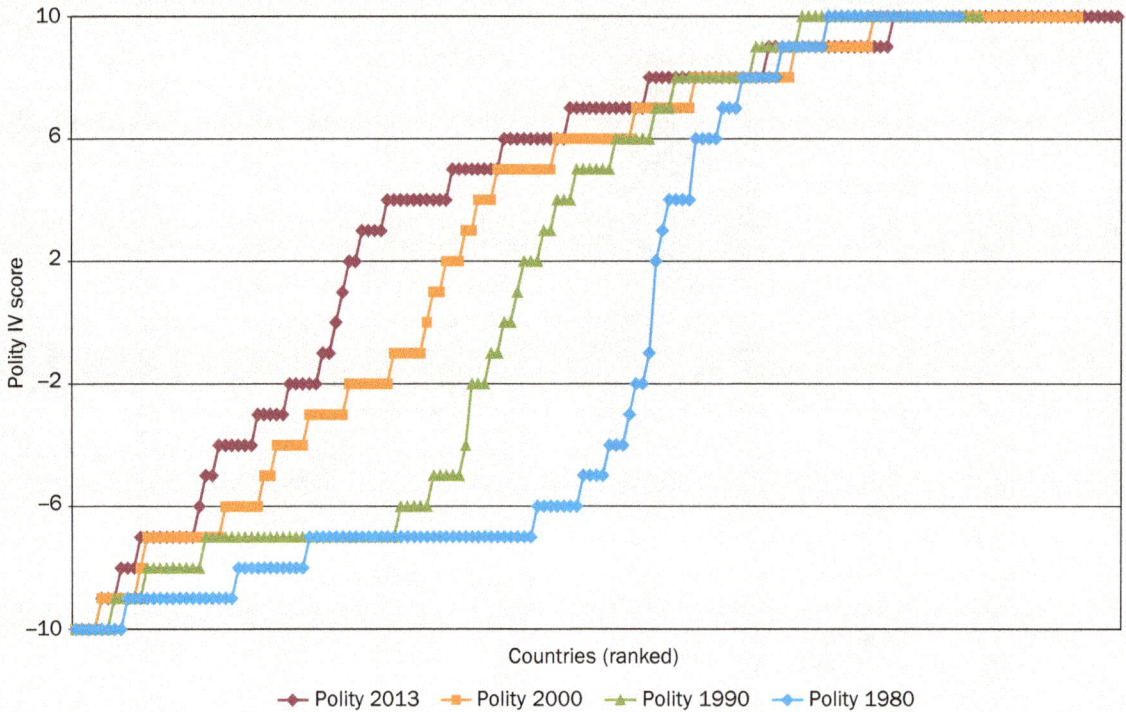

Source: Data from the Polity IV project.
Note: The Polity IV Score is a measure of state authority that is widely used in research, varying on a 21-point scale ranging from −10 (which corresponds to hereditary monarchy) to +10 (which corresponds to the Polity IV view of consolidated democracy). Higher values are associated with more democratic institutions.

Figure O.1 plots the distribution of countries ranked by the Polity IV measure of democracy, with higher values corresponding to greater space for political engagement by citizens.[5] During the past three and a half decades, the overall distribution of political institutions across countries has steadily shifted toward those institutions that allow greater political engagement. Although some individual countries have experienced reversals to more autocratic institutions or seen little change, the trend overall has been toward greater opportunities for political engagement.

Distinguishing political from non-political citizen engagement

This report emphasizes the crucial role of citizens' political engagement, distinguishing it from other non-political forms of citizen engagement.

Political engagement is a means for citizens to improve the quality of public goods they receive by selecting and sanctioning political leaders. These leaders in turn exert great influence—for good or for ill—through the many public service institutions that are responsible for providing public goods. Non-political forms of citizen engagement seek to bypass the political process. Some forms try to make public officials and frontline providers more accountable to citizens for the public goods and services they provide. Others try to increase direct citizen participation in managing public budgets and organizing service delivery. This report will argue that such forms of non-political citizen engagement can only have limited benefits when they do not address fundamental failures in the political process. Indeed, even when such forms of non-political citizen engagement improve service delivery outcomes, they may do so by letting political leaders, public officials, and frontline service providers "off the hook" and, in effect, require citizens to provide public goods for themselves.

Growing space for transparency across different institutional contexts

At the same time, greater political engagement has been supported by **greater transparency, defined as citizen access to publicly available information about the actions of those in government and the consequences of these actions.** Public disclosure policies are bringing out greater information about the functioning of government and the actions of those in power. Greater information is available not only due to disclosure by governments, but also by non-government agents, such as investigative journalists and civil society groups. New media technologies broadcast information about government performance at all levels.[6]

Established democracies tend to have independent media, but nascent and emerging democracies, as well as autocracies, are also experiencing greater media freedom. Figure O.2 shows that countries that have more democratic institutions, as measured by Polity IV indicators, also tend to have more independent media, as measured by Freedom House.[7] At the same time, even autocracies allow some degree of independence or perhaps are unable to fully control media. Indeed, new information and communications technologies (ICTs), such as high-speed Internet access, have been described as a "dictator's dilemma" (World Bank 2016). On the one hand, ICTs are important to facilitating economic growth and attracting investments, but on the other hand, these technologies increase access

Figure 0.2 Media independence across countries with different measures of democracy

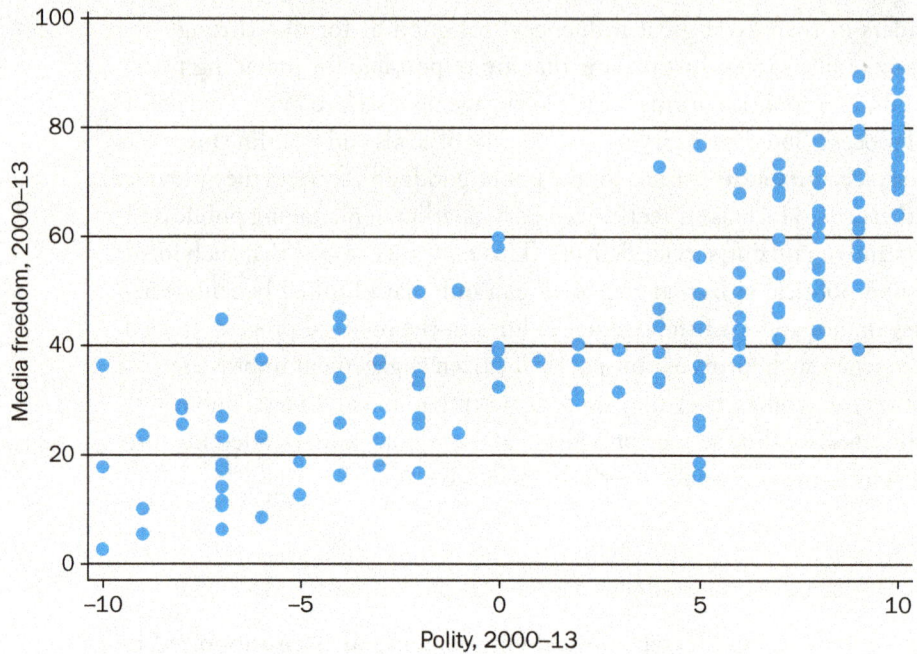

Sources: Polity IV Project for measures of democracy and Freedom House for measures of media freedom.
Note: The Polity IV measures of democracy and the Freedom House measures of media freedom are averaged over the period 2000–13.

to information and foster debate and discussion among citizens that can weaken the dictator's grip on power.

Applying research across institutional contexts

Cross-country research has examined whether national electoral institutions are correlated with better economic outcomes. While this correlation is much debated, recent research reports a robust positive association.[8] On average, this evidence suggests that political engagement through electoral institutions leads to better development outcomes. Yet clear examples can be pointed to where autocracies outperform democracies.[9] Research examining these differences in outcomes concludes that the key question that applies to both autocracies and democracies is whether leaders are selected and sanctioned on the basis of performance in delivering public goods (Besley and Kudamatsu 2008). This report is *not* about whether democratic institutions are better or worse than other institutions. It moves beyond cross-country evidence on the effects of national political systems to focus on within-country evidence on the nuances of political engagement within the same formal context and how its specific characteristics matter for governance and for development outcomes.

Political engagement happens in every institutional context, from democracies to autocracies, albeit in different ways. The main contrast examined in the literature is when there is scope for greater political engagement by a larger number of individual citizens acting as voters, and as contenders for leadership, because of electoral institutions, versus when they do not; that is, when power over leaders is instead concentrated among elites or organized groups of citizens such as political parties. The report reviews the available research to draw lessons about citizens' and leaders' political behavior and how they respond to transparency across a variety of institutional contexts. Policy makers can use this knowledge to shape public sector governance in ways that are suited to their institutional contexts. For example, national leaders across the political spectrum are concerned about monitoring and managing public officials at the local level, who are often on the front lines of service delivery. National leaders even in authoritarian regimes are considering how best to use citizen engagement and transparency to solve this "last-mile" problem, including through local elections.

The analysis in this report points to the benefits of relaxing political constraints to the adoption of technically sound policies, as opposed to choosing "second-best" solutions that are available when these constraints are taken as given. This report recommends a shift in development policy advice from one in which technical experts seek to bypass politics or lower expectations when it is a problem, to one in which they confront politics and incorporate it into the search for technical solutions to development problems. This approach does not mean prioritizing attention to political incentives or waiting until problems of politics are solved. Instead, the suggested approach opens up avenues for development practitioners to harness the current forces of political engagement and transparency, which are emergent everywhere, for better development outcomes.

Main messages

Message 1: Government failures are a consequence of "unhealthy" political engagement

The examples of government failures in box O.1, above, can be understood in the context of research on **"unhealthy" political engagement: when leaders are selected and sanctioned on the basis of their provision of private benefits rather than public goods.**[10] Unhealthy political engagement can take many forms. For example, electoral competition can involve violence, fraud, vote buying, and patronage targeted to specific groups.[11] Vote buying and fielding of candidates against whom there are serious allegations of criminality undermine the ability of citizens to use elections to hold leaders accountable for public goods provision (Khemani 2015; Prakash, Rockmore, and Uppal 2014).

Unhealthy political engagement can also result from distributive conflict among citizens. Special interest groups can mobilize to extract private benefits from public policies at the expense of the broader public interest (Grossman and Helpman 2001). Ideological beliefs among citizens about specific public policies, such as energy subsidies or immigration, can be difficult to shift with technical evidence on the costs and benefits of different policy options (Kahan et al. 2013). Distributive conflict and entrenched beliefs can lead to the selection of leaders who further polarize citizens and nurture ideological constituencies, rather than trying to find common ground to address shared problems. Polarizing leaders can prevent reformers from gaining power and pursuing appropriate public policies. Such unhealthy political engagement can occur in weak as well as strong institutional environments, and in poor as well as rich countries.

Unhealthy political engagement casts a long shadow. It not only shapes the incentives of elected leaders in adverse ways, but also the behavior of unelected public officials and of citizens. Leaders directly influence incentives and norms within public bureaucracies through the management policies they select. For example, when political leaders provide jobs in the government as political patronage, they prevent the professionalization of bureaucracies. A growing body of research provides evidence on the behavior of officials in the public sector that is consistent with the implications of such patronage politics. For example, doctors with connections to political leaders are more likely to be absent from public health clinics, and the public officials who manage these doctors are more likely to report political interference when trying to apply sanctions (Callen et al. 2014).

Unhealthy political engagement undermines the legitimacy of leaders, weakening their ability to manage complex organizations and effectively implement policies (Akerlof 2015). For example, leaders can use new technologies to monitor frontline providers, reducing opportunities for graft (Banerjee, Duflo, and Glennerster 2008; Muralidharan, Niehaus, and Sukhtankar 2014; World Bank 2016). But when leaders lack legitimacy, they may face resistance from frontline public providers to take up these technologies. For example, the time stamp machines that were installed to monitor staff attendance in public health clinics in India were sabotaged by the staff

(Banerjee, Duflo, and Glennerster 2008). Widespread electricity theft and non-payment of dues to public electric utilities in the developing world are further examples of the lack of legitimacy of the state in environments of unhealthy political engagement (Min 2015; Min and Golden 2014).

Message 2: Political engagement also functions in "healthy" ways that hold the key to addressing government failures

While unhealthy political engagement explains government failures, the solutions to these failures lie in fostering "healthy" political engagement and not in circumventing or suppressing political engagement. **Political engagement happens in "healthy" ways when leaders are selected and sanctioned on the basis of performance in providing public goods.** Healthy political engagement enables citizens to play a role in overcoming government failures by holding leaders accountable and by selecting better-quality leaders.[12] For example, corruption is lower when political leaders face reelection incentives (Ferraz and Finan 2011). Poverty is lower when political leaders come from social groups that have historically experienced greater poverty and economic discrimination (Chin and Prakash 2011). Greater political competition is associated with the selection of better-quality leaders who contribute to economic growth (Besley, Persson, and Sturm 2005).

The evidence on the adverse effects of unhealthy political engagement does *not* imply that authoritarian institutions that bypass or suppress political engagement would necessarily improve outcomes. For example, one study finds that ethnic favoritism led to distortions in public resource allocation even under authoritarian regimes in Kenya, and that periods of transition to multiparty electoral competition were in fact associated with *reductions* in these ethnicity-based policy distortions (Burgess et al. 2015). Other factors that explain unhealthy political engagement, such as the ability of political elites to punish voters through economic sanctions, violence, and coercion, can also prevent autocratic arrangements from being successful (Acemoglu and Robinson 2006; Besley and Kudamatsu 2008).

The diversity of successful institutions around the globe might tempt reform leaders to find ways of bypassing the messiness of electoral politics rather than improving it. It may even be interpreted as evidence in favor of restricting political engagement and establishing institutions run by benevolent dictators and organized elites. For example, some have attributed the East Asian growth "miracle" to institutions that restricted citizen engagement, allowing leaders to select and implement policies on technical merit.[13] This view, however, begs the question of where benevolent dictators and elites come

9

from and whether the "miracle" can be replicated in other countries. Societies in which elites do not sanction poor leaders or where elites benefit from poorly performing leaders remaining in office, are unlikely to be successful autocracies (Besley and Kudamatsu 2008). Why are some autocratic settings successful in selecting and sanctioning leaders on the basis of competence and performance, and others disastrous at it? There is little research available to guide us on this question and even less on whether messy democracies can eschew elections, however flawed they may be, and become well-functioning autocracies. Overall, however, the evidence from a large variety of institutional contexts is clear that fostering healthy political engagement rather than suppressing it is more likely to result in better development outcomes.

Table O.1 provides a typology of healthy and unhealthy forms of political engagement and behavior in the public sector. It also distinguishes between actions by individual citizens, such as voting, and actions by organized groups of citizens, such as political parties or civil society organizations.

Table O.1 Typology of political behavior
Examples of different types of political engagement and behavior in the public sector

	Individual action	Organized group action
Unhealthy: *Actions for* **Private Benefits, at the Expense of Public Goods**	• Voting on the basis of targeted benefits, such as vote buying and ethnic identity politics • Popular demand for costly policies, such as subsidies, without regard to the costs of those policies • Noncooperative behavior, such as asking for and giving bribes to avoid public interest rules and regulations	• Political parties organized around ethnic identity, or fielding criminal and corrupt candidates • Special interest groups that capture policies for their group benefit, at the expense of the larger public interest
	Interact/Reinforce	
Healthy: *Actions for* **the Public Good**	• Voting on the basis of good performance • Entry of "good" citizens as candidates for leadership • Norms of cooperative behavior in the public sector, such as abiding by public interest rules and regulations	• Local collective action to improve local public services such as at a school or health clinic • Civil society organization and programmatic political parties, such as on anticorruption platforms

Previous work has focused on the role of citizen action through groups to solve collective action problems (Grandvoinnet, Aslam, and Raha 2015; Keefer, forthcoming). This report emphasizes the role of individual citizen actions, such as voting, in solving collective action problems. Political engagement involves the interaction of both individual and organized group action. Together, individual and group actions work through political institutions to shape the incentives and quality of leaders, as well as the political beliefs and behavioral norms of citizens and public officials.

Individual citizen actions, such as voting or working through political markets, play a critical role in whether political engagement functions in healthy or unhealthy ways. Although it is an enduring puzzle to economists why people vote at all (Feddersen 2004), the evidence presented in this report suggests that citizens perceive the costs of voting as low and the potential benefits as high.[14] However, beyond the act of voting, citizens can vary in how they vote: for example, whether they are influenced by policy issues or by vote buying when deciding whether to support or evict leaders. Political leaders, both incumbents and challengers, can use different strategies, including unhealthy ones such as vote buying and violence, to influence and manipulate the votes of citizens.

The impact of organized groups such as political parties, special interests, and civil society, depends in part upon their ability to influence individual actions such as voting. Most of the available research provides examples of unhealthy organized group action that worsens the incentives and selection of leaders. For example, Satyanath, Voigtlaender, and Voth (2013) show how social groups in Germany enabled the Nazi party to mobilize voters, gain office, and subsequently subvert democracy. Research suggests that groups that can effectively organize collective action—by preventing "free-riding" by group members and by enforcing group-prescribed actions for individual members—are more likely to emerge to extract private group benefits rather than to work for the broad public interest.[15]

Well-intentioned civil society leaders can try to organize to pressure government for public goods, but for that organization to have real impact, they need strategies that work with the political incentives of government leaders to respond. There is little evidence and understanding about the impact of civil society organizations in contexts where elections are marred by vote buying or captured by special interests. However, a recent example suggests that civil society groups can make an impact when they are able to shift voting behavior. Some of the leaders of an anticorruption civil society movement in India turned their organization into a political party to contest and win elections on an anticorruption platform.[16] Such a development can improve governance by strengthening the incentives of all political parties to demonstrate competence and performance in controlling corruption, that is, by shifting the issues of political competition toward public goods.

The incentives of special interests or organized elites can become aligned with public goods when the costs of government failure become too large for these groups. When this happens, history suggests that they contribute to strengthening political incentives by increasing space for political engagement by individual citizens. For example, research suggests that a rise in demand for urban public health goods among the elite in the United Kingdom after the Industrial Revolution contributed to the movement to expand the franchise toward universal male suffrage (Lizzeri and Persico 2004). Research on the origins of state capacity has identified the emergence of citizens' demand for common-interest public goods as a driving factor (Besley and Persson 2009). When elite business groups and civil society organizations demand broad public goods, they can advance their goals by using transparency initiatives to cultivate better quality of political engagement by individual citizens.[17]

Message 3: Transparency can support political engagement in order to overcome government failures. In contrast, transparency initiatives that do not improve political engagement are unlikely to be effective

Transparency can cultivate and improve the quality of political engagement in a variety of institutional contexts.[18] Even where corruption is rampant, concrete information on the extent of corruption, as revealed by public audits of government spending, can increase the likelihood that corrupt leaders are removed from office (Ferraz and Finan 2008). Where ethnic favoritism and vote-buying practices are widespread, the use of these clientelist practices to win office by providing private benefits at the expense of public goods, can be reduced by providing greater information about the quality of leaders and their performance in delivering public services (Banerjee et al. 2011; Casey 2015; Fujiwara and Wantchekon 2013; Keefer and Khemani 2014).

Transparency, in the form of greater information and better means of communicating it, can improve what citizens demand from leaders, can influence what issues they consider when assessing candidates for leadership, and can help them determine whether to enter political markets as contenders for leadership (Campante, Durante, and Sobbrio 2013). However, in contexts in which political engagement is unhealthy, there is no clear evidence on whether transparency's impact is sufficient to get leaders to respond with sustainable or long-term improvements in outcomes, using the powers of their office to strengthen institutions.

The design of transparency is important—the nature and credibility of sources of information, and media through which it is communicated—all matter.[19] For example, a growing body of evidence, primarily from the United States, shows how the intersection of media markets and political markets shapes governance outcomes (Campante and Do 2014; Campante and Hojman 2013; Snyder and Strömberg 2010). When media markets coincide with political jurisdictions, citizens have better access to information on the actions of local leaders and their consequences for local outcomes that can be used to assess the leaders they choose. Leaders, in turn, have been found to play a role in credibly communicating information to citizens, persuading them to change their prior and typically entrenched beliefs (Glaeser and Sunstein 2013). That is, transparency as information provision alone is not enough—it needs to interact with political engagement, and the leaders selected through it, to shift behavior and beliefs.

Evidence from developing countries indicates that leaders and mass media do play the same role here as well, for example, in causing social norms related to the role of women to shift (Beaman et al. 2009; Beaman et al. 2012; World Bank 2015). This finding suggests that the effects of leaders and persuasive media programming might extend to influencing political beliefs and strengthening political behavioral norms—what policies to demand, how to behave in the public sector, what issues to consider when evaluating leaders, and whether to become a contender for leadership. Available research highlights the role of mass media as a force for persuasion, and as an institution that can address coordination problems among citizens beyond information alone (Keefer and Khemani 2014; Yanagizawa-Drott 2014).[20]

While transparency can support healthy political engagement, the evidence suggests that transparency initiatives focused on citizen engagement outside the political process are less effective. For example, citizen report cards have been used as a tool to mobilize and motivate citizens to monitor and demand accountability directly from frontline public service providers, rather than from the politicans to whom the service providers ultimately report (Banerjee et al. 2010; Bjorkman, De Walque, and Svensson 2014; Bjorkman and Svensson 2009). These types of initiatives are described as *social* accountability mechanisms because they do not rely on changes in the political incentives of leaders in government to trigger better performance on the part of providers. The evidence shows that whether a transparency initiative improves a service delivery problem depends upon the characteristics of political engagement.[21] For example, if low motivation and effort by public providers is attributable to leaders' political incentives to provide patronage jobs in the public sector, then citizen engagement for social accountability may have little effect on public service delivery (Callen et al. 2014). Consistent with this view, the evidence for the effects of citizen report cards is weakest in unhealthy political contexts.[22]

Transparency interventions, such as information campaigns about local service delivery problems, are likely to have only transient effects if they do not improve political engagement. In the absence of institutional strengthening by leaders, governance problems can be displaced to other times and other areas outside the limelight of the information campaign. For example, theft of public funds might fall when there is media coverage, only to come back with a vengeance when the news cycle is over (Bobonis, Cámara Fuertes, and Schwabe, forthcoming; Zimmerman 2014).[23] Sustained reductions in corruption and improvements in service delivery depend upon whether transparency has fundamentally changed incentives and behavioral norms in the public sector. In turn, the permanence of these changes in incentives depends upon whether leaders are selected and sanctioned on the basis of good performance.

Message 4: Building effective government institutions requires changes in political behavior—investments in formal capacity and innovative technologies are not enough. Political engagement and transparency can bring about the needed changes in political behavior

Political engagement is a blunt instrument for accountability. For example, even when they function well, elections are designed only to hold elected officials accountable. But many of the functions of government are delegated to appointed officials rather than to elected politicians. Both elected and appointed officials exercise their powers through a myriad of working-level institutions of government, ranging from ministries and agencies all the way down to local public schools and clinics. Strong institutions of internal accountability within government, such as supreme audit institutions, and checks and balances, such as through independent judiciaries, are therefore important mechanisms to complement accountability through elections and other forms of political engagement.

The problem is how to build such institutions when they are weak to begin with. A wealth of experience with efforts to strengthen institutions has shown that programs to replicate successful rich country institutions in developing countries—by providing equipment and training to bureaucracies—often fail (Andrews, Pritchett, and Woolcock 2013; IDS 2010; Pritchett, Woolcock, and Andrews 2013). Rather, effective institutions are more likely to be homegrown, using local knowledge and tailored to local contexts (Dal Bó, Foster, and Putterman 2010; Rodrik 2000).

The literature on institutional transition in the history of nations suggests that transparency in combination with political engagement provides tipping points for change in how government institutions function (Camp, Dixit, and Stokes 2014; Glaeser and Goldin 2006; Lizzeri and Persico 2004). Working together, these forces not only can hold elected leaders more accountable, but can also improve the incentives, political beliefs, and behavioral norms of appointed officials and of citizens. Political engagement and transparency serve as "meta-institutions" for building effective homegrown institutions.[24] They influence institutional change not only by affecting the "political will" or incentives of leaders to take up formal reforms, but also by changing the informal behavioral norms in the public sector to act upon them.

In contrast, change in formal institutions alone is not sufficient to change actual behavior. Research has found that healthy and unhealthy political behaviors can coexist and vary within the same formal institutional context (Acemoglu, Reed, and Robinson 2014; Anderson, Francois, and Kotwal 2015; Banerjee, Iyer, and Somanathan 2005). The importance of informal behavior is further highlighted in research examining persistent effects of historical institutions, even when those institutions have long disappeared and been formally replaced by others.[25]

Political engagement and transparency, and the leaders selected through it, can shift political beliefs and promote cooperative behavioral norms among citizens. Leaders can play this role as "prominent agents" who signal a shift in beliefs among society at large (Acemoglu and Jackson 2015).[26] Growing experience with political engagement and the learning that comes from it, such as through frustration and indignation with bad outcomes, can contribute to endogenous changes in political behavior over time (Bidner and Francois 2013).[27]

Multiple levels for political engagement created through local electoral institutions can enable transitions to healthy political behavior by increasing the supply of leaders who have built reputations for responsible management of public resources (Myerson 2006, 2012). Both the spread of local electoral competition and instruments for transparency, such as new communication technologies, can lower barriers to entry for new political contenders (Campante, Durante, and Sobbrio 2013). The experience of political engagement at these local levels, as voters and as contenders for leadership, can play a significant role in building effective institutions.

Local elections can also operate directly as a tool for monitoring and enforcement at the local level. The need for such monitoring has grown with greater devolution of public resources in developing countries to local government, often with weak capacity. Lack of capacity, in turn, can contribute to widespread beliefs about corruption with impunity, leading to a culture of poor performance in the public sector. Such a "culture of corruption" would stem not from values but rather from rational beliefs about how others are behaving and about the probability of detection and punishment in environments with scarce resources with which to combat corruption. Local institutions for political engagement supported by transparency can help solve this coordination failure by shifting beliefs and behavioral norms.

Innovative technologies can play an important role in monitoring and managing funds flows and reducing opportunities for graft (for example, Muralidharan, Niehaus, and Sukhtankar 2014; Sacks, Ensminger, and Clark 2014; World Bank 2016). By strengthening incentives and the quality of leaders, transparency in combination with political engagement can potentially be leveraged to complement technological solutions and increase the likelihood of their take-up. In the process, transparency and political engagement, along with innovative technological solutions, may together contribute to shifting the political beliefs that support a culture of poor performance in the public sector.

The lessons from research for solving government failures for the delivery of public goods are summarized in table O.2.

Implications for policy

Conditions in many countries where the vast majority of the poor live resemble those described in historical accounts of previous institutional transitions in advanced economies. These conditions include widespread political engagement by citizens, even the poor and less educated; broad-based demands for improvements in public services; dissatisfaction with clientelist politics; and availability of cheap and accessible mass media such

Table 0.2 How do transitions toward the public good come about?

Messages from research about citizens' political behavior and response to transparency

Individual action	Organized group action
Clear evidence that individual actions respond to information, such as voters acting to remove from office those candidates who have been revealed to be corrupt	Little theory or evidence that organized group action will respond to information. Group organization is shaped by the concentration of benefits for group members and the group's ability to exclude non-members from these benefits.
Potential for targeting transparency initiatives to influence individual citizen action and to serve as a coordination device, such as through focusing voter demand on good-quality candidates who compete on platforms of providing public goods	Impact of civil society organizations that want to promote the public good depends on whether they can sufficiently influence individual actions such as voting that are aggregated by political markets. Well-intentioned civil society can undercut the power of special interests by mobilizing and coordinating the actions of individual voters on the basis of public goods.

When political engagement is unhealthy to begin with, transitions toward the public good come about:

Through political engagement
- Growing experience with unhealthy aspects of political engagement and the learning that comes from it, such as through frustration and indignation with bad outcomes, can contribute to endogenous changes toward healthy political behavior over time.
- Changing formal institutions is not sufficient: unhealthy behaviors can persist.
- Technical capacity building is not sufficient when political engagement is unhealthy.

Through transparency that nurtures healthy political engagement
- Political engagement, particularly by individuals, responds to transparency.
- Information and mass media have to interact with political engagement to change incentives, political beliefs, and behavioral norms.
- Transparency initiatives targeted only at citizen action outside the political realm are not sufficient.

as television and radio. These conditions do not guarantee good outcomes, and there are many risks of unhealthy political engagement and repressive responses by leaders. However, deliberate policy efforts for transparency targeted at helping citizens select and sanction leaders on the basis of performance in providing public goods can try to channel these forces toward the goals of economic development.

The report focuses its recommendations on leveraging transparency and citizen engagement, taking existing national political institutions as given. This pragmatic approach recognizes the difficulty of, and the political constraints to, changing fundamental political institutions in the short run. However, it does suggest opportunities to harness the power of citizen engagement and transparency in a range of institutional settings. Targeted information enables citizens to select and sanction leaders on the basis of performance in delivering public goods, with far-reaching effects. As discussed above, it can improve the performance of political leaders who are disciplined by the threat of challengers, and it can improve behavioral norms in the public sector as a whole. It can also contribute to the reforms of other institutions of accountability in the public sector, in effective home-grown ways, by strengthening incentives of leaders to take up reforms and the behavior of public officials and citizens to support their implementation.

Policies toward transparency

Research findings suggest the following insights to inform policy actions on transparency:

- **Transparency is most effective when it supports the generation of specific, reliable, and impartial evidence on the performance of leaders tasked with the delivery of public policies.** The information provided through transparency must be specific about both policy actions and the resulting outcomes, so that citizens can use this information to select and sanction leaders. Information that is not specific in this way will erode the benefits of transparency. For example, information only on budget allocations is of limited use without information on how these allocations were spent and what the spending accomplished. Naturally, the information provided must also be reliable and must be accepted as impartial and untainted by partisan political considerations. This recommendation is supported by a body of research on the effects of providing information about the effort and performance of leaders, discussed in chapters 4 and 6.

- **Policies to strengthen the functioning of media markets can be a crucial part of governance strategies to foster healthy political engagement.** Policies in this area can promote healthy competition in media markets and can be complemented by interventions to support public interest programming that provides impartial information to cultivate citizens' political engagement. Even when media are independent from state control and markets are competitive, citizens can choose to access primarily entertaining programs that do not sufficiently inform them about public interest issues. Sponsorship of appealing programs or "infotainment" to communicate evidence on the actions of leaders and the effects of public policies, has the potential to persuade citizens to shift political beliefs in ways that strengthen demand for good leaders and good policies. This recommendation is supported by a body of research on characteristics of political engagement and the role of media that is discussed in chapters 4, 5, and 6.

- **Policies can encourage the provision of information and the access to media to be more relevant and timely to the political process.** A key dimension of relevance is jurisdictional: information on the performance of public policies needs to be targeted to the jurisdictions in which citizens select leaders. Information on public goods provision at the local level is more relevant to voters' decisions in local elections than is information at the national level. Timeliness matters as well: performance assessments of both current incumbents and of challengers, delivered regularly during a term in office but also at the time of elections, can make it easier for citizens to use information to decide on how to vote. Information that enables citizens to assess the potential of political contenders, not just incumbents, can be useful to avoid incumbency bias. Relevant information broadcast through media that citizens actually access and pay attention to can lower barriers to entry for candidates to compete on platforms of improving public policies and government performance. This recommendation is supported by a body of research discussed in chapters 4, 5, and 6 on how transparency and political engagement need to work together to enable accountability.

- **Policies can be designed in ways that are sensitive to the nature of political institutions.** The policy implications of this report depend on the design of government jurisdictions—which tasks are assigned to which leaders and who are the citizens who select and sanction them. If government jurisdictions have clearly assigned responsibilities for public goods, then it is easier to generate data on performance that can be attributed to the leaders of those jurisdictions and to communicate that information to enable citizens to hold those leaders accountable for public goods. Most places will have a complex set of political and bureaucratic institutions that share responsibilities for the provision of public goods. Higher order transparency, such as civic education about the roles of different government jurisdictions and officials, can play a role in strengthening governance. When citizens are not empowered to select and sanction leaders of government jurisdictions, then citizens are unlikely to have the capacity to use information to exact accountability.

Policies toward citizen engagement

Research findings suggest the following insights to inform efforts to strengthen citizen engagement to address government failures:

- **Policies can be designed to be more effective when they explicitly take citizens' and leaders' political behavior into account.** The success of policy initiatives to engage citizens to improve service delivery depends upon the political characteristics of the environment in which those services are delivered. If citizens are asked to monitor and provide feedback on the performance of powerful local elites who control service delivery, citizens are unlikely to act without credible assurance that they will be protected from retaliation. For example, if beneficiary feedback is solicited through local elites who are the ones capturing public resources, then citizens are unlikely to respond by providing reliable feedback to reduce local capture (Olken 2007). In contrast, when beneficiaries are informed with the purpose of strengthening their bargaining power vis-à-vis local elites, then they are more likely to demand their entitlements and complain about poor performance (Banerjee et al. 2015).

- **Policies to improve local service delivery can use local political engagement and transparency.** A number of social accountability initiatives that seek to work outside the political realm rely on catalyzing group action by citizens. They use transparency campaigns to trigger action by committees charged with monitoring public schools, health clinics, or other public spending programs. However, there is little evidence that transparency alone encourages group action through such committees. Survey evidence that these committees are typically inactive suggests that organized group action of this type can be costly for citizens. Theory suggests that this is because groups rarely organize to pursue broadly shared public goods. In contrast, individual actions of political engagement, such as voting, respond to transparency. In pursuing the engagement of citizens to hold local officials accountable, higher-tier policy makers even in authoritarian national systems may consider local elections to be the mechanism through which citizens are empowered to do so. The research findings of the responsiveness of voting behavior to transparency suggests that policy makers can craft transparency policies, such as public disclosure of local government audits and strengthening of local media markets, to improve local political engagement as the mechanism of holding local officials accountable.

Who will take up these recommendations?

In making these recommendations, this report is mindful of the fundamental dilemma that motivates the report: too often, leaders with the power to choose technically sound policies are encumbered by political constraints that prevent them from doing so. The same problem naturally applies to the recommendations here aimed at harnessing transparency and citizen engagement to strengthen governance.

Nevertheless, different policy messages considered in the report may appeal to the comparative advantage of a diverse range of policy actors, including reform leaders within government, as well as non-government agents such as civil society and international development partners, whose incentives may be more aligned with development objectives.[28] External agents can play potentially transformative roles in contexts in which they are most needed to address political impediments to development. For example, the policy messages from research emphasize the importance of relevance, credibility, and impartiality of information about the performance of leaders and their policy actions. External agents might offer these attributes when they have technical capacity to generate meaningful information from large data and when they are regarded as politically independent and non-partisan.

Structure of the report

The first part of this report, comprising chapters 1–3, discusses the main themes that motivate the report: government failures, political engagement, and transparency. Each chapter presents trends and provides the context for policy action on the basis of the research covered in the subsequent chapters.

Chapter 1 on the theme of governance describes government failures in the provision of public goods. It presents examples and evidence from research on how political incentives and norms of political behavior can be at the root of government failures.

Chapter 2 on the theme of political engagement discusses growth in the participation of citizens in selecting and sanctioning leaders. It relies on public opinion surveys as well as other sources to provide evidence on citizens' perceptions of and participation in elections. Citizens, especially the poor and less educated, report active participation in elections across a variety of institutional contexts. Even where electoral violence and fraud, vote buying, and ethnic conflict are common, citizens nevertheless express beliefs that elections matter for beneficial change, that through their vote they can improve their lives.

Chapter 3 discusses the emergence of transparency, defined as citizen access to publicly available information about the actions of those in government, and the consequences of these actions. Transparency has grown through deliberate policy efforts to improve governance by providing information about government actions and their consequences. For example, the public disclosure of information about government budgets has been proposed as a condition for international development assistance. Civil society organizations have also been making efforts to generate new information to monitor and evaluate government service provision. Finally, transparency has grown as a result of technological forces that allow different news media to generate and broadcast information about government performance. Established democracies tend to be more transparent, but there is also evidence of growing transparency in nascent or emerging democracies, as well as in autocracies, because of domestic and international pressures.

The second part of this report, comprising chapters 4–6, presents the lessons from research on how political engagement and transparency work together to improve governance. Each chapter contains different pieces of the theoretical and empirical research that come together in the messages summarized in this Overview.

Chapter 4 provides the conceptual framework for how political engagement is fundamental to incentives and behavioral norms within government. It shows how disciplining leaders and also selecting different types of leaders matters for governance and development outcomes. Transparency about both policy actions and policy consequences is essential. When information about policy consequences is lacking, transparency about policy actions may be counterproductive, leading to pandering and populism by politicians seeking to please uninformed citizens. In contrast, information about policy consequences can strengthen the ability of citizens to hold leaders accountable for outcomes.

Citizen beliefs about politicians, the political process, and public policies are relevant. Political norms that ingrain expectations of low performance perpetuate underperformance, be it corruption, shirking, or pandering. In addition, pandering is more likely when politicians are not trusted, which would occur when corruption is high. Thus, by creating a culture of distrust, corruption has the indirect effect of fostering pandering. Political engagement and the leaders selected through it can help shift political beliefs and norms of political behavior among citizens, potentially enabling societies to escape low-performance traps to improve governance in the public sector.

Chapter 5 presents lessons from the empirical evidence on the impact of political engagement. A large literature provides consistent evidence across a variety of contexts that political engagement matters for governance, policy selection, and development outcomes in highly nuanced ways. Both individual citizen action through electoral institutions and organized group action can assume either healthy or unhealthy forms.

Political engagement can improve outcomes by changing incentives and encouraging the selection of better-quality leaders. Much of the available empirical evidence focuses on testing the impact of political engagement through elections. Relatively less evidence is available on the impact of political engagement by civil society organizations outside of elections, but it suggests that the impact of organized groups has important interactions with and can work through the mechanisms of electoral institutions.

By connecting and interpreting a large literature on the impact of historical institutions on development, the chapter shows how beliefs and behavioral norms can vary within the same formal institutions and persist even when formal institutions change. Persistence in political beliefs and norms regardless of changes in formal institutions has implications for how to think about the transition from weak to strong institutions of governance. Building the capacity of formal institutions is not sufficient. Improvements in the quality of political behavior are crucial for improving governance.

Chapter 6 presents lessons from the empirical evidence on the impact of transparency. It shows how different types of information and means of communication influence the actions, beliefs, and behavior of citizens and leaders. Substantial evidence shows that political engagement responds to transparency within and across a variety of institutional contexts. Citizens and leaders change their actions in response to new information. Citizens are influenced by the framing of issues and messages broadcast by mass media. The specific design of transparency interventions matters—the nature and credibility of the information and media of communication all matter.

In contrast to the potentially transformative role of transparency when targeted at improving the quality of political engagement, other evidence on the impact of transparency initiatives outside the political realm suggests that it is not enough. The impact of transparency initiatives targeted at engaging citizens to take actions to improve service delivery really depends upon political incentives. Taken together, the pattern of evidence when transparency initiatives improve service delivery outcomes and reduce corruption, and when they do not, points to the important role of healthy political engagement.

The final part of the report (chapter 7) discusses the implications of the report's findings for policy actors. In doing so, it confronts the dilemma discussed above: too often those with the power to pursue policies that are good for development are constrained from doing so because of politics, and the same constraints may prevent actions to strengthen transparency and citizen engagement.

The bulk of development work occurs in imperfect governance environments where things need to get done and get done quickly. Still, development practitioners may not want to discount political economy analysis as a luxury or a distraction because politics has profound consequences for economic development. They may also not want to treat political constraints only as something to navigate using stealth and cunning. Treating perverse political incentives solely as fixed constraints that have to be navigated rather than relaxed may lead to second-best solutions that are not solutions at all, doing little to tackle the fundamental problems of development. The alternative approach recommended here on the basis of research on the emergent forces of transparency and political engagement is to find ways to tackle political constraints head on, harnessing these forces to relax the constraints such that "first-best" solutions are more likely to be sustainably implemented. Policy actors can target transparency to nourish the growing forces of political engagement and thereby complement other efforts to establish effective public sector institutions that avert and solve government failures.

The report has assembled a jigsaw puzzle from dispersed pieces of research to see what picture emerges and what the missing areas look like to understand and fix government failures. The co-evolution of transparency and political engagement in developing countries have implications for the design of appropriate public institutions in these environments that are likely to be distinct from the designs adopted by the rich world in its different development trajectory.[29] There are large areas of future work, building upon the findings of this report, that are highlighted as the contours of the missing pieces of the jigsaw puzzle in the following chapters. The understanding of the political behavior of citizens, frontline public officials, and leaders that is offered in this report can be used to address government failures and build public sector institutions that are capable of tackling public goods problems.

Perhaps more important than offering ideas for specific policy action (which may indeed not work in the face of insurmountable political problems), the report aims to influence how development practitioners think about politics. Practitioners may then be able to make greater contributions to incremental change by more effectively using the levers available to them to overcome political impediments. This approach includes not just getting governments to adopt good policies, but designing implementation arrangements that are more likely to succeed, based on a better understanding of political incentives and behavioral norms in the public sector. The hope in preparing this report is that it will invite future debate and policy experiments by applying the lessons here to make politics work for development rather than against it.

Notes

1. Chapter 1 on the report's theme of governance provides a discussion of corruption as a norm.
2. A series of papers focused on policy making in the United States provide evidence of how ideological polarization among citizens can lead to policy failures (Bishop 2008; Glaeser and Sunstein 2013; Kahan et al. 2013; Sunstein 2009). Gilens and Page (2014) and Grossman and Helpman (2001) focus on the role of special interests in the United States.
3. For example, various papers from the Cultural Cognition Project at Yale Law School (reviewed in chapter 1) show how citizens' previous beliefs make them resist scientific evidence. The availability of detailed evidence from the United States on citizens' beliefs regarding public policies provides lessons for understanding political impediments to the selection of good policies in developing countries.
4. Chapter 2 documents trends in political engagement.
5. Details about the Polity IV measures are available at their website: http://www.systemicpeace.org/polityproject.html. These measures, along with another from Freedom House (which is discussed in chapter 2) are widely used in the economics research literature on the role of political institutions in economic development. Acemoglu et al. (2014) and Besley and Kudamatsu (2008) are important examples and provide a review of how measures of democracy compiled by Polity IV and Freedom House are used as such in research.
6. Chapter 3 contains evidence of the trends in transparency.

7. A study by Egorov, Guriev, and Sonin (2009) is acknowledged as the source of the idea to analyze the correlation between the Polity IV and Freedom House indicators.

8. Acemoglu et al. (2014) review the past research and provide new evidence to support their argument that democratic institutions lead to greater growth in the long run, using data from both Freedom House and Polity IV. Rodrik and Wacziarg (2005) find a positive association between democratic transitions and growth. Mobarak (2005) finds a positive correlation between democracy and economic stability (measured as lower volatility).

9. Besley and Kudamatsu (2008) discuss examples of autocracies that have experienced steady and high growth.

10. Chapter 4 provides the conceptual framework for understanding government failure as a consequence of unhealthy political engagement.

11. Chapter 2 reports survey evidence on a variety of electoral malpractices. Chapter 5 reviews the evidence on the impact of unhealthy political engagement.

12. Chapter 5 reviews the evidence on the positive impact of political engagement on incentives and selection of leaders.

13. Isham, Kaufmann, and Pritchett (1997) suggest that this is the argument in a World Bank report on the growth performance of East Asian countries.

14. Chapter 2 presents evidence from public opinion surveys on trends in and attitudes toward voting. León (2011) provides evidence that the propensity to vote is quite inelastic to voting costs.

15. Grossman and Helpman (2001); Lowi (1972); Olson (1965); and Wilson (1973) focus on the role of special interests in the United States. Rajan and Ramcharan (2012) provide evidence of regulatory capture by well-organized elites, even in a country with accountable political institutions. Bardhan and Mookherjee (2000) examine the role of elite capture in developing countries that is conceptually similar to the analysis of special interests in the United States.

16. "India's Left-Leaning, Anti-Graft Party Made A Stunning Debut," *The Economist*, December 14, 2013, http://www.businessinsider.in/Indias-Left-Leaning-Anti-Graft-Party-Made-A-Stunning-Debut/articleshow/27328073.cms.

17. Chapter 2 provides examples of transparency initiatives and voter education campaigns undertaken by civil society organizations. Chapter 6 discusses the ipaidabribe.com initiative that is championed by business leaders in India.

18. Chapter 6 provides an extensive discussion of this evidence.

19. Chapter 6 draws these conclusions about the importance of the design of transparency by making connections across dispersed pieces of evidence.

20. The role of mass media in enabling coordination is examined by Yanagizawa-Drott (2014), albeit for the tragic outcomes of the Rwandan genocide.

21. See chapter 6 for a more in-depth discussion.

22. Grandvoinnet, Aslam, and Raha (2015) review the evidence and conclude that political context matters.

23. Burgess et al. (2012) show how local rent-seeking by public officials and politicians is substitutable across different activities.

24. Rodrik (2000, 3) writes: "Democracy is a meta-institution for building good institutions." Baland, Moene, and Robinson (2010, 1) write: "Understanding

how to improve governance necessitates understanding the nature of the entire political equilibrium."

25. Nunn (2014) provides a review of a large and growing literature on the persistent effects of historical institutions.

26. Beaman, Chattopadhyay, et al. (2009) and Beaman, Duflo, et al. (2012) provide evidence on how female leaders shift social norms related to gender.

27. A body of research examining regional differences in governance within Italy has attributed the presence of greater social capital and of public interest or "civic" voting to earlier experience with participatory democracy (Alesina and Giuliano 2015; Guiso, Sapienza, and Zingales 2006; Nannicini et al. 2013; Putnam, Leonardi, and Nanetti 1993).

28. Rajan and Zingales (2003) make a similar argument about the role of openness to trade in promoting good policies in financial markets. They write: "Why, according to us, is openness beneficial? The answer is blindingly simple. Openness creates competition from outsiders—outsiders that incumbents cannot control through political means" (Rajan and Zingales 2003, 307).

29. A 2010 study published by the Institute of Development Studies, "An Upside-down View of Governance," made the argument that it is important to understand local political dynamics in the worlds in which poor people live as a first step to thinking about how institutions different from the institutions in the Organisation for Economic Co-operation and Development might be needed in these contexts.

Bibliography

Acemoglu, Daron, and Matthew O. Jackson. 2015. "History, Expectations, and Leadership in the Evolution of Social Norms." *Review of Economic Studies* 82 (1): 1–34.

Acemoglu, Daron, Suresh Naidu, Pascual Restrepo, and James A. Robinson. 2014. "Democracy Does Cause Growth." NBER Working Paper 20004, National Bureau of Economic Research, Cambridge, MA.

Acemoglu, Daron, Tristan Reed, and James A. Robinson. 2014. "Chiefs: Economic Development and Elite Control of Civil Society in Sierra Leone." *Journal of Political Economy* 122 (2): 319–68.

Acemoglu, Daron, and James A. Robinson. 2006. "De Facto Political Power and Institutional Persistence." *American Economic Review*, 96 (2): 325–30.

Akerlof, R. 2015. "A Theory of Authority." Unpublished.

Alesina, Alberto, and Paola Giuliano. 2015. "Culture and Institutions." *Journal of Economic Literature* 53 (4): 898–944.

Anderson, Siwan, Patrick Francois, and Ashok Kotwal. 2015. "Clientelism in Indian Villages." *American Economic Review* 105 (6): 1780–816.

Andrews, M., L. Pritchett, and M. Woolcock. 2013. "Escaping Capability Traps through Problem Driven Iterative Adaptation (PDIA)." *World Development* 51: 234–44.

Baland, J. M., K. O. Moene, and J. A. Robinson. 2010. "Governance and Development." *Handbook of Development Economics*, vol. 5, edited by D. Rodrik and M. Rosensweig, 4597–656. Amsterdam: North-Holland.

Banerjee, Abhijit V., Rukmini Banerji, Esther Duflo, Rachel Glennerster, and Stuti Khemani. 2010. "Pitfalls of Participatory Programs: Evidence from a Randomized Evaluation in Education in India." *American Economic Journal: Economic Policy* 2 (1): 1–30.

Banerjee, Abhijit, Esther Duflo, and Rachel Glennerster. 2008. "Putting a Band-Aid on a Corpse: Incentives for Nurses in the Indian Public Health Care System." *Journal of the European Economic Association* 6 (2–3): 487–500.

Banerjee, Abhijit, Rema Hanna, Jordan C. Kyle, Benjamin A. Olken, and Sudarno Sumarto. 2015. "The Power of Transparency: Information, Identification Cards and Food Subsidy Programs in Indonesia." NBER Working Paper 20923, National Bureau of Economic Research, Cambridge, MA.

Banerjee, Abhijit, Lakshmi Iyer, and Rohini Somanathan. 2005. "History, Social Divisions, and Public Goods in Rural India." *Journal of the European Economic Association* 3 (2–3): 639–47.

Banerjee, Abhijit V., Selvan Kumar, Rohini Pande, and Felix Su. 2011. "Do Informed Voters Make Better Choices? Experimental Evidence from Urban India." Working paper. https://www.hks.harvard.edu/fs/rpande/papers/DoInformedVoters_Nov11.pdf.

Bardhan, Pranab, and Dilip Mookherjee. 2000. "Capture and Governance at Local and National Levels." *American Economic Review* 90 (2): 135–39.

Beaman, Lori, Raghabendra Chattopadhyay, Esther Duflo, Rohini Pande, and Petia Topalova. 2009. "Powerful Women: Does Exposure Reduce Bias?" *Quarterly Journal of Economics* 124 (4): 1497–540.

Beaman, Lori, Esther Duflo, Rohini Pande, and Petia Topalova. 2012. "Female Leadership Raises Aspirations and Educational Attainment for Girls: A Policy Experiment in India." *Science* 335 (6068): 582–86.

Besley, Timothy, and Masayuki Kudamatsu. 2008. "Making Autocracy Work." LSE STICERD Research Paper DEDPS48, London School of Economics, London.

Besley, Timothy, and Torsten Persson. 2009. "The Origins of State Capacity: Property Rights, Taxation, and Politics." *American Economic Review* 99 (4): 1218–44.

———, and Daniel Sturm. 2005. "Political Competition and Economic Performance: Theory and Evidence from the United States." NBER Working Paper 11484, National Bureau of Economic Research, Cambridge, MA.

Bidner, Chris, and Patrick Francois. 2013. "The Emergence of Political Accountability." *Quarterly Journal of Economics* 128 (3): 1397–448.

Bishop, Bill. 2008. *The Big Sort: Why the Clustering of Like Minded America Is Tearing Us Apart.* New York: Houghton Mifflin.

Bjorkman, Martina, Damien De Walque, and Jakob Svensson. 2014. "Information Is Power: Experimental Evidence on the Long-Run Impact of Community Based Monitoring." World Bank Policy Research Working Paper 7015, World Bank, Washington, DC.

Björkman, Martina, and Jakob Svensson. 2009. "Power to the People: Evidence from a Randomized Field Experiment on Community-Based Monitoring in Uganda." *Quarterly Journal of Economics* 124 (2): 735–69.

Bobonis, Gustavo, Luis Cámara Fuertes, and Rainer Schwabe. Forthcoming. "Monitoring Corruptible Politicians." *American Economic Review.*

Burgess, Robin, Remi Jedwab, Edward Miguel, Ameet Morjaria, and Gerard Padró i Miquel. 2015. "The Value of Democracy: Evidence from Road Building in Kenya." *American Economic Review* 105 (6): 1817–51.

Burgess, Robin, Benjamin Olken, Matthew Hansen, Peter Potapov, and Stefanie Sieber. 2012. "The Political Economy of Deforestation in the Tropics." *Quarterly Journal of Economics* 127 (4): 1707–54.

Callen, Michael, Saad Gulzar, Ali Hasanain, and Yasir Khan. 2014. "The Political Economy of Public Employee Absence: Experimental Evidence from Pakistan." Unpublished, Harvard Kennedy School, Cambridge, MA.

Camp, Edwin, Avinash Dixit, and Susan Stokes. 2014. "Catalyst or Cause? Legislation and the Demise of Machine Politics in Britain and the United States." *Legislative Studies Quarterly* 39 (4): 559–92.

Campante, Filipe, and Quoc-Anh Do. 2014. "Isolated Capital Cities, Accountability and Corruption: Evidence from US States." *American Economic Review* 104 (8): 2456–81.

Campante, Filipe, Ruben Durante, and Francesco Sobbrio. 2013. "Politics 2.0: The Multifaceted Effect of Broadband Internet on Political Participation." NBER Working Paper 19029, National Bureau of Economic Research, Cambridge, MA.

Campante, Filipe, and Daniel Hojman. 2013. "Media and Polarization: Evidence from the Introduction of Broadcast TV in the US." *Journal of Public Economics* 100 (April): 79–92.

Casey, Katherine. 2015. "Crossing Party Lines: The Effects of Information on Redistributive Politics." *American Economic Review* 105 (8): 2410–48.

Chaudhury, Nazmul, Jeffrey Hammer, Michael Kremer, Karthik Muralidharan, and F. Halsey Rogers. 2006. "Missing in Action: Teacher and Health Worker Absence in Developing Countries." *Journal of Economic Perspectives* 20 (1): 91–116.

Chin, Aimee, and Nishith Prakash. 2011. "The Redistributive Effects of Political Reservation for Minorities: Evidence from India." *Journal of Development Economics* 96 (2): 265–77.

Dal Bó, P., A. Foster, and L. Putterman. 2010. "Institutions and Behavior: Experimental Evidence on the Effects of Democracy." *American Economic Review* 100 (5): 2205–29.

Dhaliwal, Iqbal, and Rema Hanna. 2014. "Deal with the Devil: The Successes and Limitations of Bureaucratic Reform in India." NBER Working Paper 20482, National Bureau of Economic Research, Cambridge, MA.

Egorov, Georgy, Sergei Guriev, and Konstantin Sonin. 2009. "Why Resource-Poor Dictators Allow Freer Media: A Theory and Evidence from Panel Data." *American Political Science Review* 103 (4): 645–68.

Feddersen, T. J. 2004. "Rational Choice Theory and the Paradox of Not Voting." *Journal of Economic Perspectives* 18 (1): 99–112.

Ferraz, Claudio, and Frederico Finan. 2011. "Electoral Accountability and Corruption: Evidence from the Audits of Local Governments." *American Economic Review* 101 (4): 1274–311.

———. 2008. "Exposing Corrupt Politicians: The Effect of Brazil's Publicly Released Audits on Electoral Outcomes." *Quarterly Journal of Economics* 123 (2): 703–45.

Fujiwara, Thomas, and Leonard Wantchekon. 2013. "Can Informed Public Deliberation Overcome Clientelism? Experimental Evidence from Benin." *American Economic Journal: Applied Economics* 5 (4): 241–55.

Gilens, Martin, and Benjamin I. Page. 2014. "Testing Theories of American Politics: Elites, Interest Groups, and Average Citizens." *Perspectives on Politics* 12 (3): 564–81.

Glaeser, Edward, and Claudia Goldin, eds. 2006. *Corruption and Reform: Lessons from America's Economic History*. Chicago, IL: University of Chicago Press.

Glaeser, Edward, and Cass Sunstein. 2013. "Why Does Balanced News Produce Unbalanced Views?" NBER Working Paper 18975, National Bureau of Economic Research, Cambridge, MA.

Grandvoinnet, Helene, Ghazia Aslam, and Shomikho Raha. 2015. *Opening the Black Box: The Contextual Drivers of Social Accountability*. Washington, DC: World Bank.

Grossman, Gene M., and Elhanan Helpman. 1996. "Electoral Competition and Special Interest Politics." *Review of Economic Studies* 63: 265–86.

———. 2001. *Special Interest Politics*. Cambridge and London: MIT Press.

Guiso, L., P. Sapienza, and L. Zingales. 2006. "Does Culture Affect Economic Outcomes?" *Journal of Economic Perspectives* 20 (2): 23–48.

IDS (Institute of Development Studies). 2010. *An Upside Down View of Governance*. Institute of Development Studies, University of Sussex.

Isham, Jonathan, Daniel Kaufmann, and Lant H. Pritchett. 1997. "Civil Liberties, Democracy, and the Performance of Government Projects." *World Bank Economic Review* 11 (2): 219–42.

Kahan, Dan, Ellen Peters, Erica Cantrell Dawson, and Paul Slovic. 2013. "Motivated Numeracy and Enlightened Self-Government." Yale Law School, Public Law Working Paper No. 307, Yale University, New Haven, CT.

Keefer, Philip. Forthcoming. "Organizing for Prosperity: Collective Action, Political Parties and the Political Economy of Development." In *Oxford Handbook of Politics of Development*, edited by Carol Lancaster and Nicolas van de Walle.

Keefer, Philip, and Stuti Khemani. 2014. "Radio's Impact on Preferences for Patronage Benefits." Policy Research Working Paper 6932, World Bank, Washington, DC.

Khemani, Stuti. 2015. "Buying Votes versus Supplying Public Services: Political Incentives to Under-Invest in Pro-Poor Policies." *Journal of Development Economics* 177: 84–93.

León, Gianmarco. 2011. "Turnout, Political Preferences and Information: Experimental Evidence from Perú." BREAD Working Paper No. 376, Bureau for Research and Economic Analysis of Development. http://ibread.org/bread/working/376.

Lizzeri, A., and N. Persico. 2004. "Why Did the Elites Extend the Suffrage? Democracy and the Scope of Government, With an Application to Britain's 'Age of Reform.'" *Quarterly Journal of Economics* 119 (2): 707–65.

Lowi, Theodore J. 1972. "Four Systems of Policy, Politics and Choice." *Public Administration Review* 32 (4): 298–310.

Maor, Moshe. 2004. "Feeling the Heat? Anticorruption Mechanisms in Comparative Perspective." *Governance* 17 (1): 1–28.

Meagher, Patrick. 2005. "Anti-Corruption Agencies: Rhetoric versus Reality." *Journal of Policy Reform* 8 (1): 69–103.

Min, Brian. 2015. *Power and the Vote: Elections and Electricity in the Developing World.* New York: Cambridge University Press.

Min, Brian, and Miriam Golden. 2014. "Electoral Cycles in Electricity Losses in India." *Energy Policy 65:* 619–25.

Mobarak, A. M. 2005. "Democracy, Volatility, and Economic Development." *Review of Economics and Statistics, 87* (2): 348–61.

Muralidharan, Karthik, Paul Niehaus, and Sandip Sukhtankar. 2014. "Building State Capacity: Evidence from Biometric Smartcards in India." NBER Working Paper 19999, National Bureau of Economic Research, Cambridge, MA.

Myerson, R. 2006. "Federalism and Incentives for Success of Democracy." *Quarterly Journal of Political Science* 1: 3–23.

———. 2012. "Standards for State Building Interventions." Working Paper, University of Chicago. http://home.uchicago.edu/~rmyerson/research/std4sb.pdf.

Nannicini, Tommaso, Andrea Stella, Guido Tabellini, and Ugo Troiano. 2013. "Social Capital and Political Accountability." *American Economic Journal: Economic Policy* 5 (2): 222–50.

Nunn, N. 2014. "Historical Development." In *Handbook of Economic Growth*, vol. 2, edited by Philippe Aghion and Steven Durlauf, 347–402. Amsterdam: Elsevier.

Olken, Benjamin. 2007. "Monitoring Corruption: Evidence from a Field Experiment in Indonesia." *Journal of Political Economy* 115: 200–49.

Olson, Mancur. 1965. *The Logic of Collective Action.* Cambridge: Harvard University Press.

Prakash, Nishith, Marc Rockmore, and Yogesh Uppal. 2014. "Do Criminal Representatives Hinder or Improve Constituency Outcomes? Evidence from India." IZA DP No. 8452, Institute for the Study of Labor, Bonn.

Pritchett, Lant, Michael Woolcock, and Matt Andrews. 2013. "Looking Like a State: Techniques for Persistent Failure in State Capability for Implementation." *Journal of Development Studies* 49 (1): 1–18.

Putnam, R., R. Leonardi, and R. Y. Nanetti. 1993. *Making Democracy Work.* Princeton, NJ: Princeton University Press.

Rajan, Raghuram G., and Rodney Ramcharan. 2012. "Constituencies and Legislation: The Fight Over the McFadden Act of 1927 (May 30, 2012)." FEDS Working Paper No. 2012-61, Finance and Economics Discussion Series, Board of Governors of the Federal Reserve System, Washington, DC.

Rajan, Raghuram G., and Luigi Zingales. 2003. *Saving Capitalism from the Capitalists: Unleashing the Power of Financial Markets to Create Wealth and Spread Opportunity.* New York: Crown Business.

Rodrik, Dani. 2000. "Institutions for High-Quality Growth: What They Are and How to Acquire Them." *Studies in Comparative International Development* 35 (3): 3-31.

Rodrik, Dani, and Romain Wacziarg. 2005. "Do Democratic Transitions Produce Bad Economic Outcomes?" *American Economic Review* 95 (2): 50–55.

Sacks, Audrey, Jean Ensminger, and Sam Clark. 2014. "Scoping Mission—Anti-Corruption Mitigation in the Village Law Implementation, Jakarta March 23-26." Unpublished, World Bank, Washington, DC.

Satyanath, Shanker, Nico Voigtlaender, and Hans-Joachim Voth. 2013. "Bowling for Fascism: Social Capital and the Rise of the Nazi Party." NBER Working Paper No. 19201, National Bureau of Economic Research, Cambridge, MA.

Snyder, James M., and David Strömberg. 2010. "Press Coverage and Political Accountability." *Journal of Political Economy* 118 (2): 355–408.

Sunstein, Cass R. 2009. *Going to Extremes: How Like Minds Unite and Divide.* Oxford: Oxford University Press.

Wilson, James Q. 1973. *Political Organizations.* New York: Basic Books.

World Bank. 2004. *World Development Report 2004:* Making Services Work for Poor People. Washington, DC: World Bank.

———. 2011. *World Development Report 2011: Conflict, Security, and Development.* Washington, DC: World Bank.

———. 2015. *World Development Report 2015: Mind, Society, and Behavior.* Washington, DC: World Bank.

———. 2016. *World Development Report 2016: Digital Dividends.* Washington, DC: World Bank.

Yanagizawa-Drott, David. 2014. "Propaganda and Conflict: Evidence from the Rwandan Genocide." *Quarterly Journal of Economics* 129 (4): 1947–94.

Zimmerman, Brigitte. 2014. "Transparency, Sanctioning Capacity, and Corruption Displacement: Multi-Method Evidence from Local Government in Malawi." PhD Dissertation, University of California San Diego.

CHAPTER ONE

Governance

Overview

This report is about understanding and fixing government failures to provide the public goods needed for economic development. Governments play a unique role in economic development by providing the institutions that support competitive markets and by addressing those areas where markets fail. Governments also have unique powers for redistribution to complement other market-supporting policies to eradicate poverty and promote shared prosperity. Taken together, the government's role is paraphrased in the report as providing the public goods that it is uniquely positioned to provide. Governance is thus the process of pursuing policies to deliver public goods, using (and debating) the best available technical evidence for this purpose. Governments fail to provide public goods when leaders knowingly and deliberately ignore sound technical advice and adopt and implement policies that they know are costly, despite the availability of alternative policies that are likely to yield improved outcomes.[1]

One example of government failure that has been widely studied and measured consists of malfeasance and mismanagement within public bureaucracies and by political leaders. Examples include: corruption; weak management practices that condone frequent absenteeism among public sector workers; nepotism in the recruitment and career advancement of public sector workers; and crony capitalism, whereby politically connected firms receive privileged treatment by public regulators.

Proximate factors behind widespread corruption in poor countries are the lower capacity of governments to monitor public officials, enforce rules, and design contracts that strengthen the economic incentives of public officials to refrain from corruption. Significant evidence, how-ever, suggests that systemic and persistent corruption has its roots in the actions of powerful leaders to extract rents from the state and deliberately weaken internal checks and balances. Even when leaders change and are replaced by well-intentioned reformers, the reformers can face the chal-lenge of pervasive rent-seeking throughout the public sector that is sug-gestive of entrenched *norms of political behavior* to extract private benefits from public resources. Political norms are examined in this report as a subset of social norms, pertaining to the behavior of citizens and public officials specifically in the public sphere of governments. "Ordinary" citizens who hold no public office can be a part of government failure when they disregard the law and resort to bribery to avoid public interest regulations.

Corruption is not the only government failure. Even when govern-ment agencies are accountable for their actions, governance problems can originate from among citizens in the form of *what* they choose to demand and *for what* they hold government accountable. Citizens can be divided by ideological beliefs, leading to political polarization and policy gridlock. Ideological beliefs among citizens about specific public policies, such as energy subsidies or immigration, can be difficult to shift with technical evidence on the costs and benefits of different policy options. Similarly, distributive conflict among citizens, which leads special interest groups to mobilize to extract private benefits from public policies, frequently comes at the expense of the broader public interest.

Distributive conflict among, and inefficient demands from citizens, can lead to the selection of leaders who further polarize people and nur-ture ideological constituencies rather than exert effort to find common ground to address shared problems. These issues can also prevent reform leaders from pursuing appropriate public policies. Furthermore, this class of government failure is relevant for rich as well as for poor countries, and in weak as well as in stronger institutional environments, where inter-nal checks and balances are more effective in controlling corruption in government.

The next section of this chapter examines trends in corruption, one of the most widely studied government failures, and provides examples that show how persistent corruption can be rooted in adverse political incentives and perverse behavioral norms. The following section provides examples of how ideological beliefs and distributive conflict among citizens can be sources of government failures as well.

Trends in corruption

The vast majority of poor people live in countries with persistently low indicators of the control of corruption. A widely used measure in this regard is the Control of Corruption indicator of the World Bank's Worldwide Governance Indicators. The Control of Corruption measure "captures perceptions of the extent to which public power is exercised for private gain, including both petty and grand forms of corruption, as well as 'capture' of the state by elites and private interests."[2] Figure 1.1 shows that nearly all of the world's poor people live in countries that are almost unanimously ranked in the bottom half of the indices of the control of corruption.

Not only is the control of corruption low in most developing countries, but it is persistently low. Figure 1.2 shows that most countries where poor people live have similar measures of corruption in 2013 as they did in 1996, the earliest and latest years for which these data are available.

Figure 1.1 **Poor countries rank at the bottom on the control of corruption, 2013**

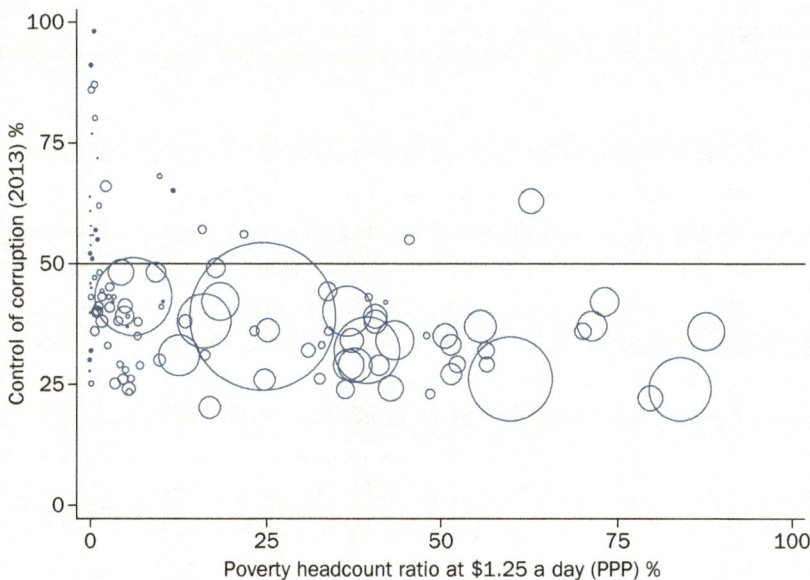

Sources: Data on the Control of Corruption are from the Worldwide Governance Indicators (WGI) 2013. Data on the size of countries' poor population are from PovcalNet, an online tool for poverty measurement produced by the Development Research Group of the World Bank.
Note: Circles reflect size of countries' poor population. Y-axis measures a country's percentile ranking in Control of Corruption. X-axis measures the Poverty Headcount Ratio at $1.25 a day (2005 PPP). PPP = purchasing power parity.

Figure 1.2   Persistence in corruption in poor countries, 2013 versus 1996

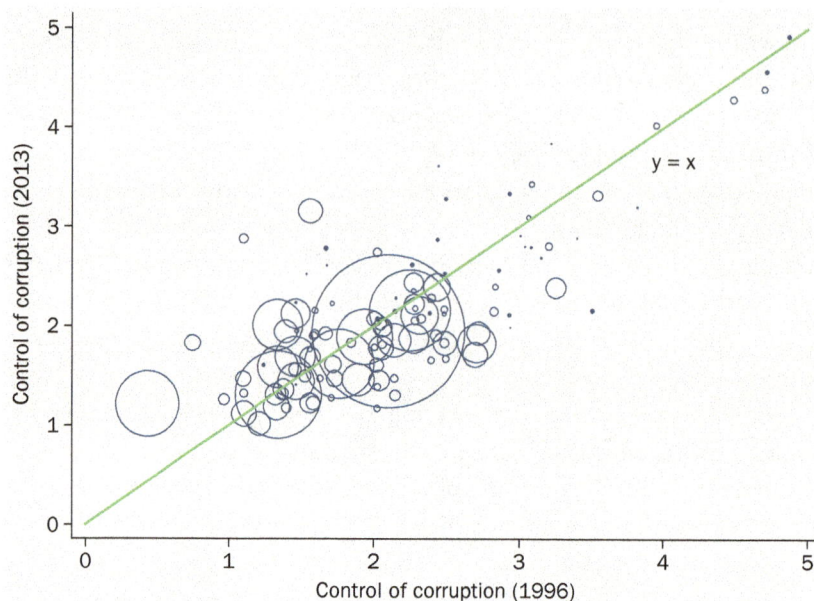

Sources: Data on the Control of Corruption are from the Worldwide Governance Indicators (WGI). Data on the size of countries' poor population are from PovcalNet (2005 PPP), an online tool for poverty measurement produced by the Development Research Group of the World Bank.
Note: WGI data have been rescaled such that the lowest value of 0 (zero) corresponds to lowest control of corruption. The line represents the 45-degree line, where y = x. PPP = purchasing power parity.

Research on corruption has generally concluded that it has pernicious consequences for both the efficiency with which resources are allocated and for equity (Mauro 1995; Olken and Pande 2012). To highlight a few examples from this large literature, Fisman and Svensson (2007) find that bribes pose a greater cost to firms than an equivalent amount in taxes. Using firm-level data from Uganda, they find that the effect of an increase in bribery on reducing firm growth is three times greater than the impact of an equivalent amount of taxes. Meanwhile, Hunt (2007) shows that in Peru, victims of misfortune rely more on public services and, in turn, are more likely than nonvictims to need to bribe public officials. The poor do not spend a higher proportion of their income on bribes, but rather public services can fail them when they need it most and they can only access it through corruption.

Corruption in politics

Systemic and persistent corruption has its roots in the actions of powerful leaders to deliberately weaken internal institutions of control within government. A striking illustration of this comes from the detailed records of bribe payments to politicians, judges, and news media maintained by Vladimiro Montesinos, the head of Peru's Intelligence Service under President Alberto Fujimori (McMillan and Zoido 2004). The average monthly amount of bribes going to politicians was US$300,000, to judges US$250,000, and to television channels US$3 million. Bribes tended to be higher if the politician was part of the opposition and lower if the politician was from Fujimori's party. The television channel with the largest viewership received US$1.5 million monthly.

Transparency International's Global Corruption Barometer (GCB) shows the extent of perceived corruption in politics. GCB is based on household surveys of more than 114,000 individuals. Patterns from the GCB in figures 1.3 and 1.4, below, reveal higher reports of corruption in political parties and the police, an instrument of the domestic coercive power of the state, compared with other institutions. The other institutions for which survey information was gathered include

Figure 1.3 Perceived corruption in political parties versus in other institutions

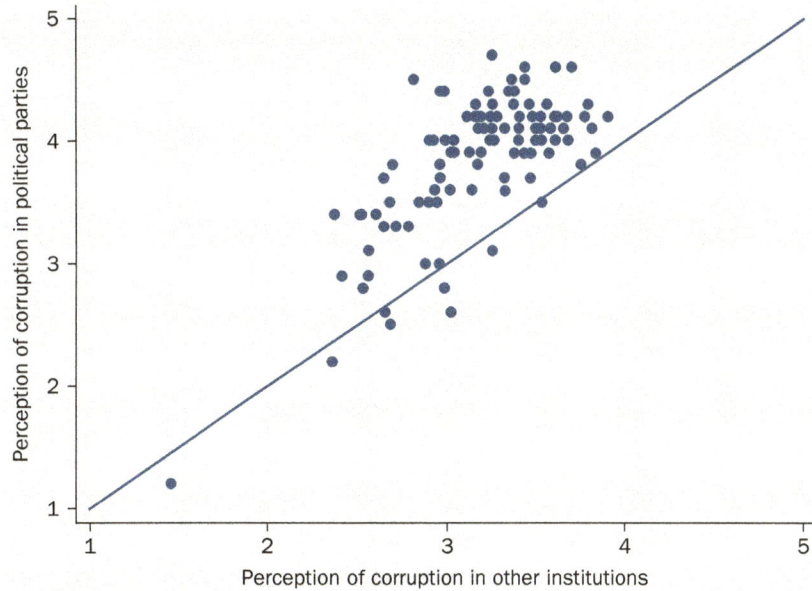

Source: Global Corruption Barometer (GCB) 2013.
Note: GCB measures perceived corruption on a scale of 1–5, with 1 reflecting "not at all corrupt" and 5 reflecting "extremely corrupt." The x-axis measures the average score of perceived corruption in the other institutions included in the GCB survey (other than political parties and the police), which are public officials/civil servants, judiciary, parliament/legislature, medical and health, education systems, military, nongovernmental organizations, media, religious bodies, and the business/private sector.

Figure 1.4 **Perceived corruption in the police versus in other institutions**

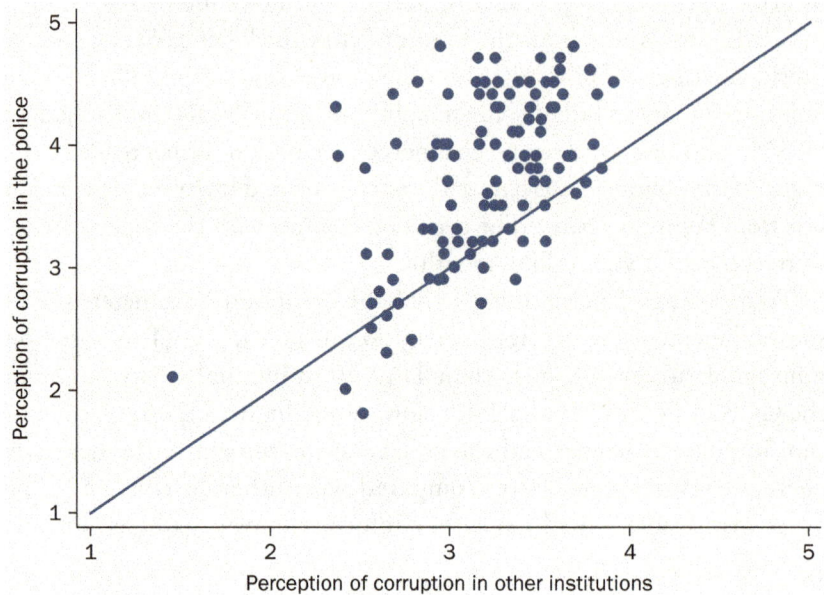

Source: Global Corruption Barometer (GCB) 2013.
Note: GCB measures perceived corruption on a scale of 1-5, with 1 reflecting "not at all corrupt" and 5 reflecting "extremely corrupt." The x-axis measures the average score of perceived corruption in the other institutions included in the GCB survey (other than political parties and the police), which are public officials/civil servants, judiciary, parliament/legislature, medical and health, education systems, military, nongovernmental organizations, media, religious bodies, and the business/private sector.

public officials/civil servants, parliament/legislature, judiciary, military, nongovernmental organizations (NGOs), the media, religious bodies, business/private sector, education system, and medical/health. The results, therefore, show that citizens systematically report greater corruption in political parties and the police than in other institutions. They suggest that corruption pervades the institutions through which leaders gain public office and wield power within government.

Political connections and corruption

Research provides evidence that political connections are used by economic agents to gain an advantage over competitors in countries with weak control of corruption. Faccio (2006) examines 20,202 publicly traded firms in 47 countries and finds that politically connected firms are more common in countries with high corruption. Moreover, political connections are significantly associated with a higher share value of firms in countries with high corruption: having a member of a firm's board or a large shareholder become a politician is associated with an increase in the firm's stock value of 4.43 percent. In contrast, there is no significant association of firm value with political connections in countries with low corruption.

These cross-country findings are bolstered by within-country research. In Indonesia, Fisman (2001) finds that the value of firms depends on the degree of their political connectedness. Following rumors of President Suharto's worsening health during 1995–97, the stock price of politically connected firms fell more than that of less connected firms. Another contrast, similar to the results in Faccio (2006) of political connections in weak versus strong institutional environments comes from Fisman et al.'s (2012) replication of the methodology used in Indonesia to estimate the value of political connections in the United States to former U.S. Vice President Dick Cheney. In contrast to political connections to President Suharto, they find no effect of connections to Vice President Cheney. Companies with personal connections to Vice President Cheney are unaffected by events that would be expected to affect Vice President Cheney's capacity to give companies preferential treatment. The authors conclude that strong institutions in the United States are effective in reining in rent-seeking through connections to high-level politicians.

Meanwhile, in Pakistan, Khwaja and Mian (2005) consider data on firms' borrowing from banks between 1996 and 2002, and find that politically connected firms, defined as those having a politician on the firm's board, borrow 45 percent more and have a 50 percent higher default rate. The effects are greater depending on whether the political party to which the firm is connected is in power. Rijkers, Freund, and Nucifora (2014) provide evidence from firm-level data in Tunisia that suggests that Tunisia's industrial policy was used as a vehicle for rent creation for President Ben Ali and his family. Diwan, Keefer, and Schiffbauer (2015) provide evidence from the Arab Republic of Egypt that entry by politically connected firms slows aggregate employment growth and skews the distribution of employment toward less productive, smaller firms.

Connections are also important at the local level. Political connections to local leaders are associated with greater absenteeism among frontline public service providers and lower motivation on the job. Callen et al. (2014) provide systematic evidence that politically connected doctors in Pakistan are more likely to be absent from public health clinics. They also find that about 40 percent of inspectors and health administrators report political interference when they try to sanction errant doctors.

39

La Forgia et al. (2014) provide case studies from India of a thriving "parallel system" for human resources management in the public health sector that is based on political connections and bribes, rather than on formal rules. Through connections and bribes, doctors are able to obtain the public clinic posts they desire, regardless of their performance on the job. Linking this study to another by Das et al. (2015) on the performance of public sector doctors in India suggests that this parallel system results in rampant underperformance. Das et al. (2015) show that doctors in the public sector in India perform significantly worse, not only compared with their counterparts in the private sector, but also when they provide services through public clinics rather than in their private practices. Furthermore, although provider effort and prices charged in the private sector are strongly and positively correlated, there is no correlation between effort and wages in the public sector.

Detailed case studies suggest that in environments with widespread rent-seeking, all types of officials in the public sector, ranging from the humble administrator and local political leader at the street level (Lipsky 1980) up to powerful politicians at the regional or national levels, can gear their discretion, ingenuity, and entrepreneurship toward finding ways to circumvent internal controls rather than solving problems in the public interest.

The point is illustrated in a quote provided by Zimmerman (2014), which is attributed to an official in the Anti-Corruption Bureau in Malawi who is discussing local corruption in the implementation of national programs:

> In the early years of the fertilizer subsidy programme, politicians would take the fertilizer bags at distributions in the presence of the people. This was discovered and there was outrage, so then fertilizer started to go missing on the journey to distributions. This was discovered and there was more outrage, so then beneficiaries who did not exist received fertilizer for a time, until this was also discovered and there was more outrage once again. Lately, the fertilizer is distributed to real beneficiaries during real distributions, but in advance the bags of fertilizer have been opened and diluted with sand. Some officials, seeing the anger over the subsidy program, have stopped their corruption there and have begun corruption in areas that do not anger the people, such as manipulating district bank accounts.

In India, Aiyar and Mehta (2015) provide examples of how local political leaders circumvent internal controls in India's flagship antipoverty program, established by the Mahatma Gandhi National Rural Employment Guarantee Act. The authors study the functioning of social audits in India, a recent institutional arrangement aimed at checking local rent-seeking by engaging citizens to directly monitor public spending. Their field work was conducted in Andhra Pradesh, a state that has been lauded for systematically investing in social audits. Aiyar and Mehta (2015) provide examples of politicians extracting large rents from this antipoverty scheme by circumventing the social audit altogether. Connections between local political elites are forged and maintained for the purpose of big-ticket theft from state funds that social audits cannot uncover.

Culture of corruption

Other evidence shows just how widespread is the practice of bribing public officials and, in that sense, the norm of behavior in the public sector in environments with high corruption. Bribe payments to public officials occur in all manner of transactions in which citizens interact with the state in poor countries, either as users of services or as owners and employers of businesses. Such interactions follow the economic dynamics of competitive markets for bribery. In a detailed empirical study of bribes paid by truck drivers in Indonesia to police and military officials to avoid harassment at checkpoints and to weigh station attendants to avoid fines for driving overweight, Olken and Barron (2009) find that the demand for illegal payments by officials adheres to standard economic models of pricing behavior.

Similarly, another study in Indonesia by Burgess et al. (2012) on the incentives of local public officials and politicians to enforce forest policy and prevent illegal logging finds evidence consistent with economic models of how officials will behave to allow deforestation, presumably in exchange for bribes. When a province is subdivided and a new district is created, greater competition among the newly created jurisdictions drives down the price for wood and increases the overall rate of deforestation in the province. Illegal logging also increases substantially in the years leading up to local elections. In a similar vein, Fan, Lin, and Treisman (2009) find that firms' reports of bribe payments to public officials are more frequent in countries with more administrative tiers of government.

The above evidence (such as in Olken and Barron [2009]) shows that the behavior of public officials is sensitive to incentives, such that there is little reason to believe in a "culture of corruption" that is rooted in mindsets and mental models that are impervious to rational incentives and hard to change. The evidence is also consistent with another view of a culture of corruption that stems from rational beliefs about how others are behaving and about the probability of detection and punishment in environments with widespread corruption and scarce resources to combat it. This analysis follows one element in the definition of "culture" in Alesina and Giuliano (forthcoming) and Greif (1994) as beliefs about the consequences of one's actions that are based on expectations of actions others will take.[3] This view suggests that a culture of corruption may not be as slow to change as other aspects of cultural beliefs and values, such as those derived from religion or inherited social norms. Instead, it may be more sensitive to experience and information in updating beliefs.

Fisman and Miguel (2007) provide evidence that both cultural norms and short-term changes in incentives in response to legal enforcement are important determinants of corrupt behavior. They find that foreign diplomats posted in New York City who come from countries with higher measures of corruption accumulated significantly more unpaid parking violations compared with their peers from better-governed countries. This finding suggests that the elite from countries with more widespread corruption have a greater proclivity to corruption than other elites in the same situation. However, they also find that the apparent norm of corruption among foreign diplomats was quickly overcome when the laws were changed to allow parking enforcement authorities to confiscate the diplomatic license plates of violators.

The quick and large impact of a change in enforcement laws observed by Fisman and Miguel (2007) was presumably facilitated by already-functioning, strong institutions of enforcement in New York City. The challenge for countries with weak institutions, and low capacity and resources for monitoring and enforcement to begin with, is how to leverage these scarce resources to tackle widespread corruption.

If prevailing incentives shape corruption, then policy initiatives can be designed to reshape those incentives to combat corruption. However, when corruption is the norm, efforts to control it through different approaches to monitoring and enforcement can be more challenging than when corruption is an aberration. Lui (1986) develops a multiple equilibrium model showing that when corruption is widespread, it is costly to reduce and difficult to detect and so the economy will remain highly corrupt. Tirole (1996) models how corruption may persist over generations. He models individual reputations as the aggregate of collective reputations and individuals' current incentives as shaped by the behavior of previous generations. The persistence of corruption among bureaucrats, for example, might reflect a corrupt reputation of previous generations and the lack of incentives to act honestly if enough bureaucrats are corrupt.[4]

Other evidence suggests that individuals with a higher proclivity to corruption might self-select into the public sector for rent-seeking motives. Hanna and Wang (2013) show that students in India who cheat on a simple task in a lab experiment are more likely to have a preference for public sector jobs. They also find that cheating on the task predicts actual corruption by government officials, consistent with the task capturing a meaningful predilection for corruption. Selection of individuals into the public sector for rent-seeking motives, or turning to corruption while in office because of the incentives and the perceived behavioral norms among colleagues, can lead to the persistence of corruption.

Citizens' attitudes to corruption

Behavioral norms to extract private benefits from public resources extend to "ordinary" citizens who hold no public office. The examples from the research discussed above not only show widespread demand for bribes among public officials but also that citizens supply bribes precisely for the purpose of deriving private rents at the expense of the greater public interest. Overweight trucks, as in the study by Olken and Barron (2009), damage public infrastructure, but truck drivers have incentives to bribe weigh station attendants to avoid regulations on weight. Greater deforestation has been associated with environmental and health problems (for example, Garg 2014), but owners of logging companies bribe local officials to get away with illegal logging (Burgess et al. 2012).

"Free-riding" among citizens can lead to lower contributions to the public good of monitoring and sanctioning public officials who engage in corruption. Few people are likely to take the costly actions needed to monitor and sanction public officials, or to desist from colluding with rent-seeking officials (as in the examples of overweight trucks and illegal deforestation), especially when they believe that others are unlikely to join them. As evidence of the free-riding problem, research has found a significant difference in citizen monitoring of different types of corruption depending on whether the monitoring would yield immediate private benefits versus more broadly shared benefits. Olken (2007) finds that community members in Indonesia are more likely to monitor and demand accurate wage payments from local officials who manage workfare projects, the benefits from which they receive individually. In contrast, community members are less likely to engage in local collective action along with others to reduce leakage in project materials costs whose benefits would accrue to the whole community.

Similarly, free-riding problems among citizens in monitoring and sanctioning public providers—for example, school teachers in India—appears in the research of Banerjee et al. (2010). The authors find that, in response to an information campaign about the poor quality of education provided in the village public schools, community members were willing to undertake private action, such as remedial instruction for their own children outside school, but not to take collective action to improve the performance of the village public school.

Citizens' behavior toward the public sector can contribute to government failures. One example is the widespread theft of electricity from public utilities, which leads to disruptions in electricity supply that cripple economic investments (Depuru, Wang, and Devabhaktuni 2011). Citizens describe such theft from the public sector in particular as justifiable, even though theft in general is considered wrong. Evidence of political leaders manipulating the electricity supply to facilitate an increase in theft at election times suggests that citizen behavior toward the state is influenced by politics (Min 2015; Min and Golden 2014). Corruption and poor service delivery can diminish the legitimacy of the state and lead citizens to organize for violent conflict (World Bank 2011). Such disregard for state institutions and laws reflects weak norms for cooperative behavior in the public sphere, which can keep societies trapped in a situation of persistent corruption and weak institutions (Basu 2015; P. Dal Bó 2007).

Government failures arising from beliefs about how others are behaving, rather than because of an inherited mindset or cultural values, can also change rapidly when people see changes in how others are behaving. A quote from an Egyptian student reflecting on people cleaning up Tahrir Square illustrates this: "We thought people didn't care and just threw their garbage on the street, but now we see that they just thought it was hopeless—why bother when it's so dirty. Why not be corrupt when everything is corrupted. But now things have changed, and it's a different mood overtaking. Even I can't stop smiling myself." (Steavenson 2011, 45).

Ideological beliefs and distributive conflict among citizens

Political impediments to selecting and implementing technically sound policies can arise even when governments are accountable to citizens and corruption is rare. Citizens' beliefs about public policies and demands for specific policies without full regard for the costs they may entail can hamper the selection of public policies on the basis of technical merit.

Different strands of research provide evidence on three channels. First, ideological beliefs about appropriate public policies can be resistant to technical evidence that is contrary to those prior beliefs. Second, lack of information or limited cognitive capacity to process information about the consequences of different policies can also lead to demand for inefficient policies. Third, special interests and distributive conflict among different groups of citizens can distort policies to benefit those who organize to pursue their interests at the expense of the greater public good. Some leaders can exploit these political beliefs and special interests to gain and remain in office by dividing citizens and polarizing constituencies rather than building common cause for public goods.

One policy area that serves to illustrate these points is that of energy or fuel subsidies. Technical evidence and wide agreement among experts indicates that fuel subsidies are inefficient and entail fiscal and environmental costs with little justification on equity grounds (Clements et al. 2013). Fuel subsidies in the developing world are highly regressive (Arze del Granado, Coady, and Gillingham 2012). In India, estimates suggest that the richest 10 percent of households receive seven times more in benefits from subsidies than the poorest 10 percent (Anand et al. 2013). A common view of the regressive incidence of energy subsidies is that costly fuel subsidies are a form of elite capture. A typical strategy used to win political support for reforms is to replace energy subsidies with cash transfers to the poor.[5] The underlying rationale is that, if people realize that the lion's share of subsidies accrues to the elite, they will punish political leaders who allocate public resources to these subsidies and reward them for allocating means-tested cash transfers to the poor.

However, if subsidies are popular because of ideological beliefs that they are "pro-poor," that governments *should* pursue price controls in addition to providing cash transfers to the poor, then even seeming reforms that curtail some subsidies may be transient and ineffective. When a price shock hits, people will be out on the streets again asking for subsidies or an increase in the cash transfer to compensate for the price increase (Clements et al. 2013). Little evidence is available to determine whether costly subsidy policies are sustained due to capture by elites or organized special interests, due to informational and cognitive constraints among citizens to recognize the costs of these policies or due to ideological beliefs about the value of such policies. However, some evidence from the United States on citizen attitudes toward combating climate change with energy policies suggests that the latter two explanations are likely to be a significant part of the story for why it is difficult to reform energy subsidies.

Dal Bó, Dal Bó, and Eyster (2013) and Sunstein (2007) provide evidence from laboratory experiments in the United States suggesting that citizens are cognitively constrained to demand policies that confer short-term benefits at the expense of long-term or "equilibrium" costs. That is, citizens fail to internalize the full impact of the demand for a particular policy.

A related but different argument is proposed by Kahan (2012) and Kahan, Jenkins-Smith, and Braman (2011). Also using laboratory experiments in the United States, these authors show that those who score highest on cognitive abilities are also the most likely to adopt ideological beliefs in defiance of technical evidence. The authors explain this as "motivated reasoning" that is adopted by people to conform to the values of the cultural groups to which they belong. Their findings suggest that public divisions over climate change are not a reflection of the public's lack of knowledge or misunderstanding of science; rather, divisions stem from conflicting interests—between an individual's interests in adopting common beliefs held by one's community versus a collective interest in making decisions to promote common welfare. Holding a viewpoint that goes against one's surrounding cultural community can exact a cost. When this cost is high, it is rational for individuals to adopt the reasoning prevailing in the group.

Together, this work substantiates the role of beliefs and behavioral norms in shaping citizens' demands for public policies. They differ in their view of the extent to which citizens' resistance to technical evidence is caused by cognitive constraints. Kahan (2012) and Kahan, Jenkins-Smith, and Braman (2011) highlight the importance of cultural norms instead of cognitive constraints, arguing that citizens engage in motivated reasoning to conform an assessment of available facts to the beliefs of the social groups to which they belong.

This research from the United States on citizens' beliefs and attitudes toward public policies suggests that rigorous scientific methods need to be

applied to develop an understanding of the sources of political impediments rather than assuming a "common sense" understanding of it. It
also has implications for communicating technical evidence to people,
highlighting the issues of social and ideological divisions and resistance to
such evidence even among educated citizens. Scientific rigor is also needed
to understand how communication can be persuasive and shift beliefs.
That is, simply providing information assuming that it will address an
information asymmetry will not work if the problem is rooted in beliefs
and behavioral norms. The following chapters of this report are aimed at
reviewing available research on how transparency and political engagement, and the leaders selected through it, play a role in shifting beliefs.

In addition to holding ideological beliefs and the existence of cognitive
capacity constraints, special interest groups and elite capture are the third
channel through which citizens' behavior poses political impediments to
the adoption of sound public policies. The theory and evidence on special
interest groups shows how citizens can organize to distort policies away
from the broad public interest and toward conferring narrow benefits to
group members (Grossman and Helpman 2001). This work focuses on
environments with strong institutional constraints such as in the United
States, showing that political impediments can arise from among citizens
even when accountability institutions function well. Gilens and Page
(2014) provide evidence to suggest that economic elites and organized
groups representing business interests substantially influence U.S. government policy. In their seminal work in the developing world, Bardhan and
Mookherjee (2000) model elite capture similarly to the modeling of special
interests in the U.S. literature.

A related strand of research provides evidence on how ideological
commitment to political parties can yield policy gridlock due to political polarization in rich countries (Glaeser and Sunstein 2013). Although
well-functioning political parties, organized around policy programs, can
solve some collective action problems (Keefer and Vlaicu 2007), they can
contribute to other problems that arise from the ideological preferences of
voters. In addition to policy gridlock in advanced institutional contexts,
partisan preferences can facilitate corruption and rent-seeking in weak
institutional environments (Bardhan and Mookherjee 2010).

Bardhan and Mookherjee (2010) find evidence suggesting that political parties can use partisan attachment among voters to pursue rents and
reduce effort rather than to deliver the policies that their party espouses.
The authors use data on a sample of villages spanning 1974–98 to

investigate the political determinants of land reform implementation in the Indian state of West Bengal. A relatively well-organized and programmatic party used to dominate the political arena in West Bengal during this period—the Communist Party of India (Marxist) with a strong political commitment to land reform. The authors find that the relationship between the party's control of local governments and implementation of land reform is consistent with both reelection concerns and rent-seeking. Villages with more closely contested elections experience more land reform. However, once the party gains a majority, land reform decreases despite the party's commitment to it.

Redistributive conflict among groups of citizens who are divided along different cleavages, such as ethnic identity, is a related source of impediments to policies for public goods. Ethnic divisions are regarded by some scholars as central to the explanation of why some regions of the world are rich and others are persistently poor (Ashraf and Galor 2013). Substantial evidence exists of an association between ethnic fragmentation and low investment in public goods (Habyarimana et al. 2009; Miguel and Gugerty 2005).

Alesina, Michalopoulos, and Papaioannou (forthcoming) find that it is not ethnic fragmentation per se that matters in explaining variations in economic development, but rather its interaction with economic inequality. Economic inequality between ethnic groups, largely arising from differences in geographic endowments across their historic homelands, is associated with lower real gross domestic product (GDP) per capita. The typical measure of ethno-linguistic fragmentation used in the literature loses its significance when the authors' measure of economic inequality between ethnic groups is included. This result is consistent with the view that redistributive conflict between groups can contribute to political failures to select and implement appropriate public policies that promote economic development.

Banerjee and Pande (2007) provide micro evidence in support of the hypothesis that redistributive conflict among citizens contributes to leaders' weak political incentives to provide public goods. They document that, in the state of Uttar Pradesh in India, political parties are organized to appeal to caste identity and regularly field candidates against whom there are allegations of corruption and criminality. The authors explain this through a model in which greater corruption arises in ethnic parties because citizens value honesty in political leaders less than reliable redistribution based on shared ethnic identity. At the same time, in other work these authors show that voter preferences regarding ethnic identity are malleable and responsive to information about the severity of allegations of transgression (Banerjee et al. 2009; Banerjee et al. 2014).

As the evidence grows on both ethnic politics in the developing world and ideological politics in the rich world, it appears that both types of divisions play a similar role of stoking conflict among citizens over the distribution of public resources, which undermines the use of these resources in addressing shared problems of public goods.

This chapter has set the stage by describing government failures that affect countries around the world and the need to solve these so that public sector institutions are capable of tackling problems of public goods. Incentives and behavioral norms among political leaders, public officials, frontline public service providers, and citizens alike can contribute to government failure. Persistent and widespread corruption in developing countries is consistent with a culture of corruption based on rational beliefs about how others are behaving in the public sector. Corruption is not the only government failure. Ideological beliefs about public policies and distributive conflict among citizens over the allocation of public resources also contribute to government failure. These problems are shared by rich and poor countries, and those with strong and weak institutions to control malfeasance and mismanagement within government.

The objective of the report is to examine how these government failures can be overcome by harnessing two forces that are spreading around the world: citizen engagement and transparency in political processes. The next two chapters examine these trends.

Notes

1. Governments can make inadvertent mistakes when they do not have the right evidence or when the state of the world changes and they need to find out what to do to tackle new problems as they emerge. Such mistakes, uncertainties, or technical debates about appropriate public policies are not part of how government failure is defined in this report. Government failure is defined on the basis of purpose, intent, and incentives of leaders to not pursue public policies in the public interest. In chapter 4, the conceptual framework of the report reviews the economic theory supporting this view of government failure.
2. Worldwide Governance Indicators, http://info.worldbank.org/governance/wgi/pdf/cc.pdf.

3. Alesina and Giuliano (forthcoming) discuss how this definition of culture overlaps with what others have described as "informal institutions." They also discuss the links between the view of culture as a set of rational beliefs with the view of "mental constructs" that generate different beliefs and can persist over time (Benabou 2008).

4. The evidence shows that even in environments with widespread corruption, when policy initiatives provide credible incentives, monitoring, and enforcement, corruption is reduced (for example, Di Tella and Schargrodsky [2003]; Muralidharan, Niehaus, and Sukhtankar [2014]). The discussion in this section is not intended to underestimate the role of technologies that reduce opportunities for corruption or of investments in monitoring and enforcement. It is aimed at including the concepts of how beliefs and behavioral norms might matter as well. This discussion is important for exploring how other policy areas aimed at strengthening political incentives and changing political beliefs and behavioral norms can complement technological solutions to governance problems and increase the likelihood of take-up.

5. An example is provided by the exchange around the following blog post: http://blogs.worldbank.org/futuredevelopment/lessons-reducing-energy-subsidies.

Bibliography

Aiyar, Yamini, and Soumya Kapoor Mehta. 2015. "Spectators or Participants? Effects of Social Audits in Andhra Pradesh." *Economic and Political Weekly* 50 (7): 66–71.

Alesina, Alberto, and Paola Giuliano. Forthcoming. "Culture and Institutions." *Journal of Economic Literature.*

Alesina, Alberto, Stelios Michalopoulos, and Elias Papaioannou. Forthcoming. "Ethnic Inequality." *Journal of Political Economy.*

Anand, Rahul, David Coady, Adil Mohommad, Vimal Thakoor, and James P. Walsh. 2013. "The Fiscal and Welfare Impacts of Reforming Fuel Subsidies in India." IMF Working Paper 13/128. International Monetary Fund, Washington, DC.

Arze del Granado, J., D. Coady, and R. Gillingham. 2012. "The Unequal Benefits of Fuel Subsidies: A Review of Evidence for Developing Countries." *World Development* 40 (11): 2234–48.

Ashraf, Q., and O. Galor. 2013. "The Out of Africa Hypothesis, Human Genetic Diversity and Comparative Economic Development." *American Economic Review* 102 (1): 1–46.

Banerjee, Abhijit V., Rukmini Banerji, Esther Duflo, Rachel Glennerster, and Stuti Khemani. 2010. "Pitfalls of Participatory Programs: Evidence from a Randomized Evaluation in Education in India." *American Economic Journal: Economic Policy* 2 (1): 1–30.

Banerjee, Abhijit, Donald Green, Jennifer Green, and Rohini Pande. 2009. "Can Voters Be Primed to Choose Better Legislators? Evidence from Two Field Experiments in Rural India." Unpublished.

Banerjee, Abhijit, Donald P. Green, Jeffery McManus, and Rohini Pande. 2014. "Are Poor Voters Indifferent to Whether Elected Leaders Are Criminal or Corrupt? A Vignette Experiment in Rural India." *Political Communication* 31 (3): 391–407.

Banerjee, Abhijit, and Rohini Pande. 2007. "Parochial Politics: Ethnic Preferences and Politician Corruption." Working Paper, Kennedy School of Government, Harvard University, Cambridge, MA.

Bardhan, Pranab, and Dilip Mookherjee. 2000. "Capture and Governance at Local and National Levels." *American Economic Review* 90 (2): 135–39.

———. 2010. "Determinants of Redistributive Politics: An Empirical Analysis of Land Reforms in West Bengal, India." *American Economic Review* 100 (4): 1572–600.

Basu, K. 2015. *The Republic of Beliefs: A New Approach to Law and Economics.* Washington, DC: World Bank.

Benabou, R. 2008, "Ideology." *Journal of the European Economic Association* 6 (2–3): 321–52.

Burgess, Robin, Benjamin Olken, Matthew Hansen, Peter Potapov, and Stefanie Sieber. 2012. "The Political Economy of Deforestation in the Tropics." *Quarterly Journal of Economics* 127 (4): 1707–54.

Callen, Michael, Saad Gulzar, Ali Hasanain, and Yasir Khan. 2014. "The Political Economy of Public Employee Absence: Experimental Evidence from Pakistan: Do Local Politics Determine the Effectiveness of Development Interventions? Why Are Service Providers Commonly Absent in Developing Countries?" Unpublished, Harvard Kennedy School.

Clements, Benedict J., David Coady, Stefania Fabrizio, Sanjeev Gupta, Trevor Alleyne, and Carlo Sdralevich, eds. 2013. *Energy Subsidy Reform: Lessons and Implications.* Washington, DC: International Monetary Fund.

Dal Bó, Ernesto. 2007. "Bribing Voters." *American Journal of Political Science* 51(4): 789–803.

Dal Bó, Ernesto, Pedro Dal Bó, and Erik Eyster. 2013. "The Demand for Bad Policy When Voters Underappreciate Equilibrium Effects." Unpublished working paper. http://faculty.haas.berkeley.edu/dalbo/demand_for_bad_policy.pdf.

Dal Bó, Pedro. 2007. "Social Norms, Cooperation and Inequality." *Economic Theory* 30 (1): 89–105.

Das, Jishnu, Alaka Holla, Aakash Mohpal, and Karthik Muralidharan. 2015. "Quality and Accountability in Healthcare Delivery: Audit Evidence from Primary Care Providers in India." Policy Research Working Paper No. WPS 7334, World Bank, Washington, DC.

Depuru, Soma Shekara Sreenadh Reddy, Lingfeng Wang, and Vijay Devabhaktuni. 2011. "Electricity Theft: Overview, Issues, Prevention and a Smart Meter Based Approach to Control Theft." *Energy Policy* 39 (2): 1007–15.

Di Tella, R., and E. Schargrodsky. 2003. "The Role of Wages and Auditing during a Crackdown on Corruption in the City of Buenos Aires." *Journal of Law and Economics* 46 (1): 269–92.

Diwan, Ishac, Philip Keefer, and Marc Schiffbauer. 2015. "Pyramid Capitalism: Political Connections, Regulation, and Firm Productivity in Egypt." World Bank Policy Research Working Paper 7354, World Bank, Washington, DC.

Faccio, Mara. 2006. "Politically Connected Firms." *American Economic Review* 96 (1): 369–86.

Fan, C. Simon, Chen Lin, and Daniel Treisman. 2009. "Political Decentralization and Corruption: Evidence from around the World." *Journal of Public Economics* 93 (1–2): 14–34.

Fisman, David, Raymond J. Fisman, Julia Galef, Rakesh Khurana, and Yongxiang Wang. 2012. "Estimating the Value of Connections to Vice-President Cheney." *BE Journal of Economic Analysis and Policy* 13 (3): 1–20.

Fisman, Raymond. 2001. "Estimating the Value of Political Connections." *American Economic Review* 91(4): 1095–102.

Fisman, Raymond, and Edward Miguel. 2007. "Corruption, Norms, and Legal Enforcement: Evidence from Diplomatic Parking Tickets." *Journal of Political Economy* 115 (6): 1020–48.

Fisman, Raymond, and Jakob Svensson. 2007. "Are Corruption and Taxation Really Harmful to Growth? Firm Level Evidence." *Journal of Development Economics* 83 (1): 63–75.

Garg, Teevrat. 2014. "Public Health Effects of Natural Resource Degradation: Evidence from Deforestation in Indonesia." Job Market Paper, Cornell University, Ithaca, NY.

Gilens, Martin, and Benjamin I. Page. 2014. "Testing Theories of American Politics: Elites, Interest Groups, and Average Citizens." *Perspectives on Politics* 12 (3): 564–81.

Glaeser, Edward, and Cass Sunstein. 2013. "Why Does Balanced News Produce Unbalanced Views?" NBER Working Paper 18975, National Bureau of Economic Research, Cambridge, MA.

Greif, Avner. 1994. "Cultural Beliefs and the Organization of Society: A Historical and Theoretical Reflection on Collectivist and Individualist Societies." *Journal of Political Economy* 102 (5): 912–50.

Grossman, Gene M., and Elhanan Helpman. 2001. *Special Interest Politics*. Cambridge and London: MIT Press.

Habyarimana, James, Macartan Humphreys, Daniel Posner, and Jeremy Weinstein. 2009. *Coethnicity: Diversity and the Dilemmas of Collective Action*. New York: Russell Sage Foundation.

Hanna, Rema, and Shing-Yi Wang. 2013. "Dishonesty and Selection into Public Service: Evidence from India." NBER Working Paper 19649, National Bureau of Economic Research, Cambridge, MA.

Hunt, Jennifer. 2007. "How Corruption Hits People when They Are Down." *Journal of Development Economics* 84 (2): 574–89.

Kahan, Dan M. 2012. "Ideology, Motivated Reasoning, and Cognitive Reflection: An Experimental Study." *Judgment and Decision Making* 8 (4): 407–24.

Kahan, Dan M., Hank Jenkins-Smith, and Donald Braman. 2011. "Cultural Cognition of Scientific Consensus." *Journal of Risk Research* 14 (2): 147–74.

Keefer, Philip, and Razvan Vlaicu. 2007. "Democracy, Credibility and Clientelism." *Journal of Law, Economics and Organization* 24 (2): 371–406.

Khwaja, Asim Ijaz, and Atif Mian. 2005. "Do Lenders Favor Politically Connected Firms? Rent Provision in an Emerging Financial Market." *Quarterly Journal of Economics* 120 (4): 1371–411.

La Forgia, Gerard M., Shomikho Raha, Shabbeer Shaik, Sunil Kumar Maheshwari, and Rabia Ali. 2014. "Parallel Systems and Human Resource Management in India's Public Health Services: A View from the Front Lines." Policy Research Working Paper No. 6953, World Bank, Washington, DC.

Lipsky, Michael. 1980. *Street-Level Bureaucracy: Dilemmas of the Individual in Public Services*. New York: Russell Sage Foundation.

Lui, Francis. 1986. "A Dynamic Model of Corruption Deterrence." *Journal of Public Economics* 31 (2): 215–36.

Mauro, Paolo. 1995. "Corruption and Growth." *Quarterly Journal of Economics* 110 (3): 681–712.

McMillan, John, and Pablo Zoido. 2004. "How to Subvert Democracy: Montesinos in Peru." *Journal of Economic Perspectives* 18 (4): 69–92.

Miguel, E., and M. K. Gugerty. 2005. "Ethnic Diversity, Social Sanctions, and Public Goods in Kenya." *Journal of Public Economics* 89 (11): 2325–68.

Min, Brian. 2015. *Power and the Vote: Elections and Electricity in the Developing World*. New York: Cambridge University Press.

Min, Brian, and Miriam Golden. 2014. "Electoral Cycles in Electricity Losses in India." *Energy Policy* 65: 619 –25.

Muralidharan, Karthik, Paul Niehaus, and Sandip Sukhtankar. 2014. "Building State Capacity: Evidence from Biometric Smartcards in India." NBER Working Paper 19999, National Bureau of Economic Research, Cambridge, MA.

Olken, Benjamin. 2007. "Monitoring Corruption: Evidence from a Field Experiment in Indonesia." *Journal of Political Economy* 115 (2): 200–49.

Olken, Benjamin, and Patrick Barron. 2009. "The Simple Economics of Extortion: Evidence from Trucking in Aceh." *Journal of Political Economy* 117 (3): 417–52.

Olken, Benjamin A., and Rohini Pande. 2012. "Corruption in Developing Countries." *Annual Review of Economics* 4 (1): 479–509.

Rijkers, Bob, Caroline Freund, and Antonio Nucifora. 2014. "All in the Family: State Capture in Tunisia." World Bank Policy Research Working Paper 6810, World Bank, Washington, DC.

Steavenson, Wendell. 2011. "Letter from Cairo: On the Square—Between the Protesters and the Military." *New Yorker*, February 28, 36–45.

Sunstein, Cass. 2007. "On the Divergent American Reactions to Terrorism and Climate Change." *Columbia Law Review* 107 (2): 503–57.

Tirole, Jean. 1996. "A Theory of Collective Reputations (with Applications to the Persistence of Corruption and to Firm Quality)." *Review of Economic Studies* 63 (1): 1–22.

World Bank. 2011. *World Development Report 2011: Conflict, Security, and Development*. Washington, DC: World Bank. https://openknowledge.worldbank.org/handle/10986/4389.

Zimmerman, Brigitte. 2014. "Transparency, Sanctioning Capacity, and Corruption Displacement: Multi-Method Evidence from Local Government in Malawi." PhD Dissertation, University of California San Diego.

CHAPTER TWO

Political Engagement

Overview

The role of citizens in influencing governance is the central theme of this report. Citizen engagement in government comes in many varieties, including non-political ways in which citizens can participate in service delivery, provide inputs and feedback at the invitation of government officials, and play a role in monitoring the performance of government agencies. This report emphasizes the crucial role of citizens' political engagement, distinguishing it from other non-political forms of citizen engagement.

Political engagement is the participation of citizens in selecting and sanctioning the leaders who wield power in government, including by entering themselves as contenders for leadership. Political engagement includes citizen actions as voters, as actual and potential challengers for leadership positions in government, and in organized groups that pressure elected politicians and appointed public officials through civil society action and public protests.

The leaders who are selected through political engagement, in turn, delegate to public officials and frontline providers the many tasks of delivering public goods and services. These leaders also choose policies for citizen engagement in the business of government.

Some forms engage citizens as "co-producers" of public goods, such as by managing and allocating budgets and delivering services, while other forms try to make public officials and frontline providers more accountable for good performance by engaging citizens to monitor their delivery of public goods. The assumption is that, even without formal powers to select and sanction officials, citizens will be able to exact accountability through social pressure. Reviews of research on the impact of social accountability initiatives conclude that their benefits are limited in the face of fundamental failures in the political process and low incentives for leaders to respond to citizens (Grandvoinnet, Aslam, and Raha 2015; Mansuri and Rao 2013). Effectiveness of social accountability initiatives will depend on the incentives of leaders to take citizen monitoring, feedback, and complaints seriously and use their formal powers over public officials to ultimately hold them accountable. This point will be supported by the research reviews contained in the latter chapters of this report.

This chapter presents evidence of growing trends in political engagement across and within countries, through electoral institutions, public protests, and civil society organizations.

Political engagement through elections

Political engagement happens in every institutional context, from democracies to autocracies, albeit in different ways. A variety of formal political institutions are found around the world that structure the degree to which the power to select and sanction leaders is diffused across many citizens acting as individual voters versus concentrated among elites or organized groups such as political parties. Even when formal institutions restrict the power of "ordinary" citizens, who hold no public office and are not organized into influential groups, research suggests that leaders are nevertheless constrained by the informal powers of non-elite citizens to engage in protests or revolts. At the same time, formal electoral institutions have spread across and within countries, expanding the power of individuals to select and sanction leaders as voters. Citizen responses to public opinion surveys provide evidence of citizens' perceptions of and participation in elections. Citizens, especially the poor and less educated, report active participation in elections across a variety of institutional contexts. Even where electoral violence and fraud, vote buying, and ethnic conflict are common, citizens nevertheless express their beliefs that elections matter for beneficial change and that through their vote, they can improve their lives.

Figure 2.1 plots the distribution of countries ranked by the Polity IV measure of democracy, with higher values corresponding to greater space for political engagement by citizens.[1] During the past three and a half decades, the overall distribution of political institutions across countries has steadily shifted toward those that allow greater political engagement.

Figure 2.1 Global shift toward democratic institutions for political engagement

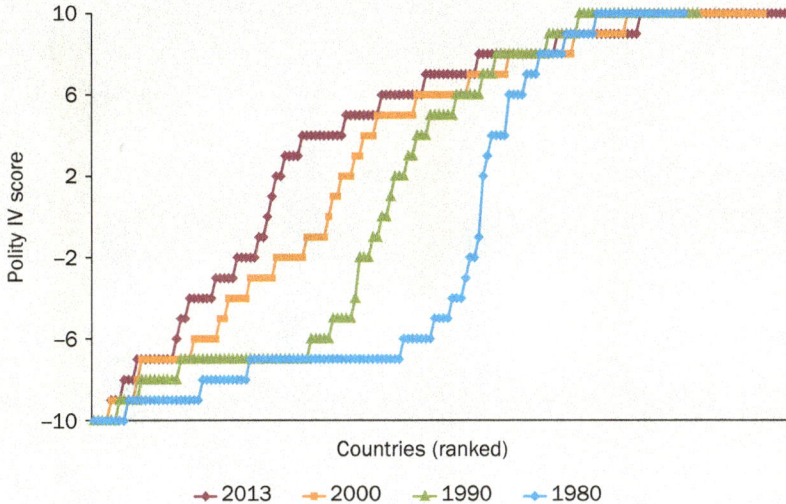

Source: Data from the Polity IV project. The Polity IV Score is a measure of state authority that is widely used in research, varying on a 21-point scale ranging from −10 (which corresponds to hereditary monarchy) to +10 (which corresponds to the Polity IV view of consolidated democracy). Higher values are thus associated with more democratic institutions.

Although some individual countries have experienced reversals to more autocratic institutions or have seen little change, the overall trend has been toward greater opportunities for political engagement.

Figure 2.2 shows that between 1980 and 2013, the fraction of democratic countries measured by Polity IV doubled from 28 percent to 56 percent and the fraction of autocratic countries declined from 54 percent to 12 percent.[2] Another initiative that measures opportunities for political engagement, Freedom House, provides indicators that are consistent with the Polity IV trends. Rather than assessing the characteristics of government institutions, as in the case of Polity IV, Freedom House measures the freedoms enjoyed by individuals. Figure 2.2 also shows that the fraction of countries rated as "free" by Freedom House increased over the same period from 31 percent to 46 percent, while the fraction of "not free" countries declined from 37 percent to 26 percent.[3]

Figures 2.1 and 2.2 show a clear trend toward greater space for political engagement by citizens. However, scrutiny of recent years indicates that such trends have plateaued with comparably negligible gains in recent

Figure 2.2 Countries categorized as "free" and "democratic," 1980 and 2013

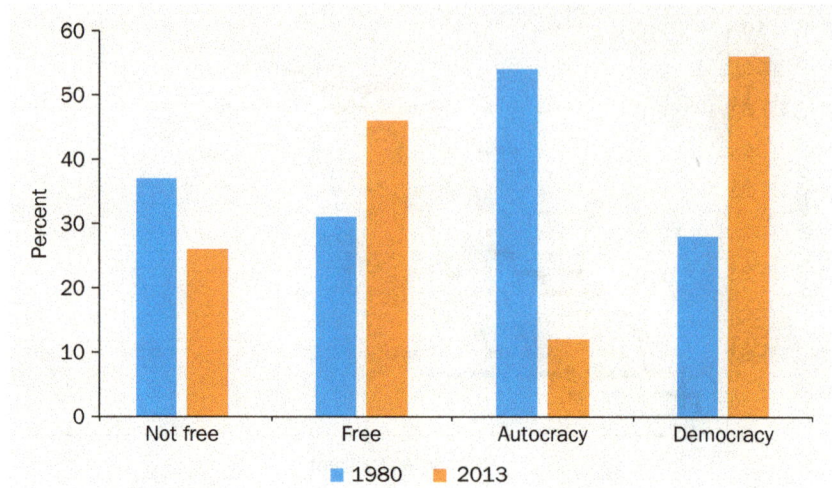

Source: Based on Freedom House and Polity IV data.
Note: Data representing "not free" and "free" are from Freedom House, while "autocracy" and "democracy" are from Polity IV.

times. Freedom House has documented declines in overall political rights and civil liberties. During 2014, nearly twice as many countries saw downturns as gains in democratic indicators, a trend that was not confined to any geographic area (Puddington 2015).

Self-reported voter turnout and interest in elections

Public opinion surveys—the World Values Survey, the Gallup World Poll, and the Afrobarometer—provide evidence of citizens' perceptions and participation in elections. Citizens report active participation in elections across a variety of institutional contexts (figure 2.3). More than 85 percent of all respondents in the regions of Europe and Central Asia, Latin America, and in the Organisation for Economic Co-operation and Development (OECD), report voting in the most recent election in their country. In the regions where most of the poorest people live, Africa and South Asia, more than 70 percent of respondents report voting. In these regions, citizens with less than a primary education, and therefore likely to be relatively poor, are *more* likely to report voting. For example, citizens in Africa with less than a primary education report voting 7 percentage points more than others and in South Asia 10 percentage points more than others.

Self-reported voting rates need to be interpreted cautiously due to the well-known problem that reported voting is likely to be greater than actual

Figure 2.3 Self-reported voting rates, by region

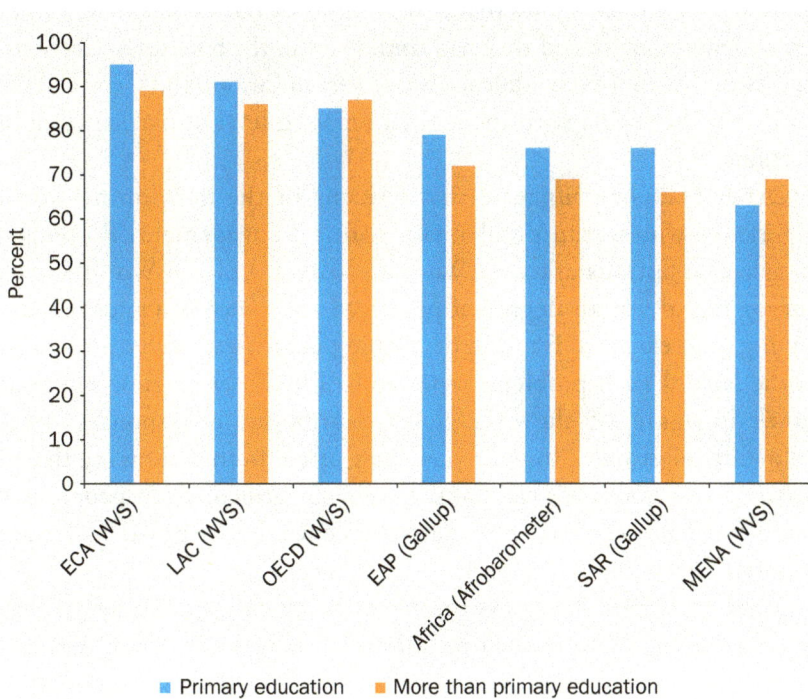

■ Primary education ■ More than primary education

Sources: Afrobarometer Survey, Gallup World Poll, and World Values Survey (WVS).
Note: Reported voter turnout rates in national elections by education and region. For each region, the source was chosen based on which one had a larger number of countries represented. EAP = East Asia and Pacific; ECA = Europe and Central Asia; LAC = Latin America and the Caribbean; MENA = the Middle East and North Africa; OECD = Organisation for Economic Co-operation and Development; SAR = South Asia.

voting. For example, although Afrobarometer survey data show that more than 80 percent of Ugandans report voting in the February 2011 elections, actual turnout reported by the election committee was slightly less than 60 percent. Yet, the pattern reported in figure 2.3 of less-educated citizens voting at higher rates than more educated citizens in some of the poor regions of the world is supported by other research evidence. Pande (2011) estimates that in many developing countries, less-educated and income-poor citizens tend to be more politically active than those with greater education and income. In contrast, in developed countries, the richer and more-educated citizens are clearly more politically active. Evidence also suggests that in autocratic institutional environments, more-educated citizens are likely to "deliberately disengage" from political processes because they are more critical of the legitimacy and effectiveness of those processes (Croke et al. 2015).

Surveys also reveal that citizens question the fairness and integrity of elections. Figure 2.4 shows that according to Gallup, fewer than half of respondents globally said they had confidence in the honesty of elections. Interestingly, reported confidence was lowest in Europe and Central Asia, yet that is the region with the highest reported level of participation in elections.

Other evidence suggests that citizens in the developing world experience widespread problems in political engagement. Responses to several questions asked in Wave 6 (2010–14) of the World Values Survey reveal a high degree of perceived incidence of violence, vote buying, and electoral fraud in developing countries, in sharp contrast to the lack of such problems reported in OECD countries. The four panels in figure 2.5 show the global distribution of responses to the following questions: "In your view, how often do the following things occur in this country's elections: Voters are bribed? Rich people buy elections? Voters are threatened by violence at the polls? Votes are counted fairly?"[4]

Panel a of figure 2.5 shows the extent to which respondents perceive voters as being bribed in their countries. In countries in South Asia and

Figure 2.4   Confidence in the honesty of elections, by region

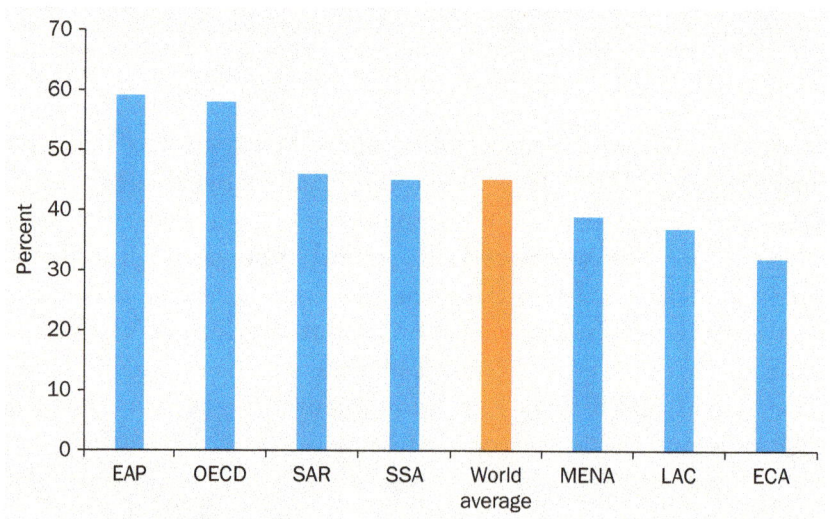

Source: Gallup World Poll 2007–13.
Note: Percent responding "yes" by region to the question, "Do you have confidence in the honesty of elections?" EAP = East Asia and Pacific; ECA = Europe and Central Asia; LAC = Latin America and the Caribbean; MENA = the Middle East and North Africa; OECD = Organisation for Economic Co-operation and Development; SAR = South Asia; SSA = Sub-Saharan Africa.

Sub-Saharan Africa, 56 percent and 42 percent of respondents, respectively, report their view that voters are bribed "very" or "fairly often," compared with only 12 percent in OECD countries. The average in the East Asia and Pacific region, at 39 percent, is lower than that of South

Figure 2.5 Citizens' views on electoral malpractice

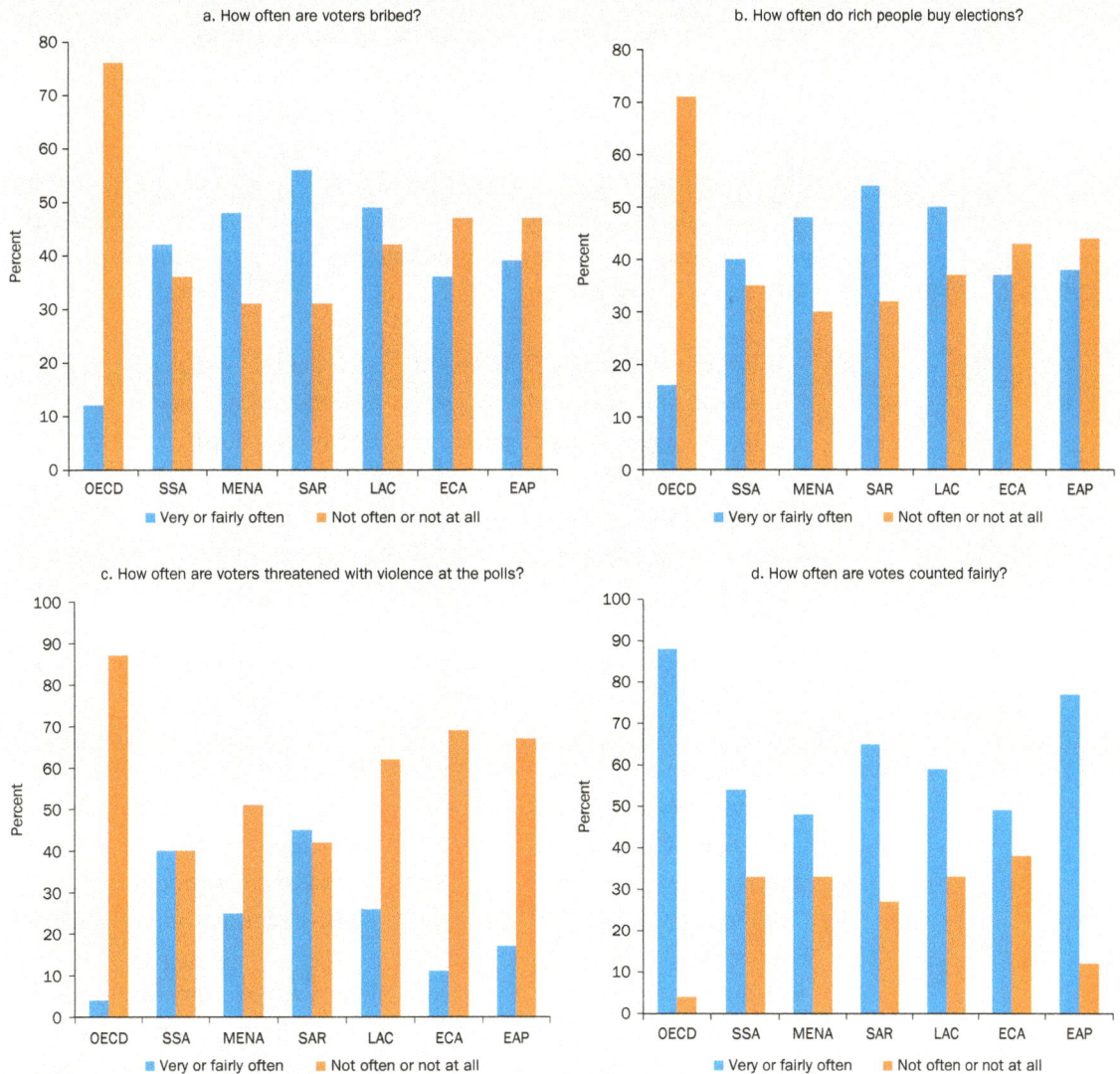

Source: World Values Survey (Wave 6 undertaken over 2010–14).
Note: EAP = East Asia and Pacific; ECA = Europe and Central Asia; LAC = Latin America and the Caribbean; MENA = the Middle East and North Africa; OECD = Organisation for Economic Co-operation and Development; SAR = South Asia; SSA = Sub-Saharan Africa.

Asia and Sub-Saharan Africa. Consistent with the pattern of responses on the voter-bribing question, respondents in the poorer regions of the world are more likely to believe that the economic elites in their countries can purchase election outcomes for their benefit (figure 2.5, panel b).

Panel c of figure 2.5 shows the prevalence of violence in elections in the developing regions of the world, compared with the OECD countries. Similarly, responses to the questions on whether the government agencies responsible for the conduct of elections perform their functions to support free and fair elections show a pronounced difference between the poor and richer regions of the world (figure 2.5, panel d).

Experience with violence, electoral fraud, vote buying, and ethnic conflict in the developing world has prompted several investigative journalists and commentators to question the value of elections in weakly governed societies and the capacity of poor and uneducated voters to exercise their franchise responsibly. Rodrik and Wacziarg (2005, 50) provide the following quotes in this regard:

> Robert D. Kaplan (2000 p. 62) states that "If a society is not in reasonable health, democracy can be not only risky but disastrous." Fareed Zakaria (2003, p. 98) points out that "although democracy has in many ways opened up African politics and brought people liberty, it has also produced a degree of chaos and instability that has actually made corruption and lawlessness worse in many countries." Amy Chua (2002, p. 124) argues that: "'... in the numerous countries around the world with a market-dominant minority, adding democracy to markets has been a recipe for instability, upheaval, and ethnic conflagration."

In contrast to the above opinions among external observers of electoral malpractice, citizens still tend to believe that elections matter for beneficial change, that through their votes they can improve their lives. The two panels of figure 2.6 show the share of individuals by region who described elections as being very or rather important on a personal and national level, respectively.

Similar patterns were obtained from two Afrobarometer surveys that were undertaken in Uganda and Nigeria on the eve of their elections in 2011 and 2007, respectively. In these surveys, about 80 percent of respondents in Uganda and 70 percent in Nigeria said that they believed the way they voted could make things better (figure 2.7). Those respondents who are likely to be poor, with low education, and reporting food insecurity, are just as likely as others to express the belief that the way they vote could make things better.

Figure 2.6   Citizens' views of the importance of elections

a. Does having honest elections make a lot of difference in your and your family's lives? Percentage of respondents answering "very" or "rather" important

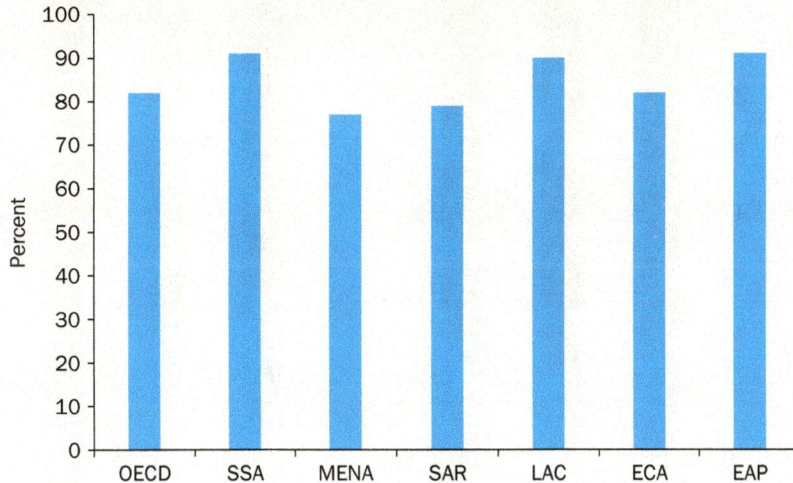

b. How important is having honest elections for whether the country develops economically?

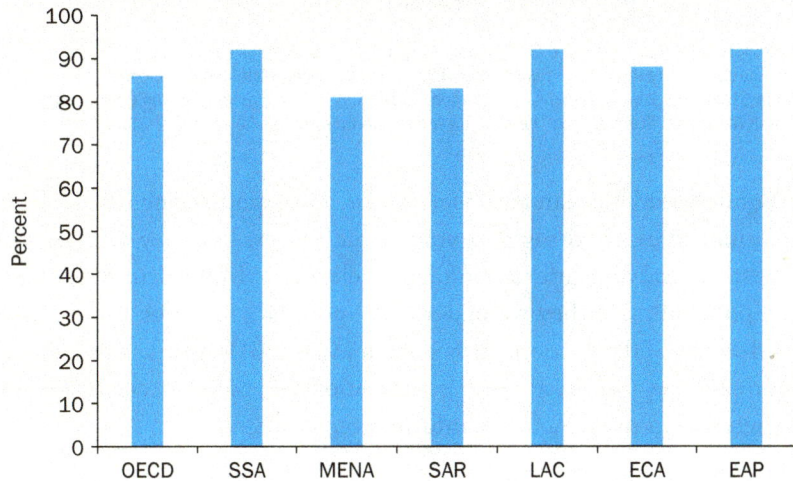

Source: World Values Survey (Wave 6 undertaken over 2010–14).
Note: EAP = East Asia and Pacific; ECA = Europe and Central Asia; LAC = Latin America and the Caribbean; MENA = the Middle East and North Africa; OECD = Organisation for Economic Co-operation and Development; SAR = South Asia; SSA = Sub-Saharan Africa.

Figure 2.7 Citizens' beliefs about whether the way they vote could make things better, Uganda (2011) and Nigeria (2007)

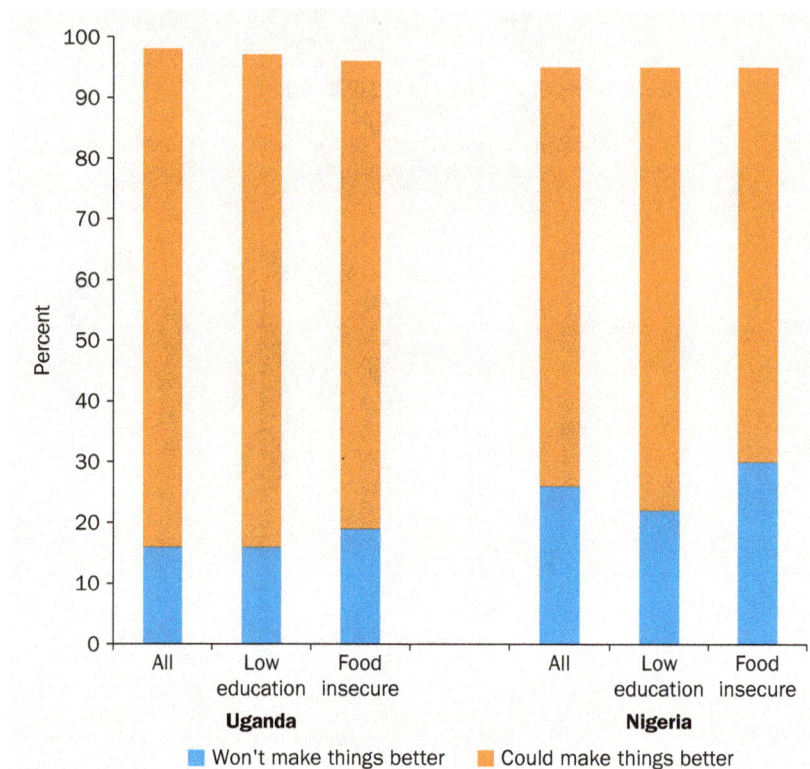

Source: Afrobarometer Round 4.5.2 (Uganda 2011), Round 3.5 (Nigeria 2007).
Note: The survey question is the following: "Which of the following statements is closest to your view? Choose Statement 1 or Statement 2. Statement 1: No matter how you vote, it won't make things any better in the future. Statement 2: The way you vote could make things better in the future."

Not only do Ugandan and Nigerian citizens report strong beliefs about the importance of voting and vote at high rates, but they also express interest in receiving information about elections. More than 80 percent of respondents said they wanted a little more or a lot more information ahead of the 2007 elections in Nigeria and the 2011 elections in Uganda (figure 2.8). Again, those with less education and food insecurity are just as interested in receiving more information as others.

Subnational electoral institutions

Evidence also indicates that political engagement is growing within countries, even in countries with low scores on Polity IV. This engagement is

Figure 2.8 How much more information do citizens want in order to decide how to vote, Uganda (2011) and Nigeria (2007)

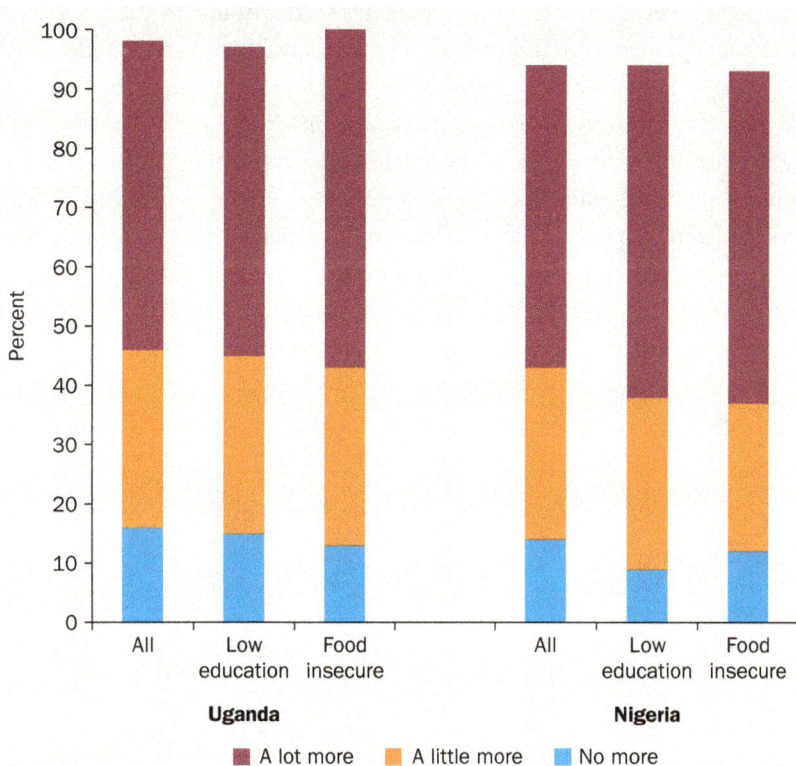

Source: Afrobarometer Round 4.5.1 (Uganda 2011), Round 3.5 (Nigeria 2007).
Note: The survey question is the following: "In order to decide how to vote in the upcoming elections, how much more information would you like to have?"

happening through the spread of elections at local levels of government, widespread citizen participation in these elections as voters and as contenders for leadership, and the rise of civil society organizations. Changes in political engagement at the local level could potentially translate into larger changes at the national level, with local levels serving as the training ground for citizens to develop their political beliefs and political behavioral norms (Giuliano and Nunn 2013). The local level can also serve to develop a supply of good leaders who have built reputations for responsible management of public resources (Myerson 2006, 2012).

This section provides case studies of the spread of local electoral competition in three different contexts—India, Indonesia, and Uganda—to illustrate the growth of political engagement within countries with different national political institutions. During the past three decades, these three countries have had dissimilar trajectories in institutional reform and political change, as reflected in their respective Polity IV trends in figure 2.9. India has maintained functioning representative democratic institutions, reflected in its Polity score of 8 until 1995, and thereafter 9. Meanwhile, Indonesia represents a transitional case, having jumped from –7 to 8 in the time frame of seven years following the end of President Suharto's rule. Finally, Uganda has seen comparatively smaller changes in measures of regime authority, shifting upward from –7 to –1. Each of these country cases, therefore, illustrates a distinct regime at the national level—consistently strongly democratic (at least as measured on Polity IV), rapidly transitional, and slow institutional change out of weak democracy (again, as measured by Polity IV).

Despite such contrasting measures of institutional trends at the national level, political engagement at the subnational level has been growing in all

Figure 2.9 Polity IV trends in India, Indonesia, and Uganda, 1986–2012

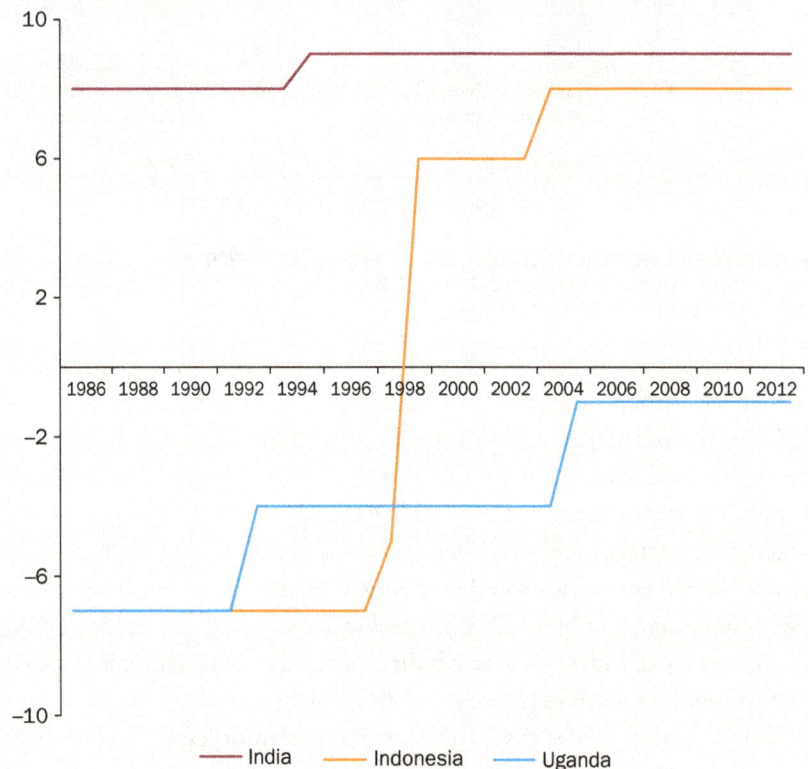

Source: Data from Polity IV.

three countries. In Indonesia and Uganda, for example, space for political engagement has grown as the result of proliferation of new subnational political units. And India has seen a marked increase in contending political parties in state elections.

The case of India

Changes in political engagement within India appear to take the form of more citizens engaging as contenders for leadership rather than greater participation as voters. Figure 2.10 shows the rise of political parties in India that contest elections at the state level. This trend is directly linked to a fall in the number of political candidates who are registered as "independents," demonstrating increasing political organization of parties. Figure 2.10 also shows that voter turnout has been relatively stable over time.

At the same time, however, India exhibits substantial volatility in the vote shares accruing to different political parties. Electoral volatility

Figure 2.10   **Number of contending political parties and voter turnout in Indian states, 1985–2014**

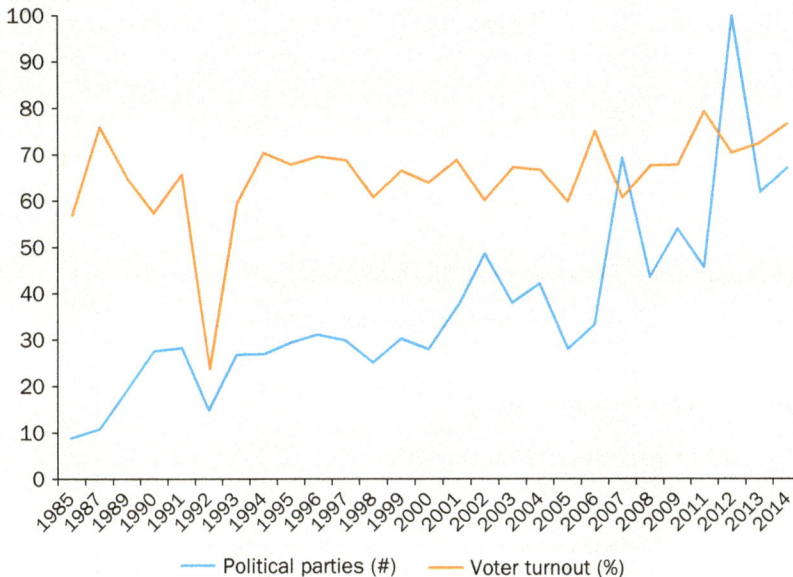

Source: Election Commission of India (http://eci.nic.in/eci/eci.html).
Note: Number of parties and turnout are each averaged over the following 14 states of India: Andhra Pradesh, Bihar, Gujarat, Haryana, Karnataka, Kerala, Madhya Pradesh, Maharashtra, Odisha, Punjab, Rajasthan, Tamil Nadu, Uttar Pradesh, and West Bengal.

in India is orders of magnitude higher than in any other country that experiences regular and contested elections (Nooruddin and Chhibber 2008).

All together, the patterns for India, the largest and poorest democracy in the developing world, suggest vigorous political competition resulting from political engagement by citizens. Citizens contribute to competition for leadership in government by engaging as critical voters who shift their votes across multiple political parties and as contesting candidates.

The case of Indonesia

Indonesia's "big bang" decentralization in 2001 substantially increased the number of jurisdictions in which citizens can engage to select and sanction the leaders who manage those jurisdictions (table 2.1). The number of districts increased from 336 in 2001, to 477 in 2010 (Skoufias et al. 2014).

Table 2.1   Large number of jurisdictions for political engagement in Indonesia

National level	
People's Representative Council (DPR) – 560 seats	Regional Representative Council (DPD) – 132 seats
Provincial level	
Provincial Legislative Assembly (DPRD) – one in 33 provinces (35-100 members)	Head: Governor
District level (consists of 398 regencies and 98 municipalities)	
House of Representatives (20-50 members)	Head: Regent (*bupati*) and Mayor (*walikota*)
Subdistricts (6,093 *kedamatans*)	
Head: *Camat*, appointed by Regent or Mayor	
Administrative village	
Kelurahan (7,878 within municipalities) – head *lurah* appointed by subdistrict head	*Desa* (65,189 within regencies) – civilian head *kepla desa* directly elected by villagers every 6 years

Source: Data on number of jurisdictions from Fitrani, Hofman, and Kaiser (2005).

A significant element of decentralization was the introduction of regional autonomy and the proliferation of local governments at the district level, with the avowed intent of improving public service delivery and government effectiveness.

Beginning in 2001, local governments in Indonesia were able to lobby the central government to split their districts. Pierskalla and Sacks (2014) consider the underlying motivations behind this district proliferation. More important than efficiency in public goods provision, Pierskalla and Sacks (2014) argue that ethnic homogeneity is a chief reason for district growth. Beyond ethnic considerations, this study also indicates that local elites' political capacity to lobby for new districts is an important determinant of local government growth. These findings update research by Fitrani, Hofman, and Kaiser (2005), who consider a similar question in a more limited time period, 1999–2004. They identify three determinants of district growth in Indonesia: geographic considerations, ethnic clustering, and relative size of government.

The decentralization reforms in Indonesia included a provision requiring members of the local legislature to be elected by popular vote rather than be appointed. In 2005, parliamentary elections for district heads were replaced by direct elections, known as *pilkada*.[5]

Figure 2.11 panel a illustrates the striking fact that no district in the first local election was uncontested, and, on average, four candidates contested each district. Figure 2.11 panel b shows the distribution of the share of votes received by the winner. The modal winning vote share was

Figure 2.11 Number of candidates running and share of votes won by the winner, per district, in the first local election, Indonesia

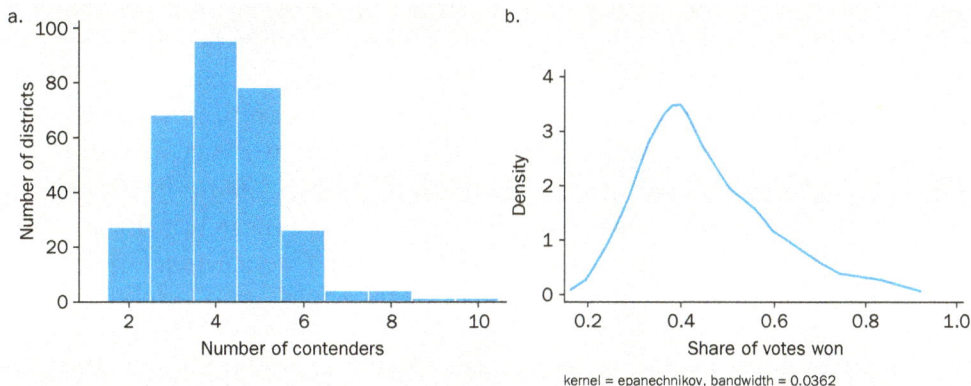

Source: Indonesian Election Commission (KPU) (http://www.kpu.go.id/).

roughly 40 percent, indicating that elections were competitive with few overwhelming margins of victory.

The proliferation of local jurisdictions in which leaders can be elected is significant because it provides space for citizens to engage not only as voters but also as contenders for leadership. Competition at this level can serve as an incubator for candidates at the national level. For example, Indonesian President Joko Widodo served as mayor of Surakarta, a city of 520,000 in Central Java Province, and then as governor of Jakarta, a city of more than 8 million, before becoming president of the country. President Widodo's trajectory from the local to the national level reflects this broadening of the political arena.

Competition is a feature of elections in Indonesia at all levels. Indonesia's 2014 legislative elections occurred on a strikingly large scale. Seats contested in the legislative elections, including the national, provincial, and district levels, numbered 19,699, for which there were 235,637 candidates or, an average, nearly 12 contestants per seat. Some 6,608 candidates competed for 560 seats in the lower house of the national assembly, again corresponding to roughly 12 contestants per seat (Rachman 2014).

The case of Uganda

In Uganda, the rise of the National Resistance Movement in the 1980s led to the implementation of decentralization reforms. Direct popular elections were mandated at all levels of local government, and the Local Government Act of 1997 increased the powers of local councils, such as power over the recruitment and firing of local civil servants (Green 2010). There are five tiers of local authority. The primary unit of local government is the district council, which contains within its boundaries between one and five second-tier county and municipal councils. These, in turn, contain third-tier subcounty and town councils, which are subdivided into fourth-tier parish councils. At the lowest, fifth-tier level of local government are village (rural) or ward (urban) councils. Districts are responsible for managing transfers from the central government and are able to impose taxes and legislate bylaws. Following decentralization reforms, the number of districts in Uganda increased from 39 in 1995, to 70 in 2005, to 112 in 2011 (figure 2.12).

As in Indonesia's 2014 legislative elections, Uganda's 2011 elections saw the country's largest number of electoral seats being contested:

Figure 2.12 District growth and average district population, Uganda, 1960–2009

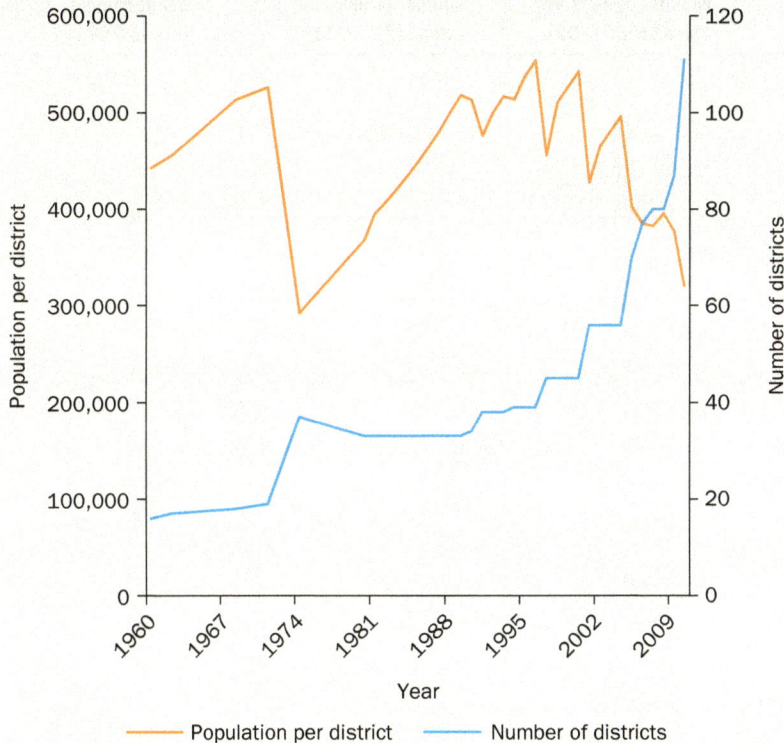

Sources: Data on a number of districts are from the Electoral Commission of Uganda (http://www.ec.or.ug/). Population data are from the World Development Indicators.

375 members of parliament; 112 district chairpersons and their 2,817 district councilors; 27 municipality or city division chairpersons and 3,586 councilors; and 1,327 subcounty, town, or municipal division chairpersons and 20,524 councilors (Uganda Electoral Commission). The number of electoral areas in Uganda increased markedly between 2001 and 2011. For example, table 2.2 shows that the number of district chairpersons doubled, while the number of directly elected district councilors increased nearly 40 percent. Between Uganda's 2006 and 2011 elections, an additional 14 counties and 9 municipalities were created, which became new parliamentary constituencies. Figure 2.13 shows that there was an average of 3.5 contenders for each position and only 21 district councilors ran uncontested, out of 355 positions. Meanwhile, the average share of votes won by the winning district councilor was 54 percent.

Table 2.2   Change in number of electoral areas, Uganda, 2001/02 to 2010/11

Category of electoral area	Number of electoral areas (2001/02)	Number of electoral areas (2010/11)	Percent change (2001 to 2011)
President	1	1	0
Parliamentary, directly elected	214	238	11
District chairpersons	56	112	100
District directly elected councilors	967	1,339	38
Municipality or city division mayors	18	27	50
Municipality or city division directly elected councilors	254	385	52
Subcounty, town, or municipal division chairpersons	956	1,321	38
Subcounty, town, or municipal division directly elected councilors	5,206	7,332	41
Parliamentary district women representatives	56	112	100
District women councilors	607	921	52
Municipality or city division women councilors	166	249	50
Subcounty, town, or municipal division women councilors	4,741	6,600	39

Source: Electoral Commission of Uganda (http://www.ec.or.ug/).

Figure 2.13   Number of candidates running for district councilor and share of votes received by the winner, Uganda, 2011

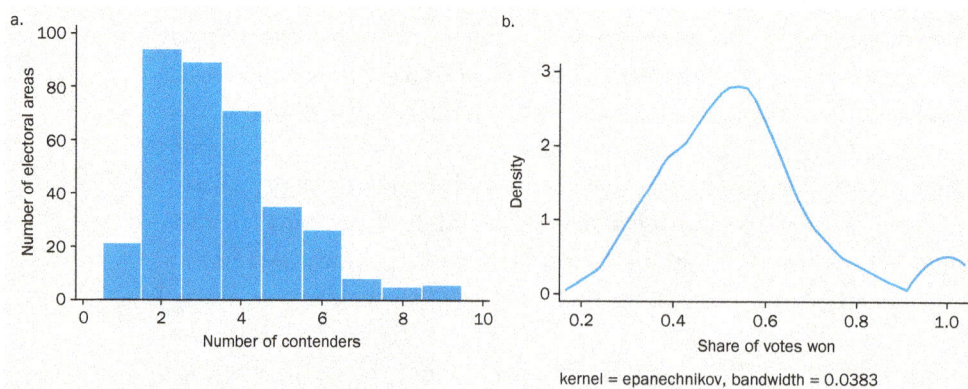

Source: Electoral Commission of Uganda (http://www.ec.or.ug/).

The creation of new local governments and rising competition for legislative positions raise questions about the causes behind the formation of new districts, which could influence the nature of electoral contestation in these new jurisdictions. The spread of local direct elections does not guarantee a commensurate increase in accountability or lowering of barriers to entry for new leaders. In fact, decentralization of political and administrative authority might increase capture of local government and raise barriers to entry if local interest groups collude. The net impact of local government proliferation on regional development and fragmentation is not evident (Mookherjee 2015).

Similar to findings in Indonesia, Grossman and Lewis (2014) show that counties in Uganda are more likely to secede and form a new district when they are underrepresented in district committees that oversee the allocation of intra-district resources. Moreover, in counties where the largest ethnic group differs from that of the district, the county is more likely to secede. From a national perspective, elevating a county to the level of a district is associated with greater political support in that county for the national ruling party. Green (2010) argues that as reforms have dried up national-level channels of patronage, new districts have provided alternate channels. For example, in the 2005 presidential election, the vote share in favor of the national ruling party in newly created districts was 74 percent in comparison with the national Ugandan average of 60 percent (Green 2010). These patterns in the data on district creation in Uganda are consistent with the theoretical arguments in Khemani (2015) about how creation of local political jurisdictions can enable leaders to maintain clientelist relationships of vote buying and patronage. While the motivation behind the spread of local electoral institutions might not be encouraging about the prospects of healthy political competition, nevertheless, these three case studies show that space has grown at the local level for citizens to engage in political processes both as voters and as contenders for leadership. This spread of electoral institutions at the local level provides a fertile context to apply the lessons distilled in the following chapters of the report on leveraging transparency to improve the quality of local political engagement.

Political engagement by civil society

Political engagement happens not only through individual citizen's actions in elections alone, but also through the activities of organized groups in civil society across different national political systems. For example,

Ortiz et al. (2013) report that nonelectoral forms of political engagement such as public protests are growing over time. In the social accountability literature, political engagement by civil society groups outside of elections has been regarded as part of "social" accountability. [6] Civil society organizations carry out a diverse repertoire of activities that seek to pressure public officials through, for example, participatory monitoring and feedback, public complaint and grievance redress mechanisms, and participation in resource allocation decisions (Fox 2014; Malena, Forster, and Singh 2004). [7] Social accountability scholars have acknowledged, however, that there is little substantive distinction from political engagement, as defined in this report, when civil society activities are directed toward seeking accountability from leaders who wield power in government. McGee and Gaventa (2011, 8), for example, write, "The fact that these transparency and accountability initiatives are 'social' and 'citizen-led' rather than political or bureaucratic in nature should not eclipse the deeply political nature of the stakes." Claasen and Alpín-Lardiés state that social accountability "is about how citizens demand and enforce accountability from those in power" (2010, 3).

There are few sources of reliable data available to examine growth in citizen organizations. Part of the data gathering challenge lies in how citizen organizations are defined. An extensive literature in sociology makes a distinction between "civil society organizations" and "nongovernmental organizations" (CSOs and NGOs), with NGOs being typically associated with foreign-aid financed delivery of services and development programs (Lewis and Kanji 2007; Mercer 2002; Pearce 2000). While NGOs may be engaged first and foremost for the purpose of service delivery, under contract with international donors and government ministries, they can be a latent force for political engagement should they choose to extend their organizational capabilities to making demands upon and sanction leaders in government.

The United Nations (UN) provides data on the number of organizations that are registered with their national governments as NGOs, and as having an official headquarters, a democratically adopted constitution, and a transparent accounting system. These organizations have official consultative status with the UN. The UN data show a steady rise of these NGOs with consultative status, from 1,226 in 1996, to 4,045 in 2014 (figure 2.14). The numbers appear to be conservative compared with other estimates of the numbers of CSOs operating in countries, but without official status with the UN. According to data on CSOs compiled by the Quality of Government (QOG) initiative at the University of Gothenburg, Africa has 5,811, Latin America 3,504, South Asia 2,281, and East Asia

Figure 2.14   Growth in citizen organizations, 1996–2014

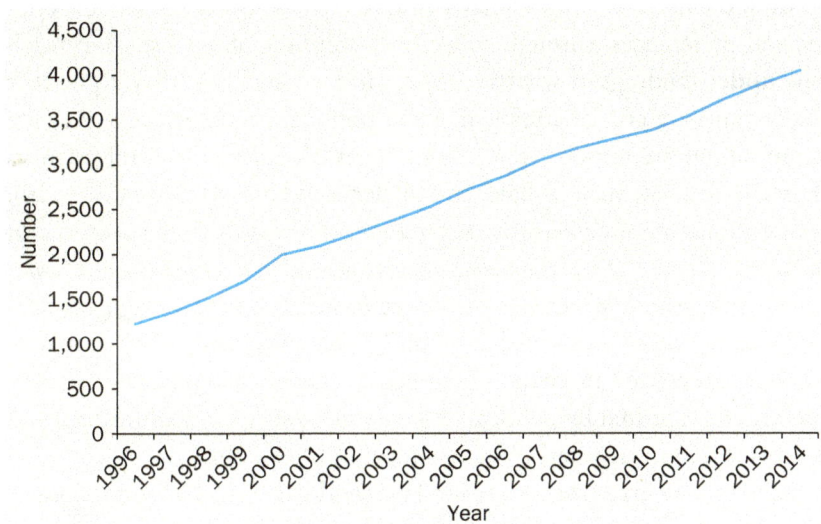

Source: United Nations, Department of Economic and Social Affairs, csonet.org.

1,516 CSOs, as of 2014.[8] However, the QOG data are only available for a cross-section of countries rather than over time.

Using a broader definition of citizen organization, the Johns Hopkins Center for Civil Society has gathered data on nonprofit NGOs. In their estimates, using data for 22 countries, the NGO sector is worth $1.1 trillion and employs more than 19 million people (Salamon et al. 1999). In other words, if the nonprofit sector in these countries were a separate national economy, it would be the eighth largest economy in the world, ahead of Brazil, the Russian Federation, Canada, and Spain. In Sub-Saharan Africa, about 79,000 national NGOs are in operation and are growing at a rate of 12 percent annually. There are approximately 54,000 national NGOs in South Asia and 68,000 in the Middle East and North Africa (both growing at 8 percent annually).[9]

Scholarship in sociology has highlighted the role of civil society in "deepening democracy" and influencing politics (Fox 1994; Heller 2009). First, it is argued that, "*civil society can facilitate the mobilization of underrepresented groups, who despite enjoying formal rights of citizenship, cannot process their claims through institutionalized channels. New collective actors in civil society can help to break through the self-reinforcing equilibrium of representative democracy in which those who have privilege (in terms of formal rights or heightened capacity to use those rights) can use politics to reinforce that privilege*" (Baiocchi, Heller, and Kunrath Silva 2011, 142). Second, the literature argues that a vibrant civil society can generate better societal preferences, through collectively thinking about issues, to reach new understandings of what society should value. Thus, they argue that associations are crucial complements to political parties because they are potentially more responsive to the inherent diversity of societal interests (Fox 1994). As defined in Baiocchi, Heller, and Kunrath Silva (2011, 20), "*in its ideal typical democratic incarnation, civil society is characterized by voluntary forms of association that are constituted by and protective of communicative power and seek to exert their influence by specifically engaging with and seeking support in the public sphere.*"[10] However, some of the available evidence, reviewed in chapter 5, suggests that in practice, civil society can also be captured by political and elite interests (Acemoglu, Reed, and Robinson 2014; Satyanath, Voigtlaender, and Voth 2013).

Civil society organizations around the world are undertaking actions to directly influence political engagement through electoral institutions. In Nigeria, Action Aid campaigned against political violence in 12 villages before the 2007 elections, effectively increasing voter turnout and reducing the incidence of electoral violence. Action Aid's country office in Nigeria partnered with other state-level local CSOs, carrying out town meetings and public theaters, and distributing informational posters to reduce politicians' ability to intimidate voters (Collier and Vicente 2013).

Similarly, in Mozambique, a national CSO consortium, *Observatorio Eleitoral*, together with a free newspaper company, @Verdade, provided citizens with similar information through a newspaper, mobile phones, and leaflets, and established a mobile phone hotline for reporting problems (Aker, Collier, and Vicente 2013). In Uganda, the Africa Leadership Institute, a Kampala-based CSO, partnered with Columbia and Stanford universities to compile information about the legislative performance of political leaders. A parliamentary scorecard was developed to influence how citizens assess the performance of members of parliament (Humphreys and Weinstein 2012). In the Philippines, the Parish Pastoral Council for Responsible Voting distributed information to voters about the existence of a major spending program and the mayor's promises just ahead of the 2013 mayoral elections (Cruz, Keefer, and Labonne 2015).

CSOs have also organized themselves into political parties to contest elections on the basis of platforms of good governance. India's Aam Aadmi Party, which won the Delhi state elections by a landslide, was born out of an anticorruption movement in 2011. Registered only in late 2012, the party was created by a group of civil society leaders who felt that political formation was needed to reinforce their ideas of fighting corruption (Palshikar 2013). The Middle East similarly witnessed a rise of several Islamist parties such as the Justice and Development Party in Turkey, Hamas in Gaza, the Justice and Development Party in Morocco, and the Muslim Brotherhood in the Arab Republic of Egypt, all of which have organized as civil society actors under conditions of political repression. Cammett and Luong (2014) argue that it is primarily their "reputation for good governance" that wins them political support rather than popular explanations such as social service provision, organizational capacity, or ideological hegemony.

In sum, the trends discussed in this chapter suggest that political engagement by citizens, as voters, as candidates for public office, and through civil society groups, is gaining strength around the world, across a variety of institutional contexts. The next chapter presents evidence of trends in transparency that goes together with political engagement in large parts of the world.

Notes

1. Details about the Polity IV measures are available at their website: http://www.systemicpeace.org/polityproject.html. These measures, along with another from Freedom House (discussed in this chapter), are widely used in the economics research literature on the role of political institutions in economic development. Acemoglu et al. (2014) and Besley and Kudamatsu (2008) are important examples and provide a review of how measures of democracy compiled by Polity IV and Freedom House are used as such in research.
2. Not all countries are included in each year of the Polity IV index. There were 144 countries in 1980, 147 in 1990, 163 in 2000, and 167 in 2013. These figures include countries with scores of –66, –77, or –88.
3. Countries' Freedom House status (free, partially free, or not free) is the average of scores for two indicators: political rights, including measures of electoral processes, political pluralism and participation, functioning of government; and civil liberties, including measures of freedom of expression and belief, associational and organizational rights, rule of law, personal autonomy, and individual rights.
4. These are question numbers V228A–I in Wave 6 of the World Values Survey.
5. Direct elections were repealed in September 2014, in a bill passed in the final days of the outgoing Indonesian Parliament, but were reinstituted in early 2015.

6. The following discussion on the rise of civil society organizations and their role in political engagement draws on background research prepared by Thapa (2012).

7. The social accountability literature makes the point that the "social" mechanisms of exacting accountability differ from (1) political mechanisms (for example, constitutional constraints, separation of powers, the legislature, and legislative investigative commissions); (2) fiscal mechanisms (for example, formal systems of auditing and financial accounting); (3) administrative mechanisms (for example, hierarchical reporting, norms of public sector probity, public service codes of conduct, rules and procedures regarding transparency, and public oversight); and (4) legal mechanisms (for example, corruption control agencies, ombudsmen, and the judiciary), in that it takes place through direct citizen engagement with state bureaucrats (McNeil and Malena 2010).

8. For more information, see http://www.qog.pol.gu.se.

9. These data were obtained from the Johns Hopkins Center for Civil Society.

10. For Habermas (1984), who coined the term, it is in the *public sphere* that citizens argue and debate common problems keeping in mind the goals of collective welfare.

Bibliography

Acemoglu, Daron, Suresh Naidu, Pascual Restrepo, and James A. Robinson. 2014. "Democracy Does Cause Growth." NBER Working Paper 20004, National Bureau of Economic Research, Cambridge, MA.

Acemoglu, Daron, Tristan Reed, and James A. Robinson. 2014. "Chiefs: Economic Development and Elite Control of Civil Society in Sierra Leone." *Journal of Political Economy* 122 (2): 319–68.

Aker, Jenny C., Paul Collier, and Pedro C. Vicente. 2013. "Is Information Power? Using Mobile Phones and Free Newspapers during an Election in Mozambique." CDG Working Paper 328, Center for Global Development, Washington, DC.

Baiocchi, Gianpaolo, Patrick Heller, and Marcelo Kunrath Silva. 2011. *Bootstrapping Democracy: Transforming Local Governance and Civil Society in Brazil.* Palo Alto, CA: Stanford University Press.

Cammett, Melani, and Pauline Jones Luong. 2014. "Is There an Islamist Political Advantage?" *Annual Review of Political Science* 17: 187–206.

Chua, Amy. 2002. *World on Fire: How Exporting Free Market Democracy Breeds Ethnic Hatred and Global Instability.* New York: Doubleday.

Claasen, Mario, and Carmen Alpín-Lardiés, eds. 2010. *Social Accountability in Africa: Practitioners' Experience and Lessons.* Cape Town: IDASA/ANSA Africa.

Collier, Paul, and Pedro Vicente. 2013. "Votes and Violence: Evidence from a Field Experiment in Nigeria." *Economic Journal* 124 (574): 327–55.

Croke, Kevin, Guy Grossman, Horacio Larreguy, and John Marshall. 2015. "Deliberate Disengagement: How Education Decreases Political Participation in Electoral Authoritarian Regimes." Working Paper No. 156, Afrobarometer.

Cruz, Cesi, Philip Keefer, and Julien Labonne. 2015. "Incumbent Advantage, Voter Information and Vote Buying." Unpublished.

Fitrani, Fitria, Bert Hofman, and Kai Kaiser. 2005. "Unity in Diversity? The Creation of New Local Governments in a Decentralising Indonesia." *Bulletin of Indonesian Economic Studies* 41 (101): 57–79.

Fox, Jonathan. 1994. "The Difficult Transition from Clientelism to Citizenship." *World Politics* 46 (2): 151–84.

———. 2014. "Social Accountability: What Does the Evidence Really Say?" *World Development* 72: 346–61.

Giuliano, Paola, and Nathan Nunn. 2013. "The Transmission of Democracy: From the Village to the Nation-State." *American Economic Review* 103 (3): 86–92.

Grandvoinnet, Helene, Ghazia Aslam, and Shomikho Raha. 2015. *Opening the Black Box: The Contextual Drivers of Social Accountability.* Washington, DC: World Bank.

Green, Elliott. 2010. "Patronage, District Creation, and Reform in Uganda." *Studies in Comparative International Development* 45: 83–103.

Grossman, Guy, and Janet Lewis. 2014. "Administrative Unit Proliferation." *American Political Science Review* 108 (1): 196–217.

Habermas, Jürgen. 1984. *The Structural Transformation of the Public Sphere: An Inquiry into a Category of Bourgeois Society.* Cambridge, MA: MIT Press.

Heller, Patrick. 2009. "Democratic Deepening in India and South Africa." *Journal of Asian and African Studies* 44 (1): 97–122.

Humphreys, Macartan, and Jeremy Weinstein. 2012. "Policing Politicians: Citizen Empowerment and Political Accountability in Uganda—Preliminary Analysis." International Growth Centre Working Paper, International Growth Centre, London.

Kaplan, Robert D. 2000. *The Coming Anarchy: Shattering the Dreams of the Post Cold War.* New York: Random House.

Khemani, Stuti. 2015. "Buying Votes versus Supplying Public Services: Political Incentives to Under-Invest in Pro-Poor Policies." *Journal of Development Economics* 177 (November): 84–93.

Lewis, David, and Nazneen Kanji. 2007. *Non-Governmental Organizations and Development.* London: Routledge.

Malena, Carmen, with Reiner Forster, and Janmejay Singh. 2004. "Social Accountability: An Introduction to the Concept and Emerging Practice." Social Development Paper 76, World Bank, Washington, DC.

Mansuri, Ghazala, and Vijayendra Rao. 2013. *Localizing Development: Does Participation Work?* World Bank Policy Research Report. Washington, DC: World Bank. https://openknowledge.worldbank.org/handle/10986/11859.

McGee, Rosie, and John Gaventa. 2011. "Shifting Power? Assessing the Impact of Transparency and Accountability Initiatives." IDS Working Paper 383, Institute of Development Studies, Brighton, UK.

McNeil, M., and C. Malena, eds. 2010. *Demanding Good Governance: Lessons from Social Accountability Initiatives in Africa.* Washington, DC: World Bank.

Mercer, Claire. 2002. "NGOs, Civil Society and Democratization: A Critical Review of the Literature." *Progress in Development Studies* 2 (1): 5–22.

Mookherjee, Dilip. 2015. "Political Decentralization." *Annual Review of Economics* 7: 231–49.

Myerson, Roger. 2006. "Federalism and Incentives for Success of Democracy." *Quarterly Journal of Political Science* 1: 3–23.

———. 2012. "Standards for State Building Interventions." Working Paper, University of Chicago. http://home.uchicago.edu/~rmyerson/research/std4sb.pdf.

Nooruddin, I., and P. Chhibber. 2008. "Unstable Politics: Fiscal Space and Electoral Volatility in the Indian States." *Comparative Political Studies* 41 (8): 1069–91.

Ortiz, Isabel, Sara Burke, Mohamed Berrada, and Hernan Cortes. 2013. "World Protests 2006–2013." Friedrich Ebert Stiftung and Institute for Policy Dialogue, New York.

Palshikar, Suhas. 2013. "Of Radical Democracy and Antipartyism." *Economic and Political Weekly* 48 (10): 10–13.

Pande, Rohini. 2011. "Can Informed Voters Enforce Better Governance? Experiments in Low-Income Democracies." *Annual Review of Economics* 3: 215–37.

Pearce, Jenny. 2000. "Development, NGOs, and Civil Society: The Debate and Its Future." In *Development, NGOs, and Civil Society*, edited by Jenny Pearce and Deborah Eade, 15–43. Oxford, U.K.: Oxfam GB.

Pierskalla, Jan H., and Audrey Sacks. 2014. "Research Note: Political Budget Cycles in Indonesian Districts." Unpublished.

Puddington, Arch. 2015. *Discarding Democracy: Return to the Iron Fist—Freedom in the World 2015*. Washington, DC: Freedom House.

Rachman, Anita. 2014. "By the Numbers: Just How Big Are Indonesian Elections?" *Wall Street Journal*, March 27.

Rodrik, Dani, and Romain Wacziarg. 2005. "Do Democratic Transitions Produce Bad Economic Outcomes?" *American Economic Review* 95 (2): 50–55.

Salamon, Lester, Helmut Anheier, Stefan Toepler, and S. Wojciech Sokolowski, and Associates. 1999. *Global Civil Society – Dimensions of the Non Profit Sector*. Baltimore, MD: Johns Hopkins Center for Civil Society.

Satyanath, Shanker, Nico Voigtlaender, and Hans-Joachim Voth. 2013. "Bowling for Fascism: Social Capital and the Rise of the Nazi Party." NBER Working Paper No. 19201, National Bureau of Economic Research, Cambridge, MA.

Skoufias, E., A. Narayan, B. Dasgupta, and K. Kaiser. 2014. "Electoral Accountability, Fiscal Decentralization and Service Delivery in Indonesia." Policy Research Working Paper No. 6782, World Bank, Washington, DC.

Thapa, Dikshya. 2012. *Reproducing Development: Donors, States, and NGOs in the Fight for Symbolic Legitimacy*. Unpublished Doctoral Dissertation, Department of Sociology, Brown University, Providence, Rhode Island.

Zakaria, Fareed. 2003. *The Future of Freedom: Illiberal Democracy at Home and Abroad*. New York: Norton.

CHAPTER THREE

Transparency

Overview

Transparency is defined in this report as citizen access to publicly available information about the actions of those in government and the consequences of these actions. Public disclosure policies are bringing out greater information about the functioning of government and the actions of those in power. Greater information is available not only due to disclosure by governments, but also by non-government agents, such as investigative journalists and civil society groups. New media technologies broadcast information about government performance at all levels. The public availability of information, for all to see, is a fundamental part of the many prevailing definitions of transparency and is the basic concept used in this report.

Several initiatives that seek to promote transparency go beyond the availability of information to include in its definition its specific content, how it should be available, and for what purposes it should be used. The use of transparency as a tool to engage citizens to hold public officials and frontline providers accountable is prominent among these initiatives.[1] This report examines research evaluating the contention that transparency—defined as citizen access to publicly available information—improves political engagement and government accountability.

Sorting out causality between transparency, political engagement, and governance is challenging. Transparency can be an outcome of political engagement and the governance environment as much as a lever to influence governance. Government agencies' provision of information is subject to the same political economy and governance problems that transparency advocates often intend to solve.[2] The quality and quantity of economic data released by governments are significantly correlated with measures of governance and political engagement (Hollyer, Rosendorff, and Vreeland 2011; Islam 2006; Lebovic 2006; Williams 2009), again likely reflecting causation in both directions.

Whether governments allow other nongovernment agencies of transparency, such as civil society and an independent press, to flourish is also an outcome of political incentives. The example provided in chapter 1 of the bribing of accountability institutions by Vladimiro Montesinos, the head of Peru's intelligence service under President Alberto Fujimori, is relevant here. McMillan and Zoido (2004) analyze the unique data obtained from the detailed records maintained by Montesinos to find that bribe payments to purchase the acquiescence of media owners was an order of magnitude greater than those paid to politicians and judges. They further describe how Montesinos was unable to purchase the support of one television channel, which continued to criticize the political regime in Peru. This channel ultimately contributed to the demise of the regime by broadcasting taped evidence of Montesinos' corrupt practices.

Different government, nongovernment, and media actors can undertake transparency interventions to bring data and information into public debate. The meaning of information from different sources—what is accurate, what is not, how it should be interpreted, and what it conveys about the functioning of government and the consequences of public policies—all matter for the effects of these interventions. For example, Glaeser and Sunstein (2013) provide evidence from experiments conducted in the United States that balanced information can intensify previously held polarized opinions. If a person believes in the information's source, then the new information will trigger a rational updating and bolster previous beliefs. In contrast, if a source is perceived to be dubious, the new information will reinforce a person's original doubts. Chapter 6 distills lessons from available research on how people respond to different types of media and transparency initiatives, and how citizen actions in turn affect governance and development outcomes.

As with other aspects of governance discussed in previous chapters, transparency is difficult to measure.[3] To date, no single comprehensive index of transparency exists. In the absence of such a measure, this chapter assembles a variety of measures of different dimensions of transparency from different sources, including civil society organizations and international development partners. Transparency has spread through deliberate policy efforts to improve governance by providing information about government actions and their consequences. For example, the public disclosure of information about government budgets has been proposed as a condition for international development assistance. Civil society organizations have also been making efforts to generate new information to monitor and evaluate government service provision. Finally, transparency has also grown as a result of technological forces that allow different news media to generate and broadcast information about government performance.

The following sections describe the global emergence of transparency through a combination of government policy changes, civil society actions, and the dynamics of media markets.

Government disclosure policies

One focus of transparency efforts is on the legal framework for access to information from the government. According to the data gathered by a global network of civil society organizations that advocates for disclosure policies, freedominfo.org, 99 countries have enacted right-to-information legislation as of 2014, compared with only 29 countries that had done so by 2000 (figure 3.1).

Figure 3.1 Number of countries with Freedom of Information Legislation in 2000 and 2014, by region

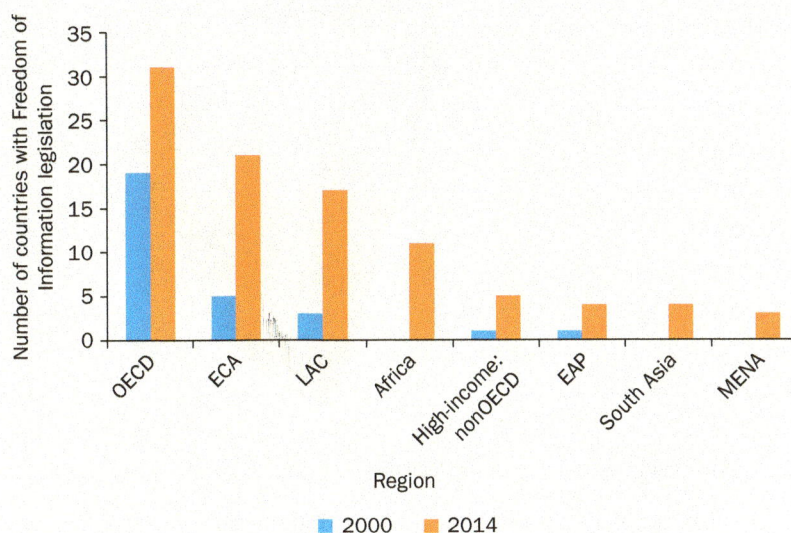

Source: Data from freedominfo.org.
Note: EAP = East Asia and Pacific; ECA = Europe and Central Asia; LAC = Latin America and the Caribbean; MENA = Middle East and North Africa; OECD = Organisation for Economic Co-operation and Development.

The existence of a right-to-information law does not guarantee that citizens are in fact able to access government information in a timely, affordable manner. As a measure of actual access, in 2010, a collection of groups—the International Budget Partnership, Centre for Law and Democracy, and Access Info Europe—organized the "Ask Your Government! The 6 Question Campaign," which made identical budget information requests to 80 governments. The requests included two questions in each of the following categories: maternal health, aid effectiveness, and environmental protection. The responses showed much progress is yet to be made (figure 3.2). Across all countries, only one in four requests was met with the full amount of information; nearly 40 percent provided no response at all. Not surprisingly, countries with right-to-information laws were much more responsive, on average, and response rates were higher the longer the law had been in place. Newer democracies or those in the developing world in particular tended to be more transparent: Georgia, India, and Namibia, for example, complied with all six information requests. Only 2 of the top 15 respondents were western democracies—New Zealand

Figure 3.2 Results of the 6-question campaign, all 80 countries, 2011

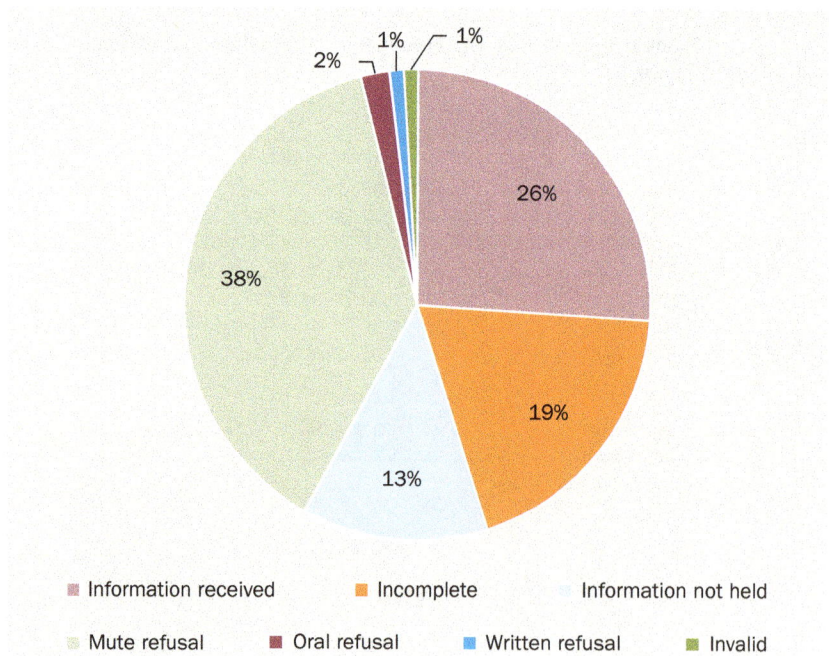

Source: "Ask Your Government! The 6 Question Campaign," A Comparative Analysis Of Access to Budget Information in 80 Countries, 2011, Access Info Europe Centre for Law and Democracy International Budget Partnership.

and Germany. In general, established democracies performed no better than other governments with right-to-information laws. The Middle East region was the worst performer in every category by a wide margin.

Another effort to measure government transparency is the International Budget Partnership's Open Budget Index (OBI), a biennial expert assessment of the availability, timeliness, and quality of central government budget documents. The measure has expanded in scope from 59 countries when it was launched in 2006, to about 100 countries in 2015. The OBI assigns countries a transparency score on a 100-point scale using a set of survey questions that focus on whether the government provides the public with timely access to information contained in eight key budget documents in accordance with international good practice standards.

Efforts to measure budget transparency extend to the local government level. Survey data from Afrobarometer indicate that more than half of the respondents in Africa are unhappy with how well their local councils are providing citizens with information about their budgets (figure 3.3). Such survey evidence on citizens' experience with accessing information about government budgets suggests scope for much improvement in the effectiveness of transparency policies.

Figure 3.3   **How well the local council is providing information about its budget, Africa and selected countries**

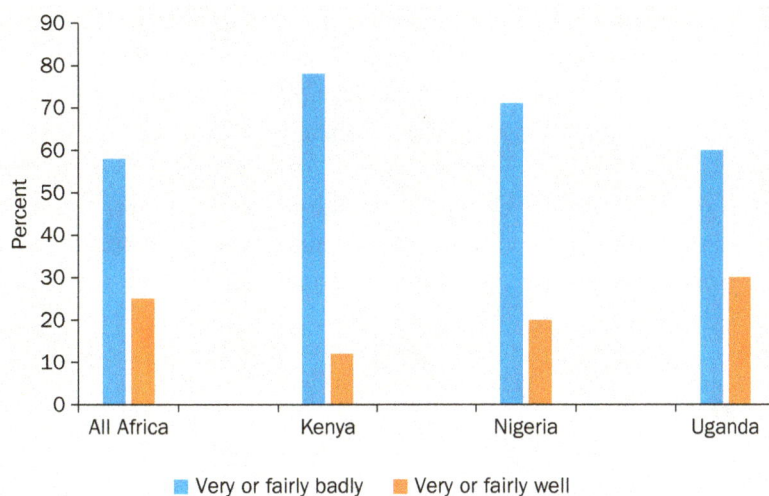

Source: Afrobarometer Round 4, 2008–09.
Notes: The survey question is as follows: "How well or badly do you think your Metropolitan, Municipal or District Assembly is practicing the following procedures? Or haven't you heard enough to have an opinion: Providing citizens with the information about the Assembly's budget (i.e., revenues and expenditures)?"

One specific aspect of transparency that has been emphasized in international policy dialogue is the disclosure of how revenue from natural resources is managed. The Resource Governance Index (RGI) measures the quality of governance in the oil, gas, and mining sectors of 58 countries. The RGI scores and ranks the countries using a questionnaire completed by researchers with expertise in the extractive industries. The questionnaire is designed to assess the quality of the institutional and legal setting, reporting practices, safeguards, and quality controls. It also includes information on state-owned companies, natural resource funds, and subnational revenue transfers that are common channels for revenue flows from natural resources.

The Extractive Industries Transparency Initiative (EITI) is a global coalition of governments, companies, and civil society working together to improve openness and further accountable management of revenues from natural resources. As a membership requirement, countries must fully disclose taxes and other payments made by oil, gas, and mining companies to the government in an annual, actively promoted report. Participation is voluntary, and as of 2014, 35 countries had produced at least one report.

Even the transparency of international organizations is subject to measurement. One World Trust's 2006, 2007, and 2008 Global Accountability Reports include a measure of how consistently international organizations publicly disclosed information and responded to information requests. Scorecards prepared by the Global Transparency Initiative have likewise rated international financial institutions' disclosure policies and information request procedures. The Aid Transparency Index produced by Publish What You Fund annually rates the level of transparency for about 70 bilateral and multilateral agencies, climate finance funds, humanitarian agencies, development finance institutions, and private foundations. In 2014, the World Bank Group's International Development Association was ranked 7th overall with noted commitment to the International Aid Transparency Initiative, while the International Finance Corporation, came in 39th.[4]

Civil society and the private sector as sources of information

Governments are not the only providers of information about their actions and performance. Civil society organizations, the private sector, investigative journalists, researchers, and international development and global agencies use enhanced technologies and research methodologies to directly observe government actions, gather data, and draw conclusions about the consequences of government actions for development outcomes. For example, researchers have used satellite imagery data compiled by the U.S. Air Force Defense Meteorological Satellite Program's Operational Linescan System to generate new information on the performance of governments in delivering electricity to villages, finding that voting patterns of villages are a significant predictor of whether the village receives electricity (Baskaran, Min, and Uppal 2015).[5]

Civil society organizations have also been making efforts to generate new information to monitor and evaluate government service provision. For example, Uwezo in East Africa and the Annual Status of Education Report in India measure education service delivery and learning outcomes on a large scale, enabling performance measures to be computed at disaggregated jurisdictional levels, such as districts, that are managed by directly elected leaders.

Global Integrity is an example of an international nongovernmental organization that works with local partners in developing countries to generate data about government performance through the participation of local civil society and investigative reporters.[6] One of the areas of governance measured through their methodology is the extent to which legal frameworks for anticorruption policies in countries are effectively implemented, both at the national level and in select local governments.

In addition to civil society organizations, multilateral efforts are under way to promote transparency, notably the Open Government Partnership, which includes 65 countries. Member countries are required to make available information on governmental activities and to support civic participation. As a complement to broader commitments to transparency and good governance, several countries have implemented open data initiatives to provide greater coordination and share resources between civil society organizations to take advantage of open government data (Bayern 2015).

Media markets and technological forces

New technologies and communications media are being harnessed to widely distribute information. The Internet is perhaps the most obvious example of such technology. Figure 3.4 shows the growth in the number of Internet

Figure 3.4   Internet users, by region, 1990–2013

Growth in number of Internet users globally, by region, 1990–2013

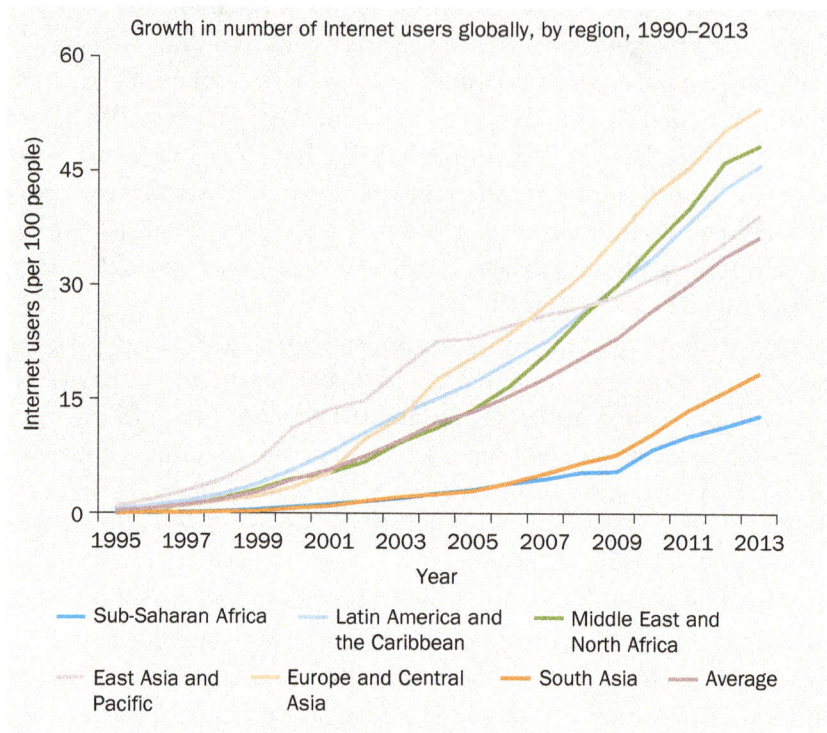

—— Sub-Saharan Africa	—— Latin America and the Caribbean	—— Middle East and North Africa
⋯ East Asia and Pacific	—— Europe and Central Asia	—— South Asia	—— Average

Source: International Telecommunication Union, World Telecommunication/ICT Development Report and database, and World Bank estimates.

users by region. The *World Development Report 2016: Digital Dividends* (World Bank 2016) finds that the Internet has reached developing countries much faster than previous technological innovations. Technological convergence or the move to a common digital platform is transforming the media globally. A significant trend is what has been called "the mobile wave," that is, the increasing role of mobile technology in the delivery and consumption of news, current affairs, and entertainment, even in developing countries.

The leading technology companies, such as Google, Facebook, and Amazon, are playing a bigger role in the packaging and delivery of information, including news and current affairs, around the world. They are creating information curation services and even hiring journalists to help them manage these services. For instance, Facebook drives about 20 percent of the traffic to news sites (Somaiya 2014).

Google, Facebook, and Microsoft, among others, have projects around the world that are aimed at bringing Internet access to remote communities. For instance, Facebook introduced Internet.org to make it easier for any mobile operator to sign up to offer free Internet access and basic online services. Internet.org was first launched in Africa, but has since expanded and is now available in 17 countries—including countries with very large populations such as India—spanning three continents, but only works with select operators. Facebook is now attempting to encourage more mobile operators to join the program, announcing a dedicated portal through which operators can sign up.[7]

Google has announced path-breaking projects to expand Internet access such as Project Loon, a network of balloons traveling on the edge of space, designed to connect people in rural and remote areas to the Internet.[8] Project Loon's efforts first began in June 2013, when Google launched several balloons to heights of about 65,000 feet above Earth's surface (Barr and Greenwald 2015). Another example is Microsoft's support for closing the digital divide in India. According to Microsoft, its White-Fi technology, which uses the unused spectrum in frequencies used for broadcasting television signals, can provide free Wi-Fi connectivity to tackle the problem of last-mile broadband connectivity in India.

More and more state-owned news organizations are active globally. Several countries are setting up powerful news organizations, stretching their public diplomacy efforts into many corners of the world. The British Broadcasting Corporation is the global leader in news and current affairs programming targeting the world. Germany and France offer Deutsche Welle and France 24, respectively. The European Union has its own transnational news network, Euronews. The United States is a giant in the field, deploying Voice of America, Radio Free Europe, Radio Liberty, Radio Free Asia, Radio and TV Marti, Worldnet, and Middle East Broadcasting Networks. The Russian Federation has RT. China has deployed Chinese Central Television and Xinhua, China's state-run news agency. All these public diplomacy instruments are broadcasting in more and more languages in more and more countries. They also have powerful online presences. This trend implies that there are no hermetically sealed national media environments; agendas from a variety of sources are being pushed into different media markets.

Satellite broadcasting is now a major feature of the global media space, allowing programming to be beamed across national boundaries. Among the big players are SES (Luxembourg) with a global fleet of 53 geostationary satellites that together cover 99 percent of the world's population, Intelsat (Luxembourg), Eutelsat (France), Telesat Canada, and JSAT (Japan).

Satellite broadcasting is not only a massive cultural force (as a purveyor of entertainment programming), but also a force for transparency about government actions because they beam news and current affairs programming from different sources into a variety of countries. For instance, satellite broadcasting has created a virtual pan-Arab media space. According to the latest report from Digital TV Research on the Middle East and North Africa (2015),[9] there are 34.3 million Arabic-speaking, free-to-air, satellite TV homes in the region.

Deregulation and commercialization have reduced the number of state media monopolies, especially broadcast monopolies. At independence, most developing countries inherited state media monopolies. In the 1970s, broadcast monopolies loyal to the government of the day were the norm. But in the 1980s and 1990s, a wave of media deregulation spread around the world. Perhaps because of the democratization wave or simply because state broadcasters became too expensive for many developing country governments to maintain, space began to be opened up for commercial broadcasters, first in radio, then television. Some of this movement could be described as deregulation to trusted friends, where authoritarian governments gave broadcast licenses to allies of specific regimes (Carpentier 2014; Das and Parthasarathi 2014). This trend has had a transformational impact in many countries, opening up media systems and promoting a diversity of voices. In contrast, public service broadcasting and community radio are not thriving. The trends noted above have led to more commercial broadcasting. More citizens in more countries have numerous media options, reducing the demand for public service broadcasting.

Citizens' reports on the media they use

Data from the Gallup World Poll, the World Values Survey, and the Afrobarometer survey provide insights into the types of media citizens use to access information. Cell phone penetration is about 85 percent worldwide. Even in Sub-Saharan Africa, the rate of cell phone ownership is greater than 60 percent (figure 3.5, panel a). Landline penetration is far lower worldwide and practically nonexistent in Africa and South Asia (figure 3.5, panel b). Since landline technology is older, these regions have "leapfrogged" that technology and directly adopted the new technology once they reached the level of development at which it became practical. The use of social media over cell-phone-based platforms in the Arab Spring provides an example of how technology is enabling citizens to access information through different sources, bypassing the hurdles that might be put in place by repressive regimes.

In contrast, rates of access to a computer and to the Internet are quite low in all regions outside of the high-income Organisation for Economic Co-operation and Development (OECD) countries (figure 3.5, panels c and d). This fact is important when designing transparency initiatives. Although it may seem tempting from the perspective of many development practitioners to make information available online because of the pervasiveness of that platform in the OECD, in fact there may be other media

Figure 3.5   Households' access to information technology, by region, 2007–13

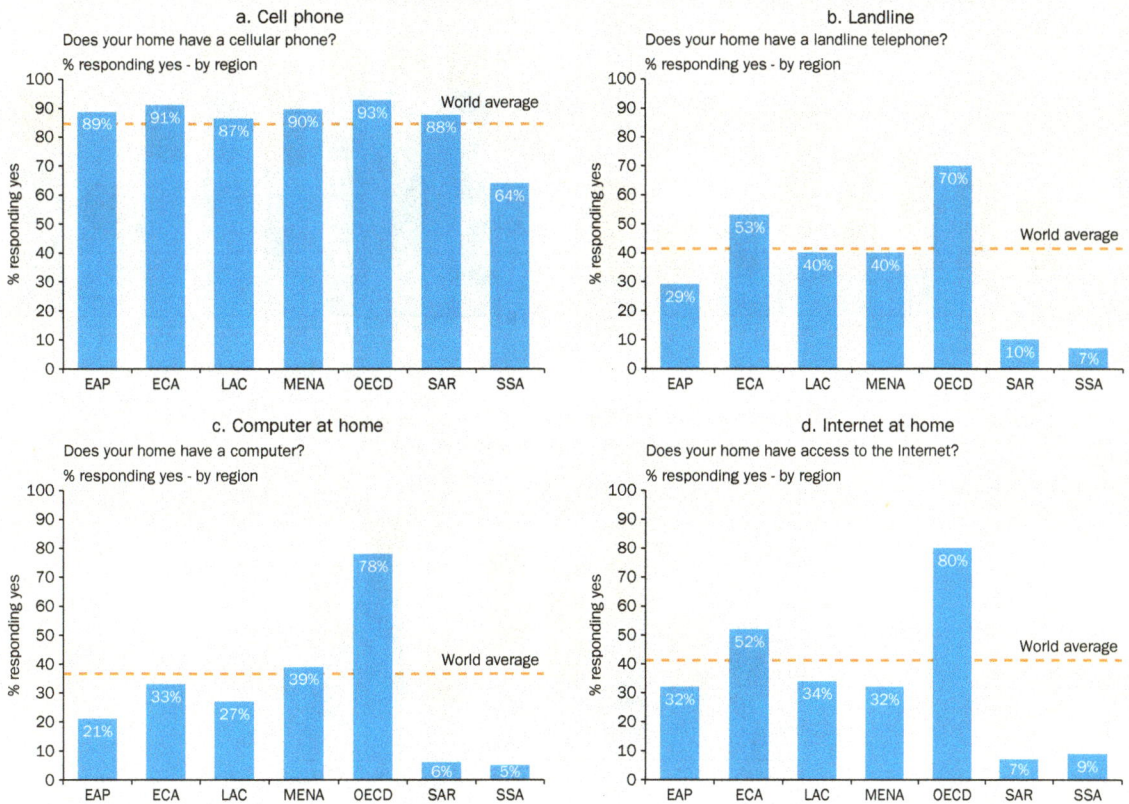

Source: Gallup World Poll.
Note: EAP = East Asia and Pacific; ECA = Europe and Central Asia; LAC = Latin America and the Caribbean; MENA = Middle East and North Africa; OECD = Organisation for Economic Co-operation and Development; SAR = South Asia Region; SSA = Sub-Saharan Africa.

better suited to disseminating information to citizens in regions with highly limited access. However, cell-phone-based platforms may enable citizens to access the Internet. Furthermore, those who *do* have access to the Internet in poorer regions may play a role in disseminating the information through older and more traditional media such as radio. In this way, new technologies can enhance the capacity of older and cheaper communications technologies that are widely used in poorer areas of the world.

The Gallup surveys suggest a striking diversity in media use across regions. Television and radio are the sources most people rely on (figure 3.6, panels b, c), with almost 80 percent of respondents in Asia

Figure 3.6   Citizens' consumption of different news media

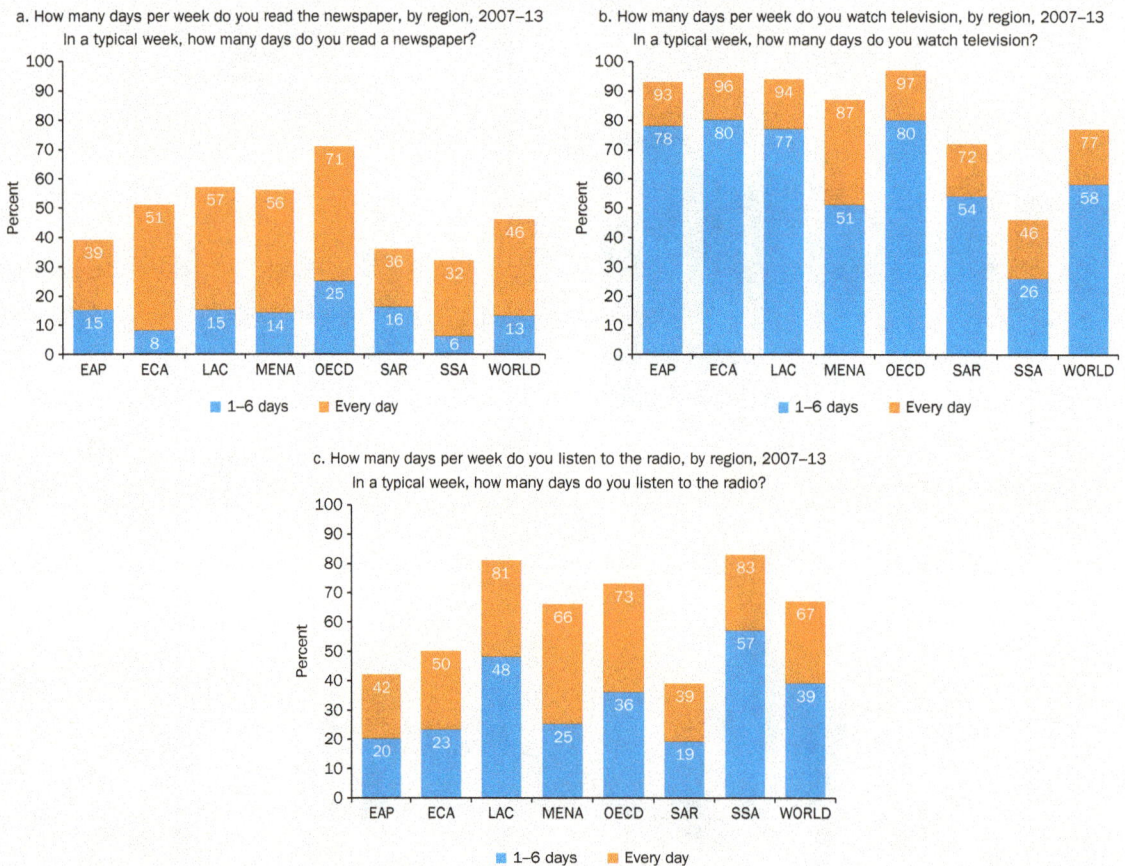

a. How many days per week do you read the newspaper, by region, 2007–13
In a typical week, how many days do you read a newspaper?

b. How many days per week do you watch television, by region, 2007–13
In a typical week, how many days do you watch television?

c. How many days per week do you listen to the radio, by region, 2007–13
In a typical week, how many days do you listen to the radio?

Source: Gallup World Poll.
Note: EAP = East Asia and Pacific; ECA = Europe and Central Asia; LAC = Latin America and the Caribbean; MENA = Middle East and North Africa; OECD = Organisation for Economic Co-operation and Development; SAR = South Asia Region; SSA = Sub-Saharan Africa.

and Latin America saying they watch TV every day. Radio is much more popular in Africa, where nearly 60 percent of people listen every day and more than 80 percent listen at least once a week. Newspaper readership, in contrast, is low, with daily readership rates of less than 20 percent worldwide (figure 3.6, panel a).

Figure 3.7 shows responses to a Gallup World poll question about the source people deem most important for becoming well-informed about events in their countries. Domestic (national) television is cited by a majority of people in all regions but Sub-Saharan Africa, where radio dominates. Radio is the most significant source of information for 61 percent of African respondents.

Although domestic sources are the most important in all regions, international radio and television also hold a degree of importance, particularly in the Middle East and North Africa, where nearly a quarter of respondents said international TV was their most important news source about domestic events. One hypothesis is that if citizens are dissatisfied with the quality of information provided domestically, they may be willing to look abroad to find more trustworthy sources. It is notable in this regard that confidence

Figure 3.7 Most important media that citizens report using for news, by region

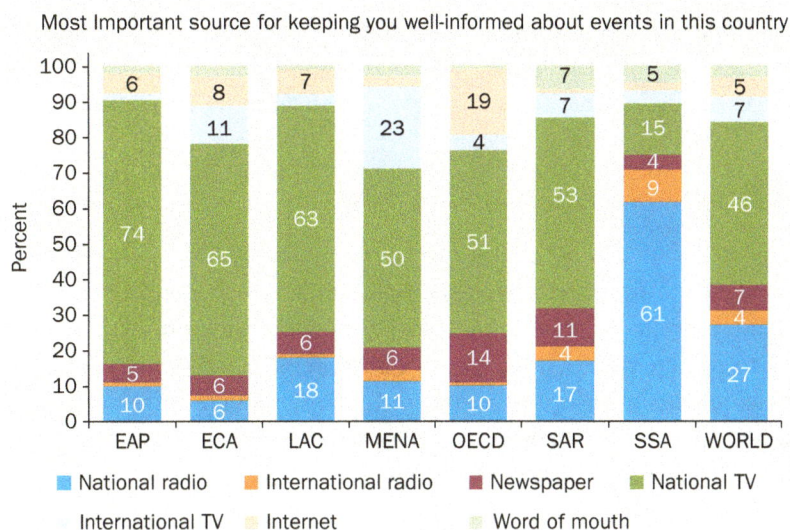

Most Important source for keeping you well-informed about events in this country

Legend:
National radio, International radio, Newspaper, National TV, International TV, Internet, Word of mouth

Source: Gallup World Poll.
Note: EAP = East Asia and Pacific; ECA = Europe and Central Asia; LAC = Latin America and the Caribbean; MENA = Middle East and North Africa; OECD = Organisation for Economic Co-operation and Development; SAR = South Asia Region; SSA = Sub-Saharan Africa.

93

Figure 3.8 Citizens' confidence in the quality and integrity of the media, by region, 2007–13

Do you have confidence in the quality and integrity of the media?

% responding yes - by region

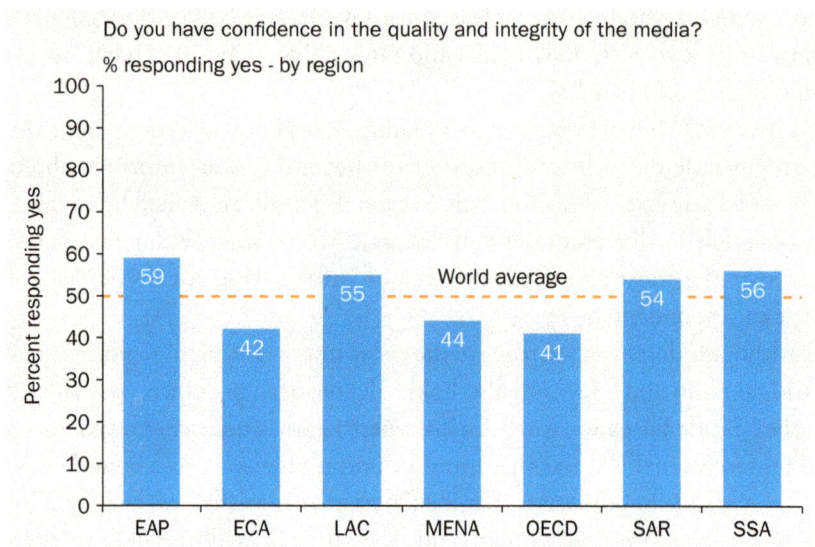

Source: Gallup World Poll.
Note: EAP = East Asia and Pacific; ECA = Europe and Central Asia; LAC = Latin America and the Caribbean; MENA = Middle East and North Africa; OECD = Organisation for Economic Co-operation and Development; SAR = South Asia Region; SSA = Sub-Saharan Africa.

in the media is lowest in Eastern Europe and Central Asia, the Middle East and North Africa, and the OECD countries (figure 3.8), which are the three regions with the highest reported rates of reliance on international sources or the Internet (which is a global source) for news (figure 3.7).

Independence and plurality in media markets

Because the media can play a large role in transparency by monitoring government officials, informing citizens, and serving as a forum for public debate, plurality of media sources and independence from state control can to some extent also serve as a barometer for transparency itself. Developments in communications technology provide citizens across the world with access to different types of news and social media. However, the quality of the available information is likely to be shaped by who owns and controls these media. Djankov et al. (2003) consider 97 countries and find that in nearly all cases, ownership is concentrated in the national government or a few private family-firms who own the largest media. Government ownership is more common in broadcasting than in print media. Based on total circulation and share of viewing, state ownership of the top five media firms is 29 percent for newspapers, 60 percent for television stations, and 72 percent for the top radio stations. Government ownership of media is higher in poor countries as well as in nondemocracies. In cross-country regressions, Djankov et al. (2003) find that government ownership of media firms is associated with less press freedom, more corruption, weaker property rights, and worse health and education outcomes.

Press "freedom" is another dimension on which several organizations rate governments. Reporters Without Borders, for example, incorporates quantitative measures such as imprisonment and the death of journalists and citizens in its press freedom index, along with qualitative information reported in surveys sent to nongovernmental organizations, researchers, journalists, and human rights activists.[10] The 2015 index shows that conditions for journalists are problematic, difficult, or serious in almost all regions of the world. A striking feature of these ratings is that Africa is not that different from the rest of the world. The African continent exhibits large variation, just like the rest of the world, rather than being uniformly poor on indicators of media freedom.

Freedom House also rates countries on freedom of the press. Freedom House's methodology comprises 23 questions and 132 indicators that are divided into three broad categories: the legal environment, the political environment, and the economic environment. It focuses on the "enabling environment," that is, the extent to which governments can apply pressure on the nature and flow of information and intimidate journalists.[11] The ratings of press freedom by Reporters Without Borders generally point in the same direction that press freedoms are greater in rich countries than in the developing world.

Not surprisingly, indicators of media freedom are correlated with indicators of political freedom. Figure 3.9 shows that countries that are measured as more democratic using Polity IV indicators also tend to have greater measures of press freedom, suggesting that these two forces go hand-in-hand in many countries. At the same time, countries with intermediate levels of media freedom are spread across the measures of democracy on Polity IV. That is, even countries measured as autocracies allow some degree of media freedom or perhaps are unable to fully control media.[12]

Figure 3.10 shows that there is a positive association between media freedom and the control of corruption. However, as indicated at the outset, such correlations are difficult to interpret and could reflect a direction of

Figure 3.9 **Media independence across countries with different measures of democracy**

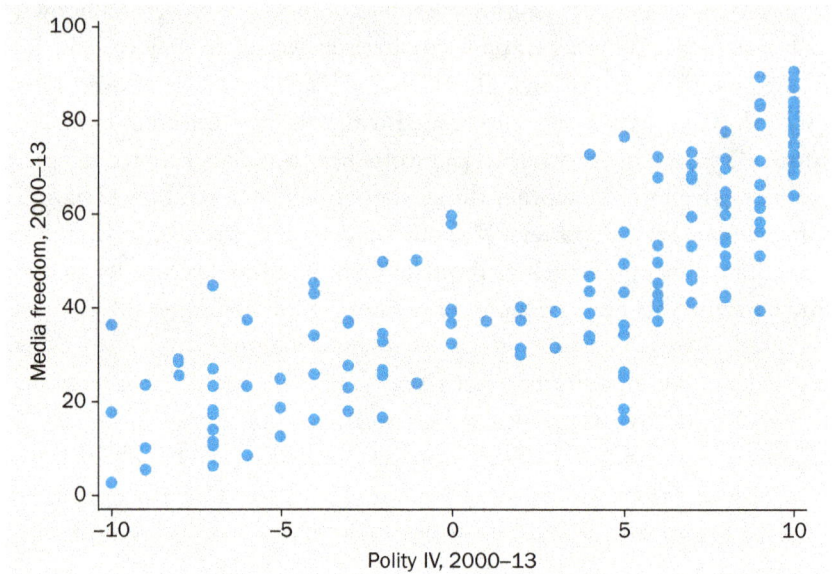

Sources: Polity IV Project for measures of democracy, and Freedom House for measures of media freedom.
Note: The Polity IV measures of democracy and the Freedom House measures of media freedom are averaged over the period 2000-13.

Figure 3.10 **Correlation between media freedom and control of corruption, 2000-13**

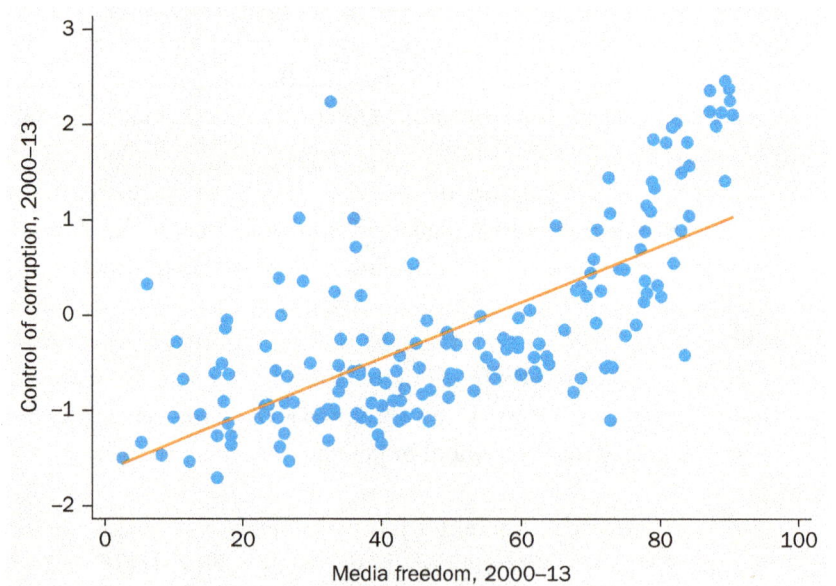

Sources: WGI for Control of Corruption and Freedom House for measures of media freedom.
Note: WGI measures of the Control of Corruption and the Freedom House measures of media freedom are averaged over the period 2000-13. WGI = Worldwide Governance Indicators.

causation from better governance to better-functioning media markets. The research evidence on the role of mass media (covered in chapter 6) is much more nuanced and is focused on situations in which it is possible to correlate exogenous changes in media access with governance outcomes.

In sum, the trends discussed in this chapter suggest transparency is on the rise across a variety of institutional contexts. Several reasons likely explain this emergence, including international and domestic political pressure, but also the spread of market forces and information and communications technology. Transparency and political engagement, in short, are together gaining strength around the world as interlinked forces that can potentially affect governance for economic development. The following chapters use available research to probe how these forces might improve governance and strengthen public sector institutions for the goals of economic development.

Notes

1. For example, the Transparency International website contains the following description of what transparency is about (http://www.transparency.org/what-is-corruption/#what-is-transparency): "Transparency is about shedding light on rules, plans, processes and actions. It is knowing why, how, what, and how much. Transparency ensures that public officials, civil servants, managers, board members and businesspeople act visibly and understandably, and report on their activities. And it means that the general public can hold them to account. It is the surest way of guarding against corruption, and helps increase trust in the people and institutions on which our futures depend." The World Bank's public sector work also uses the term transparency to refer to the greater availability of information between government departments as well as greater clarity about government processes, rules, and definitions (Trapnell 2014). This report focuses on transparency for citizens rather than between government departments to examine the role of citizens as external checks upon those who wield power within the government. This report also distinguishes outcomes (greater clarity of government processes and rules) that depend upon the political incentives, from the input of greater availability of information. For example, government processes and rules might be deliberately clouded when it serves the incentives of leaders to use their discretionary powers for rent-seeking and providing preferential treatment.
2. A recent example related to the provision of public access to information under access-to-information laws comes from the province of British Columbia in Canada, where the province's Information and Privacy Commissioner uncovered a "culture of suppression of information." This culture manifested itself in avoidance of documenting government policy

decisions and an informal policy of systemic "triple deletion" of emails (see Denham 2015). The handling of emails offers an example of mounting evidence that the introduction of information and communications technology within governments can have offsetting effects on accountability and transparency. Without proper regulatory safeguards in place, new digital forms of communication make it easier to perpetrate fraud and corrupt practices and to erase records or to avoid capturing them altogether (see Lemieux 2015). In countries with independent monitoring and oversight of public access to information and media that are aware of the issue, attempts to subvert public access to information can be uncovered, forcing the politicians to change their behavior. In many countries, however, these preconditions are not met, so such behaviors often go undetected.

3. The following parts of this chapter on measures and indicators of transparency draw on background research prepared by Scott Abrahams for this report.

4. Aid Transparency Index (http://ati.publishwhatyoufund.org/major-donor /world-bank/).

5. In constituencies that hold special elections, state governments significantly increase the provision of electricity. Manipulation of electricity provision is more pronounced when elections are closely contested and in localities where the state government only holds a small majority.

6. Global Integrity, https://www.globalintegrity.org/.

7. "One Year In: Internet.org Free Basic Services," 2015 (http://newsroom. fb.com/news/category/trends/).

8. https://www.google.com/loon/.

9. Digital TV Middle East and North Africa Forecasts (February 2015), Digital TV Research, available at: https://www.digitaltvresearch.com /products/product?id=112.

10. 2013 World Press Freedom Index—Methodology (https://en.rsf.org/IMG /pdf/2013_wpfi_methodology.pdf).

11. Freedom House Methodology (http://freedomhouse.org/report/freedom-press-2014/methodology#.VBEb32RdWDp).

12. Egorov, Guriev, and Sonin (2009) argue that autocrats will choose to allow media freedom when they need the information generated by a free press to manage the far-flung, lower-tier public officials in their countries. Media-generated information is critical, in their argument, because it enables leaders to establish strong incentive systems for lower-level officials.

Bibliography

Barr, Alistair, and Ted Greenwald. 2015. "Google Working on New Drone After 'Wing' Design Failed," *Wall Street Journal,* March 17. http://blogs.wsj.com /digits/2015/03/17/google-working-on-new-drone-after-wing-design-failed/.

Baskaran, Thushyanthan, Brian Min, and Yogesh Uppal. 2015. "Election Cycles and Economic Activity: Evidence from a Quasi-Experiment with Indian Bye-Elections." *Journal of Public Economics* 126: 64–73.

Bayern, Jessica. 2015. *Investigating the Impact of Open Data Initiatives: The Cases of Kenya, Uganda and the Philippines.* Washington, DC: World Bank.

Carpentier, Nico. 2014. "Policy's Hubris: Power, Fantasy, and the Limits of (Global) Media Policy Interventions." In *The Handbook of Global Media and Communication Policy*, edited by R. Mansell and M. Raboy, 113–28. Oxford: John Wiley & Sons, Ltd.

Das, Biswajit, and Vibodh Parthasarathi. 2014. "Media Research and Public Policy: Tiding Over the Rupture." In *The Handbook of Global Media and Communication Policy*, edited by R. Mansell and M. Raboy, 245–60. Oxford: John Wiley & Sons, Ltd.

Denham, Elizabeth. 2015. "Investigation Report F15-03 – Access Denied: Record Retention and Disposal Practices of the Government of British Columbia." Office of the Information and Privacy Commissioner of British Columbia.

Djankov, Simeon, Caralee McLiesh, Tatiana Nenova, and Andrei Shleifer. 2003. "Who Owns The Media?" *Journal of Law and Economics* 46 (2): 341–82.

Egorov, Georgy, Sergei Guriev, and Konstantin Sonin. 2009. "Why Resource-Poor Dictators Allow Freer Media: A Theory and Evidence from Panel Data." *American Political Science Review* 103 (4): 645–68.

Glaeser, Edward, and Cass Sunstein. 2013. "Why Does Balanced News Produce Unbalanced Views?" NBER Working Paper No. 18975, National Bureau of Economic Research, Cambridge, MA.

Hollyer, James, B. Peter Rosendorff, and James Raymond Vreeland. 2011. "Democracy and Transparency." *Journal of Politics* 73 (4): 1191–205.

IBP (International Budget Partnership), Centre for Law and Democracy, and Access Info. 2011. "Ask Your Government! The 6 Question Campaign: A Comparative Analysis of Access to Budget Information in 80 Countries." http://www.law-democracy.org/wp-content/uploads/2011/10/6QC-Report-Publication-version-September-2011.pdf.

Islam, Roumeen. 2006. "Does More Transparency Go along with Better Governance?" *Economics and Politics* 18 (2): 121–67.

Lebovic, James H. 2006. "Democracies and Transparency: Country Reports to the UN Register of Conventional Arms, 1992–2001." *Journal of Peace Research* 43 (5): 543–62.

Lemieux, Victoria L. 2015. "One Step Forward, Two Steps Backward? Does E-Government Make Governments in Developing Countries More Transparent and Accountable?" Working Paper, World Bank, Washington, DC.

McMillan, John, and Pablo Zoido. 2004. "How to Subvert Democracy: Montesinos in Peru." *Journal of Economic Perspectives* 18 (4): 69–92.

Somaiya, Ravi. 2014. "How Facebook Is Changing the Way Its Users Consume Journalism." *New York Times*, October 26. http://www.nytimes.com/2014/10/27/business/media/how-facebook-is-changing-the-way-its-users-consume-journalism.html?_r=0.

Trapnell, Stephanie, ed. 2014. *Right to Information: Case Studies on Implementation.* Washington, DC: World Bank.

Williams, Andrew. 2009. "On the Release of Information by Governments: Causes and Consequences." *Journal of Development Economics* 89: 124–38.

World Bank. 2016. *World Development Report 2016: Digital Dividends.* Washington, DC: World Bank.

CHAPTER FOUR

Learning from the Logic of the Theoretical Literature

Overview: Government failures as principal-agent problems

This chapter provides the conceptual framework of the report, drawing on the logic of the theoretical literature in economics. It defines the notion of government failure on the basis of economic theory, using the framework of "principal-agent" relationships between government officials who act as the agents of society or of citizens (who are the principals). Accountability problems in government are examined as a series of principal-agent problems, as follows: (i) between citizens and political leaders; (ii) between political leaders and public officials who lead government agencies; and (iii) between public officials and frontline providers. Political engagement and transparency shape all three of these principal-agent relationships.

The next section examines how political engagement is the fundamental role that citizens can play in governance. Unhealthy political engagement, when leaders are selected and sanctioned on the basis of their provision of private benefits rather than public goods, arises as a result of conflict of interest among citizens. It leads to accountability failures in the functioning of a myriad within-government principal-agent relationships between leaders, public officials, and frontline providers. Some of these accountability failures can be examined as the "inversion" of principal-agent relationships. For example, vote buying and violence in elections involves political leaders holding voters accountable for political support. Public officials and frontline providers can be organized as powerful interest groups who control political leaders and thwart citizen action to monitor their performance. Such government failures can occur in both more and less democratic settings, and depend upon whether leaders who wield power within government are held accountable for public goods or private rents.

A defining feature of principal-agent problems are informational asymmetries, which exist even when political engagement happens in healthy ways to select and sanction leaders on the basis of performance in providing public goods. Principals have imperfect information about the actions of agents and the consequences of these actions. Transparency, which provides such information, is therefore central to addressing principal-agent problems in government. The following section reviews the literature examining how transparency can improve the quality of political engagement, enabling citizens to hold leaders accountable for public goods and select better-quality leaders.

The last section examines how political engagement and transparency shape the beliefs and behavioral norms of citizens, political leaders, public officials, and frontline providers. These are topics on the research frontiers. One strand shows how political engagement and the leaders selected through it can shape norms of cooperation among citizens or in society. Another strand shows how the legitimacy of leaders matters for improving the functioning of public sector organizations and the behavior of public officials. The picture that emerges by putting together the dispersed pieces of theoretical research provides guidance for future work on how healthy political engagement, nourished by transparency, may contribute to strengthening norms and building legitimacy for effective public sector institutions.

Political engagement is the fundamental role that citizens play in the principal-agent problems of government

Political engagement directly shapes the relationship between citizens as principals and government leaders as the agents of citizens. Citizens play this role as principals in different ways across institutional contexts. For example, in countries with more democratic institutions, the power to select and sanction leaders is more dispersed among a large number of "ordinary" or non-elite citizens. In countries with less democratic or more autocratic institutions, the power is instead more concentrated among elites or well-organized citizens, such as political parties. However, even when formal electoral institutions are lacking, the threat of political engagement by nonelite citizens through informal means, such as protests and revolutions, can serve as a constraint on leaders (Acemoglu and Robinson 2000, 2006a).

Political leaders, in turn, delegate tasks to public officials who manage a myriad of agencies within the government. Political leaders are therefore the principals of a variety of lower-level public officials within the government. These public officials who lead government agencies are, in turn, the principals of frontline providers who deliver public services. Figure 4.1 illustrates this series of principal-agent relationships in government. Most government systems around the world are a complex mix of power being shared between appointed and elected officials across multiple jurisdictions. For example, responsibilities over the management of public schools can be divided between locally elected governments or elected school boards, on the one hand, and appointed administrative officers on the other hand. Theoretical research has examined how different tasks of government should be assigned to an appointed public official or to an elected politician across these multiple jurisdictions, depending on the nature of the different principal-agent problems (Alesina and Tabellini 2007).

Non-political citizen engagement has become a prominent feature of policy efforts to improve government performance. Figure 4.1 also shows how these initiatives of non-political citizen engagement fit into the principal-agent problems of government. Officials who hold leadership positions in government can engage the help of citizens in making government agencies perform better. In the principal-agent setting, non-political ways of engaging citizens to solve accountability problems include

Figure 4.1 The role of citizens in principal-agent relationships of government

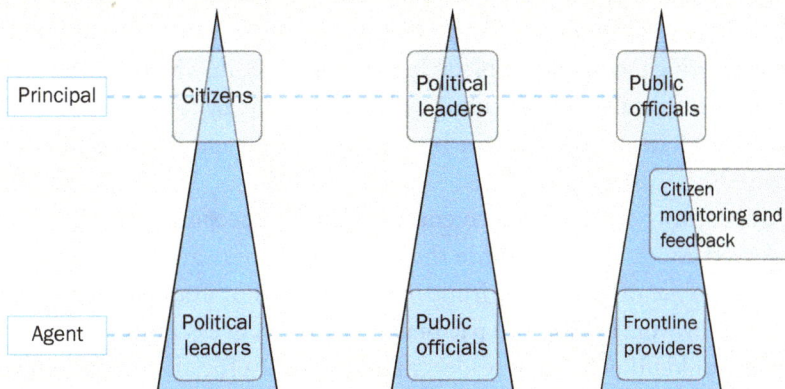

using citizens to monitor lower-level government officials and providing feedback to higher-level leaders, which these leaders can then use to solve within-government accountability problems. For example, a district executive officer with formal powers over teachers, health workers, agricultural extension workers, road works contractors, and so on, can engage civil society organizations and request feedback from beneficiaries as an input into internal management practices. Non-political citizen engagement is thus part of the management practices within government.[1]

Citizens' political engagement shapes the incentives and characteristics of leaders who, in turn, select within-government management policies to address the principal-agent problem vis-à-vis public officials and providers. Leaders and public officials also determine whether to provide citizens with any powers of monitoring and feedback on frontline providers. Citizens' political behavior—what issues they consider when selecting and disciplining leaders, and their attitudes toward the public sector—underpins the functioning of all three principal-agent relationships. Political engagement thus indirectly influences all three principal-agent relationships through how it shapes the incentives and characteristics of leaders who exercise power within government.

Unhealthy political engagement can "invert" principal-agent relationships

Unhealthy political engagement, when the leaders who wield power within government are selected and sanctioned on the basis of their provision of private benefits rather than public goods, arises out of conflict of interest among citizens. It exacerbates the accountability problem and can lead to "inversions" in each of the principal-agent relationships of government. Powerful elites with control over the coercive institutions of the state can subvert formal democratic and governance institutions. For example, the first principal-agent problem can become one in which leaders hold citizens accountable for providing political support by using violence and clientelist strategies such as vote buying (Acemoglu and Robinson 2006b; Stokes 2005).

Unhealthy political engagement can diminish accountability not only of elected leaders but also within the principal-agent relationships between leaders, public officials, and frontline providers. For example, if political norms allow vote buying and patronage to flourish in elections, those same norms would influence how leaders manage public officials and how public officials manage frontline providers. Leaders who can get away with poor service delivery during their term in office by purchasing votes at election time also tend to provide jobs to public officials and to frontline providers as political patronage and *not* hold them accountable for service delivery. When frontline providers are patronage appointees, citizens do not expect that monitoring them or providing feedback on their performance will have any effect and therefore, do not engage to improve the third principal-agent problem. Citizens' expectations of how political power is exercised within government can maintain this vicious cycle, leading to citizens' demands for private benefits and the persistence of unhealthy political engagement.

Citizens' roles as monitors in the third type of principal-agent problem is also subject to free-riding problems, when each individual citizen contributes little to the public good of monitoring. An influential strand of the literature has focused on the free-rider problems that plague collective action and how group organization and cohesion play a role in outcomes.[2] Powerful local elites can also capture civil society and invert the role of citizens in the third principal-agent problem, again, through their control over local institutions of coercion or economic resources (Acemoglu, Reed, and Robinson 2014; Anderson, Francois, and Kotwal 2015). Rather than being engaged to hold public officials accountable, citizens can be engaged to deliver public services for themselves, letting leaders and public officials abdicate their responsibilities.

Even in contexts where power is more dispersed among citizens, rather than controlled by only a few elites, there can nevertheless be a conflict of interest among citizens with pernicious consequences for accountability for public goods. Citizens are heterogeneous in their beliefs about the role of government and what they demand from public policies and government leaders. Subsets of citizens organized as special interests can capture leaders and extract private rents from public policies (for example, as examined by Grossman and Helpman [2001]). Groups can form to engage in collective action with the objective of obtaining group-specific benefits that may come at the expense of public benefits that are shared with other citizens who are not organized (this is clearly conveyed, for instance, in Grossman and Helpman [1996]). Public officials and frontline providers can each organize as special interests (for example, teacher unions) that wield political power over leaders, thus inverting the second two principal-agent relationships within government. Social conflict leads to inefficient outcomes because those in power can choose policies to serve their interest and there is no outside agency with the capacity to control them (Acemoglu 2003).

A point emerging from this discussion is that group organization may deviate from, and reconfigure, the set of political rights agreed upon ex ante and expressed in constitutional arrangements. A crucial aspect of the political process is therefore the extent to which group pressures can be accommodated in a way that maintains balance among competing interests without causing serious distortions to commonly shared interests. The Virginia school, associated with the work of Buchanan and Tullock (1962), called attention to the potential inefficiencies that emerge from the de facto political process. The Chicago school, associated with the contributions of Becker (1983) and Wittman (1989) emphasized that the democratic process embodies a strong tendency to efficiency once competition and incentives for political entrepreneurship are taken into account.

An additional point emerging from the literature on collective action is that political parties can be a vehicle for organizing citizens in a way that makes rulers more responsive to citizen needs. But the way parties interact depends on electoral and representation institutions. For example, Persson, Roland, and Tabellini (2007) analyze the way in which, by affecting the accountability regime, presidential-congressional systems generate less spending and public goods provision than parliamentary systems (see also Persson and Tabellini [2004] and references therein). Although political parties are expected to play a large role in democracies, they may also play a surprisingly important role in some nondemocracies (Keefer 2011). The main body of this chapter largely abstracts from these themes to focus on arguments that can be made in more institution-neutral principal-agent models.

The specific characteristics of political engagement therefore matter in how it shapes the three principal-agent problems between citizens and leaders within each formal institutional context. These characteristics pertain to how active and organized different groups of citizens are, to what extent elite groups are in de facto control of state institutions, and to what are citizens' beliefs about public policies and demands from governments.

Even healthy political engagement is constrained by information asymmetries

A large literature examines how, even if citizens have political power over leaders and want to hold them accountable for the delivery of public goods, they are constrained by a lack of information about the actions of leaders and the consequences of those actions. The transparency regime within which each of the principal-agent relationships plays out determines what type of information is available to citizens and voters.

The accountability problem in principal-agent relationships arises because agents pursue objectives different from that of the principal and have access to private information that the principals lack. In the absence of these factors—if agents shared the objectives of principals, or if principals had full information—there would be no principal-agent problem. Leaders, public officials, and frontline providers undertake tasks to maximize their own payoffs comprising policy interests, reelection concerns, rent extraction, and so on. The ability of voters to decide whether political leaders have delivered the right policies and, as a result, whether those politicians should be reelected, depends on what information voters have about what policy was implemented, what level of welfare they perceive, and if policy is observed, whether circumstances warranted that particular policy choice. Similarly, voters may obtain information about the quality of political leaders themselves via disclosure rules (for example, individual assets) or through the media. An important question is what types of information are beneficial to citizens and when, both to better discipline officials and to sort good ones from bad ones.

Information problems are also acute in the within-government principal-agent problems between political leaders and public officials, and between public officials and frontline providers. Government agencies typically operate in areas where markets fail, which has profound implications for accountability. Market-based indicators of performance, such as profits, which discipline firms, cannot be used to discipline agents in government. This is one of the key conditions giving rise to bureaucracy, which instead disciplines agents by keeping track of inputs and imposing procedural constraints (Downs 1965; Wilson 1989). Procedural constraints (that is, red tape) then also become a potential source of misgovernance. Because relying on market forces is infeasible, red tape may be used not just to control agents, but also to screen clients—another potential source of misgovernance (Banerjee 1997).

Within firms, more complete incentive contracts can be written that reward agents for performance. Within government, good metrics of performance may be unavailable, making incentive contracts impractical. Multitasking distortions, which occur when agents shift effort away from valuable tasks in which their performance is difficult to measure in favor of those tasks where performance is more easily measured, are more common in government. These characteristics of principal-agent problems within government mean that even well-intentioned leaders will face the challenge of designing appropriate institutions to influence incentives for some tasks, but also to shape professional norms of behavior for others where incentives alone will be insufficient (Dixit 2002).

Information is a special good. It is a public good whose use is nonrival, hence it will typically be underprovided by the market system. Government intervention can help address this market failure and help information to be provided at more satisfactory levels in markets. A problem arises when the information that must be generated is about the government itself. Information is a crucial ingredient for solving principal-agent problems of the kind discussed above that particularly plague government agencies. Like any other industry, the government may have perverse incentives to aggravate the market failures that arise in the provision of information. But unlike any other industry, the government also has the means to do so. Against this backdrop, as will be discussed in greater detail further below in this chapter, third-party actors such as the media are critical to accountability relationships because they can provide information about the government that the government may prefer remain undisclosed.

Transparency can strengthen political engagement to improve incentives of and select better-quality leaders

The theoretical literature on the role of transparency focuses on institutional contexts in which citizens can exercise electoral power to select and discipline political leaders. The first contribution on electoral discipline as a constraint on shirking and rent extraction is by Barro (1973), although this work did not include an informational advantage for the politician. Ferejohn (1986) expanded the analysis to consider a politician who has greater knowledge than do voters about economic circumstances. This asymmetric knowledge allows politicians to gain higher rents from office. In this model, policy amounts to the choice of an effort level by the politician, that is, policy is vertical, and more is always better for the citizen. As a result, information is good for the voter because it allows him or her to fine-tune the use of elections as a source of discipline. Voters do not observe actions, but only the consequences of those actions as evident in resulting welfare. This result parallels that in Holmström (1979), in which information about the agent can never hurt the principal as long as an optimal contract can always be improved to exploit that information.

In politics, however, the "contracting" environment is very limited, and electorates often face other objectives in addition to providing incentives for pure effort.

Ambiguous effects of transparency: Details matter

Unfortunately, the basic lesson that more information is always better does not generalize over many relevant political settings. A case in point arises in models in which policy can be differentiated in a horizontal rather than vertical fashion (for example, left versus right, well adapted to circumstances versus not) and voters can only choose to retain an agent or not. When politicians have "career concerns," they may want to pick policy with an eye toward generating a favorable image of themselves. An early example of this phenomenon is in models of biased advisors (Morris 2001). Harrington (1993) makes the point that when voters have strong views about what policy ought to be picked and politicians have strong office motivation, pandering will result. In other words, politicians will do what voters demand even when politicians have better private information than voters that suggests an alternative policy would be better.

Canes-Wrone, Herron, and Shotts (2001) prove this pandering tendency is present even when politicians are benevolent rather than directly office-minded, but desire to be perceived as competent so they can continue to have the chance to set good policy. Maskin and Tirole (2004) allow for office motivation but consider politicians who do not want to project competence but, instead, congruence with the electorate's tastes. In both of the last two models, pandering is eliminated if the probability that voters will observe the consequences of actions is high enough. The key distortion is that certain policy actions, which are observable, are *a priori* tied to certain types of politician (competent or congruent) who are more desirable. It is the voters' desire to use information to weed out bad incumbents that creates a cost in the form of forgone discipline.

Prat (2005) studies a situation in which the politician does not have superior information about his or her level of expertise but is concerned with the perception of competence. The politician shows that transparency about actions can distort incentives when the politician wants to increase the voters' perception of his or her competence. The key condition is that a sufficiently strong correlation be present between a certain type of politician and the actions the voters tend to consider appropriate. An ancillary yet interesting aspect of models à la Prat is that if the principal could observe the same signal that the agent observed, the agent's incentives to manipulate his or her actions would disappear. In other words, the negative effect of information on actions stems both from opacity of consequences as well as of "process." An additional distinction is between transparency of revenues versus transparency of expenditures (Gavazza and Lizzeri 2007b). Transparency of revenues may have negative effects if expenditures are not fully transparent.

In summary, the theoretical literature yields a few key insights. First, information about policy actions may distort incentives and discipline when agents want to be perceived as competent or congruent with principals. This situation happens when information about policy consequences is poor. In those circumstances, somewhat paradoxically, transparency about actions may be counterproductive. When that happens, accountability leads to a form of "excess responsiveness" in which informed agents disregard valuable information and take actions to please their uninformed principals. In contrast, information about policy consequences (as opposed to actions) is typically beneficial. Finally, direct "information on information," that is, about the agent's signal, eliminates the bad effects of information on actions, suggesting that giving citizens information about the policy-making process is beneficial.

Discipline effects versus selection and sorting effects of transparency

Papers in the Downsian tradition of economic analysis of political markets (Downs 1957) typically take the set of candidates and the set of voters as given and show how the preferences of voters, as well as the competitive nature of elections, shape policy outcomes. The typical question is whether convergence to the median voter's preferred policy occurs.

The citizen-candidate tradition (Besley and Coate 1997; Osborne and Slivinski 1996) considers endogenous entry. The nature of the electorate, the costs of running, and competition are key determinants of who runs and subsequently what policies are implemented. In other words, the rules of the democratic game affect who gets elected to office. Although it is tacit, a clear message in this work is that the composition of the electorate is important. Therefore, citizens' political engagement as voters matters directly for policy outcomes.

To the extent that partisanship and other politician characteristics have a bearing on policy, candidate self-selection and screening by voters are also relevant to outcomes. Political engagement matters for outcomes through leader selection even in strong institutional environments because leader characteristics play a role in policy selection and implementation. That is, elections do not only serve to choose between competing policies but also in the selection of the "quality" of leaders. A theoretical literature has examined the effect of various factors on political selection, for example, compensation on the quality and integrity of politicians (for example, Caselli and Morelli 2004; Messner and Polborn 2004). Other papers have considered whether candidates with good "character" are likely to arise endogenously (and be elected). Callander (2008) shows that candidates who care about policy and not just office will in equilibrium come forward and signal their genuine interest in policy by diverging from the median.[3] Myerson (2006) shows how federal electoral institutions can enable local leaders, who have built reputations for responsibly managing public resources at local levels, to emerge as credible contenders in national politics.

Abstracting from selection, Alesina and Spear (1988), Harrington (1993), and Keefer (2011) discuss the role of political parties in disciplining politicians. The key idea is that opportunistic deviations trigger some punishment of the politician. One important question is whether institutions that discipline politicians—be they parties or forms of accountability—in office can have effects on what type of politician reaches office. It has been argued that in polities in which policy makers face coercive pressures, the presence of political parties as protection or insurance devices can improve outcomes and attract better candidates (Dal Bó and Di Tella 2003).

Besley (2004) integrates the analysis of disciplining and selection effects. The key tension is that when reelection incentives lead noncongruent politicians to choose policies voters want, voters lose the ability to distinguish between congruent and noncongruent politicians. Knowledge of the politician's type is directly valuable because it allows the weeding out of noncongruent types. However, a higher rate of direct revelations about the politician's type can backfire because it weakens the incentives of a noncongruent type to mimic the policy choices of a congruent type. For example, the politicians might think, "If the media will reveal I am a crook, I might as well behave like one." The idea that more precise information about the agent's type can weaken discipline goes back to Dewatripont, Jewitt, and Tirole (1999) and Holmström (1979).

In summary, theoretical models of the role of transparency and political engagement in the selection of leaders have three main predictions. First, citizen engagement matters through citizens' direct participation as candidates, and in many contexts, the personal qualities of those who participate will translate into policy outcomes. Second, the compensation, the expected impact on policy, and the conditions surrounding policy making (for example, the protections afforded to policy makers) will affect political selection. Third, information about the (bad) quality of politicians has counteracting effects: although it may help the electorate weed out noncongruent politicians, it can also weaken discipline.

Role of the media and consequences of media slant

The media can reveal information about the effort of politicians, which is valuable because it provides incentives for politicians to exert effort that benefits citizens (as in the model in Besley and Burgess 2002), thereby mitigating the principal-agent problem between citizens and politicians. The media can also reveal information about the politician's type. This information will help the electorate weed out incumbents with preferences that are not congruent with those of voters, but will also decrease the ability of the electorate to discipline bad incumbents. If bad incumbents know they will be seen as such, they will lose the incentive to mimic the policies of more congruent types (Besley 2004). This outcome will be an acceptable trade-off for an electorate that is primarily concerned with weeding out bad incumbents (Besley and Prat 2006).

Some papers have analyzed the special properties of information in models in which voters must seek out that information (for example, Martinelli 2006). The basic lesson is that, although costly, information is acquired in a way that permits information aggregation and the correct collective decision to be made.

Another strand of papers on voting and elections incorporates the media and the possibility that media are biased in a way that affects political outcomes. The predictions for voter welfare from adding profit-oriented media are at variance with each other. For example, Bernhardt, Krasa, and Polborn (2008) consider a model in which for-profit media may suppress information to cater to partisan voters and increase profits. The result of information suppression is potentially inefficient political outcomes. Chan and Suen (2008) analyze a model in which media seeking to maximize their audience by partially informing voters leads parties to be more likely to select platforms that cater to the median voter. Prat and Strömberg (2013) synthesize approaches considering for-profit media, politicians that seek rents from office, and voters interested in selecting and disciplining politicians.[4]

A prediction of their model is that groups that are larger and have more potential as advertising markets will see more coverage of the issues in which they are interested and be able to attract more public policy efforts by officials. This finding qualifies the discoveries in Besley and Burgess (2002): officials will exert more effort to protect the vulnerable if there is media coverage of the issues pertinent to that population. But this is a big "if." On the contrary, if a profit-seeking member of the media caters to either the numerous or the elite, public policy will also. This result raises the question of how to level the playing field in issue coverage for more vulnerable sectors of the population.

Most of the political entry models (for example, citizen-candidate models) pertain to ideological selection. But the point has been made that transparency about politicians may affect equilibrium selection along a valence dimension, that is, pertaining to the competence of politicians. Caselli and Morelli (2004) show that more precise information about politicians' types leads to higher-quality politicians. This effect acts through candidates' decisions to run and is additional to the effect highlighted by Besley (2004) of voters being able to select better types among a given set of incumbents. Counterintuitive results have been found, however, wherein more transparency (meaning better information about individual talent being available to the private sector) lowers the quality of politicians, because talented individuals are more likely to move into the private sector and select out of political entrepreneurship (Mattozzi and Merlo 2007).

Prat and Strömberg (2013) derive predictions of media coverage of issues relevant to a group for the expected competence of representatives along those issues. Groups whose issues are covered more can expect to see not only more effort directed to their issues but also higher competence.

There are strong theoretical links between political selection and capture of media by powerful or special interests. Dal Bó, Dal Bó, and Di Tella (2006) derive results emphasizing negative effects on politician quality when honest policy makers are subjected to coercive pressures that the judiciary cannot neutralize, and that the captured media may be used to amplify through targeted press operations. If much of what is good in public policy occurs as the result of benevolent political entrepreneurs, this adverse selection of politicians is a first-order problem since higher media capture will diminish the availability of those benevolent political entrepreneurs. This result has the effect of harming policy and reducing the quality of politicians.

113

Rather obviously, bad incumbents prefer an opaque regime in which their types are not revealed directly; their actions, when related to rent extraction, are not observed; and the negative consequences of their actions are not known. Governments may then have incentives to suppress information. A key lesson in Besley and Prat (2006) is that a more numerous and diverse media industry, that is, more plural media, raises the costs for the government to suppress information, leading to better ability to weed out bad incumbents. Apart from government, special interest groups can also capture media in the pursuit of their group interests (Grossman and Helpman 2001). When a society faces hurdles in diversifying its internal press sources, international partners may have a potential role in helping remove the hurdles on the path toward plural media, with healthy competition among diverse sources and low risk of capture by the state or special interests.

In summary, theory predicts positive effects of transparency on effort, although in a multigroup society with for-profit media, the discipline effects may be biased in favor of specific groups for reasons other than merit. In addition, most theories predict positive effects of free media and transparency in particular, and "clean" politics (in which unhealthy practices such as violence, intimidation, and vote buying do not invert the principal-agent relationship) in general, on selection. The theoretical work on the link between transparency and selection is scarce, but the empirical work is even scarcer, suggesting the need for studies on the topic.

Importance of citizen capacity and modes of engagement in using transparency

A key question is what citizens do with information they obtain as a result of transparency, beyond individual actions of complaining or optimally choosing what part of the bureaucracy to engage with. In most of the models already reviewed, citizens use information to vote politicians in or out of office. However, a lot of the effective control takes place through civil society activities such as petitioning, lobbying, and challenging official decisions in court. Examples of this are the actions of consumer advocate organizations, unions, and business associations. As mentioned in the context of the logic of collective action, group activity may pursue particularistic objectives rather than the general interest. A good system will maintain a balance between competing special interests, and more transparency is likely to aid all groups in mutually checking each other.

Political scientists have advanced the view that transparency and accountability can be created by design in the regulation of agencies, guaranteeing a level playing field for various interests to engage with the rule-making process (McCubbins, Noll, and Weingast 1987). In this view, citizens can be empowered via the design of administrative procedures to act as monitors (in the third type of principal-agent relationship) and as principals themselves. Certain aspects of administrative procedure are directly linked to transparency, such as freedom of information acts. Another relevant concept in the United States is the Government in the Sunshine Act (1976), which limits what parts of the policy-making process can remain opaque.

Citizens' capacity to influence bureaucratic processes is unequally distributed. As stated by McCubbins, Noll, and Weingast 1987, 261), "the resources available for representation in the administrative process vary systematically and predictably among interests." This motivates the question of how groups organize and what institutions and initiatives facilitate pluralistic citizen organization along healthy lines. This question is important because, according to the Olsonian logic of collective action, endeavors that might be costly when undertaken individually may become affordable when undertaken collectively (Olson 1965). This "cost savings" is especially true for actions that resemble public goods, like generating and using information to hold leaders accountable, challenging official decisions in court, and counterbalancing another interest group.

Transparency can have ambiguous effects even with citizens as monitors. Gavazza and Lizzeri (2007a) study cases in which publicizing the best bureaus permits more efficient queuing, but may dampen the incentives of the better bureaucrats to invest in lowering waiting times.

Another mode of citizen engagement is through complaint. Prendergast (2003) studies how complaints may yield value to the management of the bureaucracy. A central government may rely on elections at the local level or even permit rioting as an additional way to monitor the performance of local governments.

One important problem in citizens' ability to hold powerful leaders accountable is the phenomena of clientelism, vote buying, and elite control over coercive state institutions. Some early contributions to the vote-buying literature expanded principal-agent models to cases wherein a special interest (a principal) sought to provide incentives to legislators, seen as agents (Groseclose and Snyder 1996; Snyder 1991). A highly stripped-down model of vote buying that aids in the understanding of influence over both committees and general electorates is analyzed in E. Dal Bó (2007), where again principals can direct payments to voters who act as agents. The analysis shows that when voters care about the outcome (rather than just about how they vote), each voter exerts a "voting externality" over the others, which causes inefficiencies to arise. This is the fundamental difference between a market for typical goods and a market for votes.

Because the market for government policies is very different from the market for goods, establishing protections for the independence of the vote can be valuable. E. Dal Bó (2007) introduces analysis of the secrecy of the ballot when vote buying is a concern and finds that secret ballots can help when voters care about the outcome (as in general elections), but may hurt when voters care about their vote per se (as with legislators voting under monitoring by their constituencies, suggesting that voting in legislatures should be public, but ballots in general elections should be secret).[5]

Dekel, Jackson, and Wolinsky (2008) consider a dynamic setup in which principals can compete for votes. They show that voters tend to be better off when vote buyers cannot directly buy votes up front, but can only make promises contingent on winning (that is, campaign promises), a result that would also recommend secret ballots. Note that secret ballots are a constraint on transparency, but may help maintain citizens as principals in the political game rather than agents. Baland and Robinson (2008) study a model in which landowners sell the votes of their workers and, in turn, offer them contracts that leave rents but stipulate their political behavior. The authors examine the introduction of the secret ballot in Chile in 1958 and show how it decreased the vote for the right wing more where there were more rural workers who were dependent on landowner contracts, suggesting that the secret ballot increased the independence of the vote.

Powerful leaders, whether landowning patrons or political leaders, may offer compensation other than direct cash. To provide two examples from the vast literature on clientelism and electoral particularism, Anderson, Francois, and Kotwal (2015) consider the exchange of insurance for votes in rural India. Lizzeri and Persico (2001, 2004) consider political elites who compete using two instruments: particularistic transfers (as in Myerson [1993]) and public goods with diffuse benefits. Conditional on the cost of producing public goods, transfers confer an advantage at courting voters because transfers can be targeted more narrowly. These papers study factors that can mitigate the underprovision of public goods. Lizzeri and Persico (2001) compare the advantages of proportional representation versus winner-take-all systems, and Lizzeri and Persico (2004) examine the extension of the franchise as an inducement toward less particularism. Lizzeri and Persico (2004) show that when voters can be courted in these ways, more political competition (a higher number of parties) can exacerbate the incentives to cultivate narrow constituencies, leading to less efficient outcomes.

Political engagement and transparency shape beliefs and behavioral norms

The analysis of norms and, in particular, of what might create informal authority and legitimacy are difficult topics in the research frontier. However, several approaches yield valuable insights. To begin with, citizen beliefs can matter to political accountability in several natural ways. In models of electoral discipline, citizen expectations about officials' performance can drive equilibria to display high or low performance (Barro 1973; Myerson 2006). But central aspects of the institutional architecture, such as federalism, can contribute to pinning down beliefs, thereby ruling out systematic bad equilibria (Myerson 2006). This implies that institutions and norms can interact, with certain types of institutions preventing "bad-norm equilibria." The beliefs of citizens can also be important in driving outcomes in settings where pandering, rather than shirking, is a possibility. Frisell (2009) studies how widespread beliefs about the corruptibility of officials make idiosyncratic policy choices seem suspect, thereby providing honest politicians with incentives to pander ("populism").[6]

Citizen norms can also affect how a particular institution (for example, unemployment benefits) affects outcomes. For example, if living off of benefits is deemed acceptable, moral hazard will be acute and taxpayers will desire low welfare benefits in political equilibrium (Lindbeck, Nyberg, and Weibull 1999). In a more abstract environment, P. Dal Bó (2007) shows that under community enforcement, beliefs can support not only cooperative equilibria, as typically characterized by folk theorems pertaining to bilateral games, but also highly unequal and "discriminatory" equilibria. These equilibria include "royal" equilibria in which one actor always defects to take an action with social cost on others, but enjoys cooperative behavior by all others, and a "caste" equilibrium in which each higher caste takes an action that imposes a cost on lower castes but enjoys cooperation from them. Thus, citizen beliefs can undergird social structures that shape basic patterns of social interaction. Can these patterns be improved? Expectations about mutual behavior do much to determine what is perceived as legitimate behavior. This situation, however, only begs the question of what exactly legitimate behavior might be and what could enhance it.

Dal Bó, Foster, and Putterman (2010) offer an experimental design that enables a view of legitimacy and legitimate behavior as what arises when people choose their own rules of the game. In their experiment, subjects can vote for a policy (or institutional) reform that will transform a prisoners' dilemma game into a coordination game. Subjects may then find themselves in the new game either as a result of their own votes (an endogenous, "organic," reform), or as a result of an arbitrary, random decision of the computer (an exogenous reform). Subjects coordinate in the good equilibrium significantly more often when they access the coordination game because of their own decision rather than the computer's, even if the information about the vote is held constant, suggesting a buy-in or legitimating effect, of the reform bestowed by the democratic process. If homegrown policies and institutions will be more effective at improving behavior, it would be important to enable healthy political engagement wherever possible to select both policies and new institutions.

Akerlof (2015) offers a model of legitimacy-based authority, that is, the level of orders that a principal can give that will be carried out by the agent because following orders is a "duty." The model can be applied to gain an understanding of performance and behavioral norms in complex public bureaucracies. Akerlof shows how the model is operationally equivalent to agents monitoring each other to ensure compliance with orders when leaders have greater legitimacy. If legitimacy is lacking, however, the agent will reject that there is a duty and revert to considering the incentives to comply, as in standard principal-agent models with moral hazard.

However, the origins of legitimacy are not modeled in Akerlof (2015). Bolstering legitimacy is treated as an investment decision of leaders. The notion of legitimacy of leadership links with the previously mentioned work on how legitimacy for cooperative behavior can arise from democratic processes (Dal Bó, Foster, and Putterman 2010).

A way to improve interactions both among people and between people and officials might be to have leaders that exemplify certain types of behavior. Hermalin (1998) provides an early analysis of how an informed leader may promote efforts by others through his or her own effort, thereby signaling the worth of a task (see also Komai et al. [2007]). The behavior of leaders can also shift political norms under which citizens feel indignant about bad performance and act to hold leaders accountable (Bidner and Francois 2013). Acemoglu and Jackson (2015) also offer a theory in which the behavior of leaders (actors whose actions are visible to all) affects norms (citizen beliefs about mutual behavior). In the last three papers, leaders can take actions that subsequently lead to citizens' adopting cooperative social or political norms.

Taken together, this body of work suggests a pathway from political changes to the strengthening of bureaucratic institutions for service delivery. If "clean" politics can bolster the legitimacy of leaders for delivering public goods and the reverse is true when politics is "dirty," cleaning up politics can be an avenue for larger changes in how bureaucratic institutions function. Bolstered legitimacy of political leaders for delivering public goods and leaders' roles in signaling a shift in behavioral norms, might translate into improvements to the culture of performance in bureaucracies. In environments in which politics is becoming cleaner, public officials and frontline service providers may be more inclined to monitor each other to comply with rules rather than bend them for private gain.

The theme of legitimacy is also raised in Basu (2015), who is motivated by the question of the interplay of laws and norms. He argues that behavioral traits as well as citizen beliefs can result in a change in the incentives of enforcers and generate multiple equilibria. In that context, the law may have an expressive component that acts as an equilibrium-selection device. Acemoglu and Jackson (2015) analyze the interplay between laws and norms through a model in which private parties choose complementary levels of a behavior before being matched with each other. The law stipulates a threshold beyond which behavior is illegal. Multiple equilibria arise; aside from actions being complementary, detection of illegality by enforcers depends on whistleblowing by the parties, which leads to mutual expectations of behavior relevant to expectations of law enforcement. In this context, tighter laws affect the prevalence of law breaking, as well as the level choices of law breakers and law abiders, in relation to prevalent mutual expectations. Thus, the effectiveness of the law at shaping behavior (and setting future norms) depends on initially prevalent norms.

Emergence of citizens' demands for public goods

The very experience of political engagement and the outcomes it produces for quality of government and service delivery, can lead to evolution in political behavior toward the larger public interest. The previously mentioned work of Bidner and Francois (2013) has this flavor, whereby citizens become frustrated with corruption and increasingly intolerant of transgressions by leaders. This situation leads to a shift in political norms toward punishing corruption. Establishing anticorruption norms among citizens is also the idea in Dixit (2015), who examines the role of the business community in reducing the supply of bribes to government officials in the award of licenses and contracts.

A rise in demand among the elite for public goods has been linked to historical episodes of institutional reform. Lizzeri and Persico (2004) explain the extension of suffrage by English elites in the mid- to late-1800s as arising from an increase in the value of urban public goods following the industrial revolution (public health infrastructure such as sewerage, waterworks, and paved roads). A majority of the franchised elite pushed for reforms to extend the suffrage so that political parties would have stronger incentives to deliver these public goods. Consistent with their explanation, the authors document that following suffrage reforms, spending by municipal corporations on public health infrastructure increased substantially.

Demand for common-interest public goods and inclusive political institutions are highlighted by Besley and Persson (2009) as part of the explanation for the origins of state capacity. The building of legal and fiscal institutions of the state, which are needed to support markets, protect property rights, and provide public goods, are linked in their model to conditions that enable citizens to come together for a common purpose.

If citizen beliefs and demands are important because of how they interact with institutions and with politicians, one avenue to improving outcomes would be to foster interventions that affect those beliefs and demands for common-interest public goods. The literature on persuasion offers guidance on how to approach that agenda[7] and is part of the review of empirical evidence in chapter 6. An important question is whether transparency may affect beliefs, and thereby change how citizens engage with institutions, leading to an interaction between transparency and modes of engagement. Transparency can increase the value of specific modes of engagement and do so in ways that increase the value of transparency.[8] Elections and mass media are two institutional elements through which transparency and citizen engagement can potentially interact as strategic complements. Both elections and media have the potential to coordinate citizen action. Fearon (2011) offers a theory in which elections coordinate voters' beliefs about compliance by the ruler and thus also coordinate their readiness to revolt when incumbents ignore the electoral calendar or results. A similar role is played by royal courts in the model by Myerson (2008), wherein a common venue allows the nobles to learn how the king is treating each of them. Yanagizawa-Drott (2014) offers a model in which media play a similar role as a coordination device. Although the effects of media in politics have been studied, disentangling pure coordinating effects from other, more direct, encouragement effects is difficult. The evidence in Yanagizawa-Drott (2014) shows that media can be used to manipulate citizens and coordinate actions, and even do so in negative directions, as in the role of radio in promoting participation in the Rwandan genocide.

This issue links back to the discussion of how media can affect political selection and incentives depending upon the nature of its programming content—whether it reflects capture by political leaders or by special interests, or whether more diverse and plural media flourish to reveal information that is relevant for accountability. Empirical advances discussed in chapter 6 suggest that the role of media is a challenging yet crucial area for governance policy. The challenges arise from how even plural media that are independent of state control can sometimes work to reduce political engagement and polarize the electorate.

Previous sections deal with the fact that politicians may gain from opacity and media slant, and may prevent all valuable information from reaching voters. The chapter also covers the fact that voters may face collective-action issues in acting on the information they do have. Problems with clientelism notwithstanding, voting is a low-cost activity and could be relied upon more when it comes to engaging citizens in decision making. But voter capacity issues arise—voters may lack the capacity to keep track of all relevant issues and metrics. A literature on political behavior[9] studies the ability of voters to compose a "political picture" by relying on partisan cues and other information-economizing heuristics. But as Caplan (2007) shows, substantial gaps remain between the policy opinions of experts and average voters. Bartels (1996) argues that voter information gaps can have large political consequences. Several voter biases have been characterized, such as antimarket and antiforeign biases. However, little is known about structural characteristics that may lead voters to error. This situation is intriguing given that the possibility of voter error is an assumption in the pandering models reviewed previously.

Dal Bó, Dal Bó, and Eyster (2013) propose a conceptual framework based on the idea that voters may underappreciate equilibrium effects, leading to a demand on their part for inefficient policies and institutions, and show experimental evidence to support this idea. According to the evidence, voters fail to democratically solve social dilemmas (such as getting out of the tragedy of the commons) because they perceive the direct effects of policy on payoffs, but not its indirect effects through the induced changes in the behavior of other players. Voters reject Pigovian taxes that help internalize externalities and improve equilibrium payoffs because their immediate, visible effect, being a tax, is to lower payoffs. The evidence suggests that experience with all policy options, or at least voter education on the relevant options, is a necessary condition for overcoming this type of voting failure. Understanding the way in which civil society can expand voter capacity is a pending assignment for future research.

This chapter has cast governance problems as a sequence of principal-agent problems, as follows: (i) between citizens and political leaders; (ii) between political leaders and public officials who lead government agencies; and (iii) between public officials and frontline providers. Political engagement and transparency shape all three of these principal-agent relationships in fundamental ways.

Citizen engagement matters to governance outcomes. Engagement involves various dimensions: whether citizens act as principals or agents, citizen beliefs and expectations, and citizens' empowerment to act on information. When citizens are engaged as agents rather than principals, for example, as a result of vote buying, this typically leads to inefficiency. This outcome is true even when candidates compete for votes, because competition may push candidates to target narrow majorities via particularistic benefits, eschewing public goods. This situation is typical of clientelist systems. The ability of different groups to engage, cooperate with each other, and achieve tighter accountability varies, sometimes with socioeconomic characteristics, but also with aspects of the design of the policy process and institutions, such as democratic mechanisms and federalism. If citizen collective action is an important component of engagement, a crucial question is how best to promote pluralistic citizen organization.

The chapter shows how disciplining leaders and selecting different types of leaders matters for governance and development outcomes. Transparency about both policy actions and policy consequences is essential. When information about policy consequences is lacking, transparency about policy actions may be counterproductive, leading to pandering and populism by politicians seeking to please uninformed citizens. In contrast, information about policy consequences can strengthen the ability of citizens to hold leaders accountable for outcomes.

Citizen beliefs about politicians, the political process, and public policies are relevant. Political norms that ingrain expectations of low performance perpetuate underperformance, be it corruption, shirking, or pandering. In addition, pandering is more likely when politicians are not trusted, which would occur when corruption is high. Thus, corruption, by creating a culture of distrust, has the indirect effect of fostering pandering. Political engagement, and the leaders selected through it, can help shift political beliefs and norms of political behavior among citizens, potentially enabling societies to escape low-performance traps to improve governance in the public sector.

Notes

1. Direct citizen participation in providing public goods is separate from this principal-agent setting because it consists of citizens directly contributing their labor and monetary resources to the maintenance of local public goods and the management of funds that are devolved to community-based organizations. Citizen engagement by public officials to provide technical inputs into the formulation of public policies, such as, for example, regulatory agencies seeking feedback from businesses in rule-making, is also separate from this principal-agent setting. These forms of direct citizen participation in the provision of public goods and in the crafting of public policies and regulations, are not within the scope of this report.
2. See, for example, the seminal work by Olson (1965).
3. On the issue of candidate character, see also Kartik and McAffee (2007) and Bernheim and Kartik (2014).
4. Their treatment draws on Strömberg (2004a, 2004b).
5. Levy (2007) considers transparency in committees where members are not targeted by vote buyers but where members care about their reputation. She shows that transparency in committees, by allowing a tighter attribution of a collective decision to individual inputs, may make committees less "conformist" and more likely to pass reforms.
6. On populism, see also Acemoglu, Egorov, and Sonin (2013).
7. See DellaVigna and Gentzkow (2010) for a review of the literature.
8. A different example of the interaction between transparency and modes of engagement is provided earlier in the chapter, in the context of information about different government bureaus that can lead to actions (queuing) that lower the value of transparency (Gavazza and Lizzeri 2007a).
9. See Bartels (2012) for a review.

Bibliography

Acemoglu, D. 2003. "Why Not a Political Coase Theorem? Social Conflict, Commitment, and Politics." *Journal of Comparative Economics* 31 (4): 620–52.

Acemoglu, D., Georgy Egorov, and Konstantin Sonin. 2013. "A Political Theory of Populism." *Quarterly Journal of Economics* 128 (2): 771–805

Acemoglu, D., and M. Jackson. 2015. "History, Expectations, and Leadership in the Evolution of Social Norms." *Review of Economic Studies* 82 (2): 423–56.

Acemoglu, D., Tristan Reed, and James A. Robinson. 2014. "Chiefs: Economic Development and Elite Control of Civil Society in Sierra Leone." *Journal of Political Economy* 122 (2): 319–68.

Acemoglu, D., and J. A. Robinson. 2000. "Why Did the West Extend the Franchise? Growth, Inequality and Democracy in Historical Perspective." *Quarterly Journal of Economics* 115 (4): 1167–199.

———. 2006a. *Economic Origins of Dictatorship and Democracy.* Cambridge, U.K. and New York: Cambridge University Press.

———. 2006b. "De Facto Political Power and Institutional Persistence." *American Economic Association Papers and Proceedings* 96 (2): 325–30.

Akerlof, R. 2015. "A Theory of Authority." Unpublished, University of Warwick.

Alesina, Alberto, and Stephen E. Spear. 1988. "An Overlapping Generations Model of Electoral Competition." *Journal of Public Economics* 37 (3): 359–79.

Alesina, Alberto, and Guido Tabellini. 2007. "Bureaucrats or Politicians? Part I: A Single Policy Task." *The American Economic Review* 97 (1): 169–79.

Anderson, Siwan, Patrick Francois, and Ashok Kotwal. 2015. "Clientelism in Indian Villages." *American Economic Review* 105 (6): 1780–816.

Baland, Jean-Marie, and James A. Robinson. 2008. "Land and Power: Theory and Evidence from Chile." *American Economic Review* 98 (5): 1737–65.

Banerjee, Abhijit. 1997. "A Theory of Misgovernance." *Quarterly Journal of Economics* 112 (4): 1289–332.

Barro, Robert. 1973. "The Control of Politicians: An Economic Model." *Public Choice* 14 (1): 19–42.

Bartels, L. 1996. "Uninformed Votes: Information Effects in Presidential Elections." *American Journal of Political Science* 40 (1): 194–230.

———. 2012. "The Study of Electoral Behavior." In *The Oxford Handbook of American Elections and Political Behavior*, edited by Jan Leighley. Oxford: Oxford University Press.

Basu, K. 2015. *The Republic of Beliefs: A New Approach to Law and Economics.* Washington, DC: World Bank.

Becker, G. 1983. "A Theory of Competition among Pressure Groups for Political Influence." *Quarterly Journal of Economics* 98 (3): 371–400.

Bernhardt, Dan, Stefan Krasa, and Mattias Polborn. 2008. "Political Polarization and the Electoral Effects of Media Bias." *Journal of Public Economics* 98 (5–6): 1092–104.

Bernheim, B. D., and N. Kartik. 2014. "Candidates, Character, and Corruption." *American Economic Journal: Microeconomics* 6 (2): 205–46.

Besley, Timothy. 2004. "Paying Politicians: Theory and Evidence." *Journal of the European Economic Association* 2 (2–3): 193–215.

Besley, Timothy, and Robin Burgess. 2002. "The Political Economy of Government Responsiveness: Theory and Evidence from India." *Quarterly Journal of Economics* 117 (4): 1415–51.

Besley, Timothy, and Stephen Coate. 1997. "An Economic Model of Representative Democracy." *Quarterly Journal of Economics* 112 (1): 85–114.

Besley, Timothy, and Torsten Persson. 2009. "The Origins of State Capacity: Property Rights, Taxation, and Politics." *American Economic Review* 99 (4): 1218–44.

Besley, Timothy, and Andrea Prat. 2006. "Handcuffs for the Grabbing Hand? Media Capture and Political Government Accountability." *American Economic Review* 96 (3): 720–36.

Bidner, Chris, and Patrick Francois. 2013. "The Emergence of Political Accountability." *Quarterly Journal of Economics* 128 (3): 1397–448.

Buchanan, J., and G. Tullock. 1962. *The Calculus of Consent.* Ann Arbor, MI: University of Michigan Press.

Callander, S. 2008. "Political Motivations." *Review of Economic Studies* 75 (3): 671–97.

Canes-Wrone, Brandice, Michael C. Herron, and Kenneth W. Shotts. 2001. "Leadership and Pandering: A Theory of Executive Policymaking." *American Journal of Political Science* 45 (3): 532–50.

Caplan, Bryan. 2007. *The Myth of the Rational Voter: Why Democracies Choose Bad Policies.* Princeton, NJ: Princeton University Press.

Caselli, Francesco, and Massimo Morelli. 2004. "Bad Politicians." *Journal of Public Economics* 88 (3–4): 759–82.

Chan, Jimmy, and Wing Suen. 2008. "A Spatial Theory of News Consumption and Electoral Competition." *Review of Economic Studies* 75 (3): 699–728.

Dal Bó, Ernesto. 2007. "Bribing Voters." *American Journal of Political Science* 51 (4): 789–803.

Dal Bó, Ernesto, Pedro Dal Bó, and Rafael Di Tella. 2006. "Plata o Plomo? Bribe and Punishment in a Theory of Political Influence." *American Political Science Review* 100 (1): 41–53.

Dal Bó, Ernesto, Pedro Dal Bó, and Erik Eyster. 2013. "The Demand for Bad Policy when Voters Underappreciate Equilibrium Effects." Unpublished working paper. http://faculty.haas.berkeley.edu/dalbo/demand_for_bad_policy.pdf.

Dal Bó, Ernesto, and Rafael Di Tella. 2003. "Capture by Threat." *Journal of Political Economy* 111 (5): 1123–54.

Dal Bó, Pedro. 2007. "Social Norms, Cooperation and Inequality." *Economic Theory* 30 (1): 89–105.

Dal Bó, Pedro, Andrew Foster, and Louis Putterman. 2010. "Institutions and Behavior: Experimental Evidence on the Effects of Democracy." *American Economic Review* 100 (5): 2205–29.

Dekel, E., M. Jackson, and A. Wolinsky. 2008. "Vote-Buying: General Elections." *Journal of Political Economy* 116 (2): 351–80.

DellaVigna, S., and M. Gentzkow. 2010. "Persuasion: Empirical Evidence." *Annual Review of Economics* 2 (1): 643–69.

Dewatripont, M., I. Jewitt, and J. Tirole. 1999. "The Economics of Career Concerns, Part I: Comparing Information Structures." *Review of Economic Studies* 66 (1): 183–98.

Dixit, A. 2002. "Incentives and Organizations in the Public Sector: An Interpretative Review." *Journal of Human Resources* 37 (4): 696–727.

———. 2015. "How Business Community Institutions Can Help Fight Corruption." *World Bank Economic Review* 29 (suppl 1): S25–S47.

Downs, A. 1957. "An Economic Theory of Political Action in a Democracy." *Journal of Political Economy* 65 (2): 135–50.

———. 1965. "A Theory of Bureaucracy." *American Economic Review* 55 (1/2): 439–46.

Fearon, J. D. 2011. "Self-Enforcing Democracy." *Quarterly Journal of Economics* 126 (4): 1661–708.

Ferejohn, John. 1986. "Incumbent Performance and Electoral Control." *Public Choice* 30 (Fall): 5–25.

Frisell, Lars. 2009. "A Theory of Self-Fulfilling Political Expectations." *Journal of Public Economics* 93 (5–6): 715–20.

Gavazza, Alessandro, and Alessandro Lizzeri. 2007a. "The Perils of Transparency in Bureaucracies." *American Economic Review, Papers and Proceedings* 97 (2): 300–5.

———. 2007b. "Transparency and Economic Policy." *Review of Economic Studies* 76 (3): 1023–48.

Groseclose, Tim, and James M. Snyder. 1996. "Buying Supermajorities." *American Political Science Review* 90 (2): 303–15.

Grossman, Gene M., and Elhanan Helpman. 1996. "Electoral Competition and Special Interest Politics." *Review of Economic Studies* 63: 265–86.

———. 2001. *Special Interest Politics*. Cambridge and London: MIT Press.

Harrington, Joseph. 1993. "Economic Policy, Economic Performance, and Elections." *American Economic Review* 83 (1): 27–42.

Hermalin, Benjamin E. 1998. "Toward an Economic Theory of Leadership: Leading by Example." *American Economic Review* 88(5): 1188–206.

Holmström, B. 1979. "Moral Hazard and Observability." *Bell Journal of Economics* 10 (1): 74–91.

Kartik, N., and R. P. McAfee. 2007. "Signaling Character in Electoral Competition." *American Economic Review* 97 (3): 852–70.

Keefer, P. 2011. "Collective Action, Political Parties, and Pro-Development Public Policy." *Asian Development Review* 28 (1): 94–118.

Komai, M., M. Stegeman, and B. E. Hermalin. 2007. "Leadership and Information." *The American Economic Review* 97(3): 944–47.

Levy, Gilat. 2007. "Decision Making in Committees: Transparency, Reputation and Voting Rules." *American Economic Review* 97 (1): 150–68.

Lindbeck, A., S. Nyberg, and J. Weibull. 1999. "Social Norms and Economic Incentives in the Welfare State." *Quarterly Journal of Economics* 114 (1): 1–35.

Lizzeri, A., and N. Persico. 2001. "The Provision of Public Goods under Alternative Electoral Incentives." *American Economic Review* 91 (1): 225–39.

———. 2004. "Why Did the Elites Extend the Suffrage? Democracy and the Scope of Government, With an Application to Britain's 'Age of Reform.'" *Quarterly Journal of Economics* 119 (2): 707–65.

Martinelli, C. 2006. "Would Rational Voters Acquire Costly Information?" *Journal of Economic Theory* 129 (1): 225–51.

Maskin, Eric, and Jean Tirole. 2004. "The Politician and the Judge: Accountability in Government." *American Economic Review* 94 (4): 1034–54.

Mattozzi, Andrea, and Antonio Merlo. 2007. "The Transparency of Politics and the Quality of Politicians." *American Economic Review, Papers and Proceedings* 97 (2): 311–15.

McCubbins, Matthew, Roger Noll, and Barry Weingast. 1987. "Administrative Procedures as Instruments of Political Control." *Journal of Law, Economics and Organization* 3 (2): 243–77.

Messner, M., and M. Polborn. 2004. "Paying Politicians." *Journal of Public Economics* 88 (12): 2423–45.

Morris, S., 2001. "Political Correctness." *Journal of Political Economy* 109 (2): 231–65.

Myerson, R. 1993. "Incentives to Cultivate Favored Minorities under Alternative Electoral Systems." *American Political Science Review* 87 (4): 856–69.

———. 2006. "Federalism and Incentives for Success of Democracy." *Quarterly Journal of Political Science* 1 (1): 3–23.

———. 2008. "The Autocrat's Credibility Problem and the Foundations of the Constitutional State." *American Political Science Review* 102 (1): 125–39.

Olson, Mancur. 1965. *The Logic of Collective Action*. Cambridge, MA: Harvard University Press.

Osborne, M., and A. Slivinski. 1996. "A Model of Political Competition with Citizen-Candidates." *Quarterly Journal of Economics* 111 (1): 65–96.

Persson, T., G. Roland, and G. Tabellini. 2007. "Electoral Rules and Government Spending in Parliamentary Democracies." *Quarterly Journal of Political Science* 2 (2): 155–88.

Persson, T., and G. Tabellini. 2004. "Constitutional Rules and Fiscal Policy Outcomes." *American Economic Review* 94 (1): 25–45.

Prat, Andrea. 2005. "The Wrong Kind of Transparency." *American Economic Review* 95 (3): 862–77.

Prat, Andrea, and David Strömberg. 2013. "The Political Economy of Mass Media." In *Advances in Economics and Econometrics: Theory and Applications, Proceedings of the Tenth World Congress of the Econometric Society*. Cambridge University Press. http://www.columbia.edu/~ap3116/papers/mediasurvey11.pdf.

Prendergast, Canice. 2003. "The Limits of Bureaucratic Efficiency." *Journal of Political Economy* 111 (5): 929–58.

Snyder, James M. 1991. "On Buying Legislatures." *Economics and Politics* 3 (2): 93–109.

Stokes, Susan C. 2005. "Perverse Accountability: A Formal Model of Machine Politics with Evidence from Argentina." *American Political Science Review* 99 (3): 315–25.

Strömberg, David. 2004a. "Mass Media Competition, Political Competition, and Public Policy." *Review of Economic Studies* 71 (1): 265–84.

———. 2004b. "Radio's Impact on Public Spending." *Quarterly Journal of Economics* 119 (1): 189–221.

Wilson, James Q. 1989. *Bureaucracy: What Government Agencies Do and Why They Do It*. New York: Basic Books.

Wittman, D. 1989. "Why Democracies Produce Efficient Results." *Journal of Political Economy* 97 (6): 1395–424.

Yanagizawa-Drott, David. 2014. "Propaganda and Conflict: Evidence from the Rwandan Genocide." *Quarterly Journal of Economics* 129 (4): 1947–94.

CHAPTER FIVE

Evidence on the Impact of Political Engagement

Overview

This chapter provides evidence from research across a variety of contexts that political engagement has profound consequences for governance, policy selection, and development outcomes, often in highly nuanced ways. Healthy political engagement, when citizens select and sanction leaders on the basis of performance in delivering public goods, can improve development outcomes by changing the incentives of and encouraging the selection of better-quality leaders. Unhealthy political engagement, conversely, create incentives for leaders to extract private rents from public resources, at the expense of the public goods needed for development. The next two sections cover this evidence on the nuanced effects of political engagement on incentives and selection of different types of leaders. Much of the available evidence focuses on testing the impact of political engagement by individual voters through elections. Less evidence is available on the impact of political engagement by elite citizens and by civil society organizations outside of elections. What is available suggests that the impact of organized groups has important interactions with and ultimately works through electoral institutions.

The next section reviews empirical research which supports the theoretical insights (in chapter 4) that the experience of political engagement and the leaders selected through it shape behavioral norms. It first reviews the evidence on how the leaders selected through political engagement themselves influence norms. Second, it reviews a literature on the impact of historical institutions of political engagement, showing that the inclusiveness of those institutions influences norms. More inclusive institutions that facilitated the engagement of larger groups of citizens are associated with norms of cooperation among citizens. A history of cooperative norms is, in turn, associated with political engagement functioning in healthy ways in current times. Conversely, exclusionary historical institutions, which concentrated power in the hands of a few elites, are associated with unhealthy political engagement and worse development outcomes.

Finally, the last section of this chapter shows that strengthening public sector institutions through formal capacity building is not enough because informal norms of political behavior play a significant role in how those institutions actually function. Persistence in norms regardless of changes in formal institutions has implications for the transition from weak to strong institutions of government. Historical accounts of how effective state capacity and institutional change comes about are consistent with the role of healthy political engagement in creating the conditions for that change. Improvements in the quality of political engagement are crucial for improving governance.

Impact of political engagement on the incentives of leaders

This section reviews the literature on the impact of political engagement on governance, policy selection, and development outcomes, which operates through its impact on the incentives of leaders. It begins by briefly reviewing cross-country evidence on the correlation between national-level indicators of political engagement and growth. It then moves on to discuss the evidence of the impact of political engagement on outcomes within countries.

Political engagement happens in every institutional context, democracies and autocracies, albeit in different ways. The main effect examined in the literature is when there is scope for greater political engagement by a large number of individual citizens acting as voters and as contenders for leadership because of electoral institutions, versus when they do not, that is, when power over leaders is instead concentrated among elites or organized groups.

Cross-country evidence

A wave of cross-country research has examined whether countries with electoral institutions exhibit different economic performance than those with nonelectoral institutions that restrict the power of citizens to discipline leaders. While the cross-country correlation between democracy and economic growth is much debated, recent research reports a robust positive association. On average, this evidence suggests that political engagement through electoral institutions leads to better development outcomes. Yet, clear examples can be pointed to where autocracies outperform democracies. Research examining these differences in outcomes concludes that the key question that applies to both autocracies and democracies is whether leaders are selected and sanctioned on the basis of performance in delivering public goods. That is, the variation across countries shows that the impact of political engagement on economic outcomes depends on whether it is healthy or unhealthy.

Acemoglu et al. (2014) provide robust evidence that democratic institutions lead to greater growth in the long run, using data from both Freedom House and Polity IV. They study the effect of democratization within countries over time, controlling for forms of institutional variation across countries other than democracy. They report extensive robustness tests, using different measures of democracy and different methods of estimation, including to account for the dynamics inherent in how gross domestic product (GDP) changes over time. Their finding is that democratization contributes to a sustained positive impact on economic growth.

Other recent work examining the political determinants of variation across countries in economic growth is consistent with the results and conclusions of Acemoglu et al. (2014). Papaioannou and Siourounis (2008) look at the growth effects of permanent democratic transitions, building on the Polity IV data. They find that transitions to democracy are associated with a roughly one percent increase in annual real per capita GDP growth. Rodrik and Wacziarg (2005) also identify transitions to democracy using Polity IV data. They find that transitions to democracy do not take place at the expense of economic growth and often lead to short-term boosts in growth and reductions in economic volatility. Mobarak (2005) uses Polity IV data and finds a negative correlation between democracy and economic volatility. Rodrik (2000) provides a range of evidence—that democracies have more stable and predictable growth, handle adverse shocks better, and deliver better distributional outcomes—to support the contention that democracies are able to build better institutions that are suited to local conditions, to support economic outcomes.

Andersen et al. (2014) link the democracy measures in Polity IV to corruption outcomes. The authors find that changes in the world price of oil, resulting in exogenous shocks to petroleum rents, lead to an increase in hidden wealth abroad (measured by bank deposits in offshore financial centers) in petroleum-rich autocracies, but with no similar effect for petroleum-rich democracies. They interpret this evidence as follows: political elites are more easily able to turn petroleum rents into political rents in countries that lack political constraints, as measured using Polity IV data.

Easterly (2011) examines the notion of a "benevolent autocrat" that has been regarded in some public policy quarters as a way of achieving economic development goals. In fixed-effects regressions decomposing growth variation into variation between leaders and within leaders, Easterly (2011) finds no results supporting growth effects for autocrats. He reports that the effect of leaders accounts for more of the variation in growth in democracies than in autocracies. He further argues that the notion of a benevolent autocrat as a leadership paradigm is in large part rooted in cognitive biases. For example, trends in newspaper coverage show considerably more reporting of successful autocrats compared with unsuccessful ones. As a result of overreporting and relatively abundant information, individuals' perceptions of an autocrat achieving high growth rates may be upwardly biased.

The above-reviewed evidence does not mean that democracies invariably produce better outcomes. In fact, Besley and Kudamatsu (2008) and Keefer (2011) provide evidence that some autocracies are more successful than many democracies. Besley and Kudamatsu (2008) model the conditions under which autocracies can produce better outcomes than democracies. Their main argument is that if an autocracy is governed by a selectorate (that is, a group of presumably elite citizens with the power to select the leader), and if the selectorate exercises control to discipline poor performance, then the autocracy will promote good policies. Societies in which elites do not have norms and capacity to sanction leaders, or where elites benefit from leaders staying in office despite poor performance, would not satisfy the criteria for successful autocracies. Empirically, the authors characterize successful autocracies as those that had a growth rate above the 80th percentile of the distribution. Consistent with their theoretical explanation, they show that autocracies that are successful according to their definition of high growth are associated with more leadership turnover.

Keefer's (2011) argument is conceptually similar. He shows that organized political parties can solve collective-action problems by holding leaders accountable for performance. The analog to the selectorate in his work is the organized party. Empirically, he finds that measures of party organization outperform measures of democracy in explaining variation in governance and growth across countries. Keefer (2007) provides other evidence of differences between nascent and established democracies that is consistent with the importance of organized political parties in democracies in holding leaders accountable. Younger democracies are more corrupt; exhibit less rule of law, lower levels of bureaucratic quality, and secondary school enrollment; and spend more on public investment and government workers.

A common thread in this literature that applies to both democratic and autocratic institutional arrangements, is whether leaders are selected and sanctioned on the basis of performance. Besley and Kudamatsu (2008) show how the performance of both democracies and autocracies depends on the political environment within which each system of government is implemented. They show that although a successful autocracy performs better than a polarized democracy in which elections do not reward public interest policies, the autocracy is, in turn, outperformed by a well-functioning democracy in which public interest policies are politically salient. The worst of all systems in their model are autocracies in which leaders are able to maintain their grip on power despite bad performance. Consistent with their model and with other work (Mobarak 2005; Rodrik 2000), they document a high degree of variance of growth under autocracies compared with democracies.

Within-country evidence

This report is *not* about whether electoral institutions at the national level are better or worse than other national political systems. It moves beyond cross-country evidence on the effects of national political systems, to focus on within-country evidence on the nuances of political engagement within the same national context and how its specific characteristics matter for governance and for development outcomes.

Research is growing on the impact of electoral institutions within countries across the spectrum of national political systems. One body of evidence uses institutional variation in term limits across local political jurisdictions to examine the effects of reelection incentives on leaders' behavior. Besley and Case (1995) pioneered this literature, showing that term limits affect the fiscal policies chosen by U.S. governors. Between 1950 and 1986, per capita taxes were higher during the final term of term-limited governors who did not have to face voters again. This shows that in a context where taxation, or the size of government, is the most salient policy issue in political competition, as in the United States political engagement shapes leaders' incentives toward that policy. List and Sturm (2006) build upon Besley and Case (1995) to provide evidence that electoral incentives influence other policy areas in the United States as well, which are not as salient as taxation, such as environmental policy.

The methodology for estimating the impact of electoral institutions has been fruitfully applied to a wide variety of developing countries. Several papers examine variation across municipalities within Brazil when directly elected mayors face term limits versus when they are eligible for reelection. Ferraz and Finan (2011) show that reelection incentives reduce corruption. Comparing mayors who are in their first terms with those who are in their second terms and can no longer be reelected, they find that second-term mayors have greater indicators of corruption. Second-term corruption is more pronounced among municipalities with less access to information and where the likelihood of judicial punishment is lower.

De Janvry, Finan, and Sadoulet (2012) examine whether reelection incentives affect the performance of a decentralized conditional cash transfer program in Brazil. They too exploit the variation in reelection incentives induced by term limits. They show that although this federal program successfully reduced school dropout rates by 8 percentage points, the program's impact was 36 percent larger in municipalities governed by mayors who faced reelection possibilities compared with those with lame-duck mayors. First-term mayors with good program performance were much more likely to get reelected. These mayors adopted program implementation practices that were not only more transparent, but also were associated with better program outcomes.

Burgess et al. (2015) and Casey (2015) provide evidence of the importance of electoral competition in Sub-Saharan Africa where ethnic favoritism distorts economic policies. They find that electoral competition can reduce ethnicity-related policy distortions. Burgess et al. (2015) quantify ethnic favoritism in public investment, in particular, road construction in Kenya. They show that during the 1963–2011 period, districts in Kenya that shared ethnicity with the president received twice as much expenditure on roads and had four times the length of paved roads built. They further show that this patronage took place mostly during autocratic periods and not during the periods of multiparty political competition. Casey (2015) examines whether local elections, where voters may have more information about local candidates compared with national-level elections, helps relax ethnic and partisan loyalties in Sierra Leone. She finds that in local elections, citizens exhibit greater willingness to cross ethnic-party lines.[1]

Evidence is also available from China—where elections are held at the village level. Martínez-Bravo et al. (2011) argue that local elections in China support accountability of local leaders to citizens. In a companion paper, Martínez-Bravo et al. (2014) argue that local electoral institutions can improve local government performance in delivering public goods, compared with bureaucratic monitoring through upper-level governments. For this work, the authors construct a panel data set of village administrative records to document the history of political reforms and economic policies for more than 200 villages. The research design relies on the staggered timing of the introduction of village elections to identify its effects.[2]

Other results are available on the role of local elections within autocratic national political systems. Martínez-Bravo (2014) examines the behavior of local officials during the transition to democracy in Indonesia after 1999. Specifically, she examines whether local officials' incentives differ depending on whether the local officials are appointed or elected. The method of selecting local officials varies across Indonesia. The country is divided into two types of villages: *desa*, where the village head is elected by villagers; and *kelurahan*, where the village head is appointed by the district mayor. Martínez-Bravo (2014) finds that President Suharto's party was 5.5 percentage points more likely to win in villages that had appointed heads, relative to villages that had elected heads. The results suggest that in villages where the people elected their local leaders, they were more able to vote against the dominant party in contrast to where the local leaders were appointed by that party. The results also show that elected leaders can influence governance through their control over appointed public officials. Within districts where the main opposition party won by a tight margin, the villages where President Suharto's party won experienced a 7.4 percentage point higher probability of turnover of their appointed village heads than did the villages where another party won. Similarly, within districts where President Suharto's party won by a tight margin, the probability of appointed village head turnover was 19 percentage points lower in villages where President Suharto's party won than in villages where another party won.

The above studies undertaken in the contexts of local elections within nondemocratic national regimes are linked to the results of Enikolopov and Zhuravskaya (2007), who show that appointing local politicians rather than electing them does not improve the results of fiscal decentralization.

That is, local electoral institutions through which citizens select leaders, rather than appointments by higher-tier authorities, makes a significant difference for local accountability across a variety of national political systems.

Evidence of the importance of electoral institutions for accountability also comes from a strand of literature that finds that restrictions on political engagement by individual voters—because of limited suffrage laws, or voter capacity constraints, or because of elite control of economic resources—are associated with worse outcomes than when larger numbers of citizens are effectively enfranchised.

Miller (2008) examines the effects of enfranchisement on policy outcomes in the United States. He uses the staggered introduction of women's suffrage in the United States to show that suffrage laws were followed by immediate shifts in legislative behavior and sudden large increases in local public health spending. This growth in public health spending fueled large-scale door-to-door hygiene campaigns, and child mortality declined by 8–15 percent (or 20,000 annual child deaths nationwide).

Contrasting the impact of women's suffrage with the continuing disenfranchisement of black southerners in the United States, Carruthers and Wanamaker (2015) provide further evidence of the importance of voting for public service outcomes. They find that female voter enfranchisement can account for up to one-third of the 1920–40 rise in public school expenditures. Yet, these increases in school resources were disproportionately targeted at white schools, where gains far outpaced those for schools serving the black population. As a result, the authors conclude that women's suffrage exacerbated racial inequality in education expenditures and substantially delayed relative gains in black human capital observed later in the century.

Fujiwara (2015) studies the introduction of electronic voting in Brazil and finds that it improved health services by effectively enfranchising poor and less educated voters. Electronic voting was introduced at scale in the 1998 elections. But because of a limited supply of devices, only municipalities with more than 40,500 registered voters used the new technology. Using a regression discontinuity design, Fujiwara finds that electronic voting reduced residual votes, or those that are not counted because of irregularities at the polling booth, in state legislature elections by a magnitude larger than 10 percent of total turnout, thus effectively enfranchising millions of voters. Consistent with the hypothesis that these voters were more likely to be less educated, the effects are larger in municipalities with higher illiteracy rates. Moreover, electronic voting raises the vote shares of left-wing parties. These results are not driven by the (nonexistent) effects on turnout or candidate entry. The author finds that electronic voting was associated with a rise in the number of prenatal visits by health professionals and a drop in the prevalence of low-weight births (below 2,500 grams) by less educated women, but not for the more educated. The effects on health outcomes are striking, but should be treated with caution because the variables are measured at the state level, with consequently lower power of the empirical test to identify the impact of electronic voting at the municipal level.

Kudamatsu (2012) finds that the emergence of democracy in Sub-Saharan Africa in the post–Cold War period reduces infant mortality by 1.2 percentage points or 12 percent of the sample mean. He compiles indicators of political competition and leader turnover, and links it to a Demographic and Health Survey retrospective panel of mother-level fertility and infant mortality data to study 11 episodes of democratization since 1990. He compares the survival of infants (up to 12 months) born to the same mother before and after democratization. He shows that this association is robust to a variety of controls including the possible effects of official development assistance, mother age at the birth of the child, country-specific birth order, time and other trends, mother asset ownership and education level, and country-level GDP.

Elections are not the only way through which large groups of nonelite citizens can impact the incentives of leaders. Public protests and "revolutions" are also means through which citizens can discipline leaders, the theory of which was discussed in chapter 4. Empirical evidence is lagging that theory, but is beginning to emerge. Aidt and Jensen (2014) provide econometric support for the theory, showing that the threat of revolution leads to extension of franchise. Acemoglu, Hassan, and Tahoun (2014) find a negative correlation between the size of street protests in the Arab Republic of Egypt and the stock market value of politically connected firms, suggesting that protests can restrict the ability of connected firms to profit from corruption and favoritism. The authors conduct a series of event studies around the Arab Spring. They find that in the nine trading days following Mubarak's fall, the value of firms connected to the National Democratic Party fell by about 13 percent relative to the value of nonconnected firms. They then use information from Egyptian and international print and online media to construct a daily estimate of the number of protesters in Tahrir Square and analyze the effect of these protests on the returns of firms connected to the group then in power. Their specifications estimate the differential changes in the stock market values of different types of connected firms relative to nonconnected firms as a function of the size of the protests. They find that a turnout of 500,000 protesters in Tahrir Square lowered the market valuation of firms connected to the incumbent group by 0.8 percent relative to nonconnected firms.

Other evidence on the impact of organized groups outside of elections shows that their impact interacts with and works through electoral institutions. Madestam et al. (2013) examine the Tea Party movement in the United States and provide evidence of the effects of political protests on policy making through changes in voting behavior. The paper analyzes the effects of the 2009 nationwide Tax Day Rallies of the Tea Party movement. On April 15, 2009, members of the nascent movement held more than 500 protests in cities all across the United States. The authors investigate whether the size of these protests increased public support for the Tea Party position and led to more Republican votes in the 2010 midterm elections. To causally identify these relationships, the authors use rainfall on the protest day as an instrument. The authors show that the size of the protest led to more campaign contributions and changes in voting behavior and policy stances of incumbent politicians.

Unhealthy political engagement can weaken incentives of leaders

Political competition can involve the practices of vote buying, electoral fraud, violence, and appeals to ethnic identity, with pernicious consequences for public goods. Unhealthy political engagement is not confined to voting by individual citizens in elections but can also characterize the actions of organized groups. For example, the findings in Burgess et al. (2015), discussed earlier, that ethnic favoritism in public investment in Kenya occurred particularly under authoritarian regimes, with reductions in ethnicity-based policy distortions during periods of multiparty electoral competition, suggest that groups can organize around ethnic identity to extract targeted benefits.

The effects of unhealthy political engagement extend well beyond what individual research papers are in a position to assess. For example, the impact of political engagement around ethnic groups is unlikely to be restricted to the distribution of road investments in Kenya. Theory and available analysis of comparative development in the history of nations (which will be reviewed in the next section), suggest that these political behaviors can accumulate for far-reaching effects across the economy through the poor functioning of public sector institutions.

Elite control over institutions of violence and coercion can account for unhealthy political engagement and is associated with worse outcomes. Acemoglu and Robinson (2006a) provide accounts from Colombia and the U.S. South of the persistence of elite capture of state institutions despite the de jure extension of voting rights. They show how political elites use violence against opponents, and coercion and economic sanctions against voters, to maintain their hold on power despite the formal existence of electoral institutions and despite poor performance.

Acemoglu, Reed, and Robinson (2014) use variation in the colonial organization of chieftaincy in Sierra Leone to show that chiefs face fewer constraints and less political competition in chiefdoms with fewer ruling families. Places with fewer ruling families have significantly worse development outcomes today—in particular, lower rates of educational attainment, child health, nonagricultural employment, and asset ownership. Similar results are provided by Anderson, Francois, and Kotwal (2015) from India: variation across villages within a state in the domination of landed, high-caste elites is associated with variation in the provision of public investments to fight poverty. Elite domination is likely to lead to lower levels of antipoverty spending.

However, the above examples from Sierra Leone and India of the persistence of elite control in some parts of the country also show that in other parts of the same country, electoral competition has enabled citizens to weaken elite power. To the extent that government performance in these other parts, where elite control is presumably weak, continues to exhibit high levels of corruption and mismanagement, other explanations are needed for why political engagement does not further improve outcomes. This is where other research comes in showing widespread electoral malpractices that can weaken the ability of voters to hold leaders accountable (Collier 2009; Vicente and Wantchekon 2009).

A large body of political science research documents how political rights of voters, particularly among poor people, are undermined through the practice of vote buying at election time (Kitschelt and Wilkinson 2008; Schaffer 2007; Stokes 2005, 2007). The offering of "gifts" or money in exchange for votes has been found to be widespread in poor democracies, despite the existence of secret ballots. Khemani (2015) shows that vote buying is associated with lower provision of broadly delivered pro-poor public services in health and education.[3] The central finding is that in places where households report greater vote buying (in direct response to questions about offers of money in exchange for votes at the time of elections), village facility records show lower investment in basic health services for mothers and children. Furthermore, in places with greater vote buying, a higher proportion of children are severely underweight, possibly as a result of the lower public investments.

To corroborate the evidence from the Philippines in other countries, Khemani (2015) turns to survey data from the Afrobarometer initiative. In round 5 of the Afrobarometer surveys, respondents were asked whether they had been offered something in exchange for their vote in the most recently concluded elections. A separate and standardized module on experience with service delivery asked about the quality of public schools and health clinics—whether households had experienced any problems in schools and health facilities. Among the 33 countries for which variables measuring both vote buying and service delivery are available, three-quarters of them, or 25, exhibit a robust association between experiencing vote buying and experiencing problems in service delivery. Pooling the data across countries, and including country fixed effects, also yields a highly significant and robust association between vote buying and problems in public schools and health clinics.

Anderson, Francois, and Kotwal (2015) similarly show that weakening enfranchisement through clientelist relations between land-owning elite families and agricultural households in Indian villages is associated with lower public investments in social safety nets and antipoverty programs. In related results, Baland and Robinson (2008) find historical evidence that the introduction of the secret ballot in Chile was associated with a decline in votes for right-wing parties and a drop in the price of land (both of which are consistent with a reduction in the power of clientelist relations).

Banerjee and Pande (2009) show that caste- or ethnicity-based political parties in India, which mobilize support primarily on the basis of identity appeals, are associated with greater corruption. The economic effects of the ethnic conflict that occurred after Kenya's 2008 election are examined by Ksoll, Macchiavello, and Morjaria (2014). They put together a rich data set on Kenya's flower exports market. The authors use daily data on exports from 2004 through 2010 for 104 producers (representing about 90 percent of Kenya's floriculture market). They combine these data with a firm-level survey conducted after the electoral violence to uncover mechanisms through which the electoral violence affected economic outcomes. They use data from the Red Cross to discern the areas of Kenya where electoral violence broke out. They then estimate a difference-in-differences model comparing firms located in areas affected by the violence with firms located in areas unaffected by the violence over time. The authors find that the effects of violence reduced export volumes by about 40 percent. The main mechanism for this drop was a reduction in the labor force (as opposed to disruption in transportation). At the peak of the violence, work absence reached close to 50 percent.

Callen and Long (2015) examine electoral fraud in Afghanistan. First, they show that fraudulent practices are greater among electoral officials with political connections. Second, they show how available technology can support electoral institutions to reduce elite power. The authors implement an experiment to estimate the causal effect of "photo quick count"—a technology that allows monitoring of voter tally sheets at polling stations both prior to and after their aggregation into final vote counts that would determine the winner of the election. This technology is intended to reduce fraud in the counting of votes. They provide evidence on the response of fraud to the credible threat of discovery through monitoring by announcing photo quick-count measurements to election officials. Photo quick-count announcements reduced the damaging of election materials by candidate representatives to 8.1 percent from 18.9 percent. It reduced votes for politically powerful candidates at a given polling location from about 21 percent to about 15 percent. This evidence suggests that technology can play a role in reducing unhealthy political practices. Although technology and capacity building are likely needed and play crucial roles in improving outcomes, investments in technical solutions alone can be undermined by political incentives and behavioral norms, as further discussed later in this chapter.

Impact of political engagement through the selection of different types of leaders

The previous section shows that political engagement can improve governance and development outcomes by making leaders accountable to citizens. Political engagement can also improve outcomes through the selection of leaders with better characteristics. For example, political engagement by disadvantaged social groups can lead to the selection of leaders who are more likely to provide health, education, and targeted benefits for poverty reduction. Another strand of evidence shows that political engagement can enable more competent leaders to be selected, who perform better in governing public resources.

Isolating the political engagement effects on economic outcomes through the mechanism of improving leader characteristics, separately from the effect on incentives, is challenging because it requires data on leader characteristics. The bulk of the literature from developing countries is focused on issues of identity—whether being a woman or of a particular caste or religion matters for policy actions of leaders in office. Plausibly exogenous variation in the identity of politicians is often available because of changes in political reservations, creating "natural experiments" from which to draw reliable lessons. The existence of policy instruments that target benefits to specific social groups also makes it possible to measure policy outcomes that are preferred by particular groups to which leaders belong.

Empirical work on leader selection is lagging behind theoretical developments. For example, Bernheim and Kartik (2014) and Caselli and Morelli (2004) provide models in which adverse selection of dishonest and incompetent candidates as leaders plays a key role in determining government performance. Yet little empirical work is available that measures such attributes directly and examines the conditions under which selection can improve. Some strides have been made in the realm of measuring the characteristics of public officials and frontline providers (Banuri and Keefer 2013; Dal Bó, Finan, and Rossi 2013; Hanna and Wang 2013). This work can be extended to political leaders and to understanding the interaction between the selection of leaders and public officials. Future work also needs to examine the influence of platforms of political competition—whether they consist of broad public goods programs—on the selection of public officials and the environment in which they work.

With these caveats in mind, the following discussion suggests that leaders matter and political competition can be important in selecting better-quality leaders. Furthermore, other work suggests that attention to selection is important because elections are a blunt tool for accountability. Good performance of government relies on the capacity of institutions to select leaders who have intrinsic motivation to use their public office for the public good (Besley 2005).

The characteristics of leaders matter

A body of evidence shows that the characteristics of leaders matter. Jones and Olken (2005) use the deaths by natural causes of leaders while in office as a source of exogenous variation in leadership, and show that leaders have an impact on growth. The effects of individual leaders are strongest in autocratic settings where there are fewer constraints on a leader's power. Besley, Montalvo, and Reynal-Querol (2011) build on Jones and Olken (2005) and extend the data set to include more than 1,000 political leaders between 1875 and 2004. They show that the individual characteristics of leaders, particularly education, are important for growth.

Using data on the composition of central government expenditures in a panel of 71 democracies for the period 1972–2003, Brender and Drazen (2009) test whether changes in leadership induce significant changes in spending composition. They find that the replacement of a leader tends to have no significant effect on expenditure composition in the short run. In the medium term, leadership changes are associated with larger changes in expenditure composition, mostly in developed countries.

Lee, Moretti, and Butler (2004) provide evidence supporting the notion that the ideological beliefs of leaders matter in what policies they decide to support. The evidence shows that successful leaders from the Democratic party in the United States who win closely contested elections cast similar votes in congressional proceedings as Democrats who win by large margins. The authors show how this pattern is consistent with leaders voting for policies according to their own ideological position rather than responding to the different preferences among their voters in closely contested versus safe districts. Similarly, they find that Democrats and Republicans who win by extremely narrow margins are as dissimilar in their voting patterns as those who win by large margins.

Alt, de Mesquita, and Rose (2011) build upon Besley and Case (1995) to try to separate the incentives effects from the selection effects that elections induce. Their argument is as follows: conditional on the number of terms, the difference between incumbents who face reelection incentives and those who do not reflects whether they are subject to the incentives effect or the accountability effect. The relative performance of term-limited incumbents in different terms reflects the competence or selection effect, since each has been reelected a different number of times but has the same incentive to take costly action on behalf of voters. The authors find that economic growth is higher and taxes, spending, and borrowing costs are lower under reelection-eligible incumbents than under term-limited incumbents, holding tenure in office constant (evidence of an accountability effect), and under second-term incumbents than under first-term incumbents, holding term-limit status constant (evidence of a selection effect). These two effects are of comparable magnitudes.

Humphreys, Masters, and Sandu (2007) conducted a field experiment in democratic deliberation in São Tomé and Príncipe. In these deliberations, meetings were moderated by discussion leaders who were randomly assigned to run meetings in 56 sites around the country. The authors show that leadership effects were extremely large, accounting for more than one-third of all variation in the outcomes of the national discussions. They also find a strong correlation between the preferences of the leaders and the outcomes of the meetings.

Political competition is associated with the selection of better-quality leaders

One strand of evidence shows that political competition is associated with the selection of better-quality leaders, typically measured as the education levels of leaders. Besley and Reynal-Querol (2011) use a data set on 1,400 world leaders between 1848 and 2004 and find that compared with autocracies, democracies select better educated leaders. Controlling for country and year fixed effects, they find that democracies are 20 percent more likely to select highly educated leaders. Besley, Persson, and Sturm (2005, 2010) investigate the effect of political competition in the United States on incentives and selection of better-quality leaders and find a positive relationship. They conclude that greater competition led to the selection of better-quality leaders who pursued better public policies for economic growth rather than extract private rents.

Martínez-Bravo (2014) provides evidence that the education of leaders matters for outcomes. She constructs a village-level panel of more than 10,000 villages on the island of Java between 1986 and 2003. She investigates the impact of a large school construction program in Indonesia on village governance and public goods provision. Between 1974 and 1978, 61,000 new schools were constructed, which doubled the existing stock of schools. This program was associated with a sharp increase in the educational attainment of village heads a decade or more later: their average number of years of schooling increased from 7.6 to 10.2. Examining the impact of the first election in which new educated cohorts run as candidates, she finds that this election led to important increases in the provision of key public goods: the number of doctors, the number of schools, and the number of kindergartens.

Galasso and Nannicini (2011) use a data set on Italian members of parliament elected in majoritarian districts from 1994 to 2006 to test whether political competition results in better politicians. They measure political contestability in two ways: the margin of victory in the previous political election, and the district-specific ratio of the number of swing voters to the difference between the numbers of ideological voters of the two main coalitions. The quality of a politician is measured by years of schooling, previous income, and experience in local government. They find that politicians with more years of schooling, higher preelection income, and more local experience tend to emerge in more competitive districts.

Inclusive political engagement yields leaders who reduce poverty and improve human development outcomes

Research on the impact of institutional reforms that made political engagement more inclusive of socially and economically disadvantaged groups shows that it yielded leaders who are more likely to reduce poverty, improve human development outcomes, and reduce social discrimination.

Pande (2003) uses political reservations in India to examine the role of mandated political representation in providing disadvantaged groups influence over policy making. The variation used in this paper is at the state level, and it exploits the fact that the extent of state-level political reservation enjoyed by a minority group varies by its population share, but is only revised during census population estimates. This situation creates discrete changes in representation even though the underlying population share is continuous. The paper finds that political reservations in Indian states that yielded more leaders from lower caste groups has increased redistribution of resources, such as increases in spending on public education programs, which benefits low-caste groups.

The impact on poverty of political reservation for disadvantaged minority groups is examined by Chin and Prakash (2011). The authors find that increasing the share of seats reserved for the most disadvantaged groups, the Scheduled Tribes of India, significantly reduces poverty. Greater space for political engagement by disadvantaged groups has a greater effect on rural poverty than urban poverty, and appears to benefit people near the poverty line as well as those far below it.

Using close election races at the state level in India from which women emerged as leaders, Clots-Figueras (2011) examines the effect of the gender of leaders on policy choices. The focus on the state level allows her to examine the effect of leader identity on a larger set of policy instruments. She finds an important interaction of gender with caste identity. Women elected for state legislative assembly seats that are reserved for historically disadvantaged low-caste groups behave differently from women elected from unreserved constituencies. In reserved constituencies, female legislators spend more on health and less on education and are more likely to support "women-friendly" inheritance laws and pro-poor land reforms compared with male legislators. Female legislators elected from unreserved constituencies are no different from their male counterparts in their support for "women-friendly" laws and are more likely than men to oppose land reforms. They are also different from male legislators in spending patterns, investing more in higher tiers of education and less on social expenditures. Taken together, these results provide significant evidence that promoting the inclusion of historically disadvantaged groups as leaders has significant impact on a range of policy choices.

Bhalotra and Clots-Figueras (2014) examine whether women state legislators in India influence health outcomes for individuals in the districts from which they are elected through the health policy levers available to them. The authors match data on health outcomes, health-related behaviors, and village-level access to health facilities for a large representative sample of individuals to the gender composition of state legislators around the time of their birth and in the district of their birth. They find that greater representation of women in the state legislature in the birth year and in the two years preceding birth is associated with a significant reduction in neonatal mortality. Additional evidence supports the finding that the mechanism of impact is greater public health investments by women leaders. Female political leaders are more likely to invest in village-level public health facilities, whereas male leaders are associated with greater availability of financial (and telecommunications) infrastructure. Female leaders are also associated with higher probabilities that women attend antenatal care, take iron supplements during pregnancy, give birth in a government facility as opposed to at home, and initiate breastfeeding early. Correlation of women leaders with outcomes that are not dependent upon public health infrastructure, such as breastfeeding, suggests that female leaders are more likely to promote health outreach and education campaigns.

Chattopadhyay and Duflo (2004) use political reservations for women in India to study the impact of women's leadership on policy decisions. There are two key features of this study: first, since the mid-1990s, one-third of village council head positions have been randomly reserved for a woman, which allows for causal interpretation of the results. Second, the study conducted a survey to elicit women's preferences on public goods. The main finding is that policy decisions better reflected the preferences of women when the village council head was a woman.

Rehavi (2007) uses variation in the number of female state legislators created by the outcomes of close elections in the United States to examine the impact of the leader's gender. The analysis finds that the increase of women in U.S. statehouses over the past quarter-century was responsible for a significant 15 percent share of the rise in state health spending. There was no effect on the share of spending on education.

Ferreira and Gyourko (2011) examine the effects of female leadership using a data set of U.S. mayoral elections from 1950 to 2005. They find no effect of gender of the mayor on policy outcomes related to the size of local government, the composition of municipal spending and employment, or crime rates. Although female mayors do not implement different policies, they do appear to have higher unobserved political skills, given that they have a 6–7 percentage point higher incumbent effect than a comparable male.

Washington (2008) shows that U.S. members of Congress who have daughters tend to vote more liberally on women's issues bills. She uses congressional voting record scores compiled by the American Association of University Women and the National Organization for Women, and exploits the fact that the gender of a child is exogenous conditional on family size. She finds that, conditional on total children parented, each female child parented is associated with a score increase that is approximately one-quarter of the difference in the score accounted for by a congressperson's own gender.

Unhealthy political engagement yields bad-quality leaders

Other research shows that when political parties and special interest groups are organized to extract private rents, they support the selection of bad-quality leaders. Political parties in India that are organized on the basis of ethnic identity and win support by targeting private benefits to members of their ethnic groups are also more likely to field candidates against whom there are serious criminal allegations (Aidt, Golden, and Tiwari 2011). Political parties in India are more likely to select alleged criminal candidates when confronting greater electoral volatility and in parliamentary constituencies with lower literacy. Prakash, Rockmore, and Uppal (2014) provide evidence that there are large economic costs of electing criminally accused politicians.

Daniele and Geys (2015) examine the role of organized crime groups in Italy in influencing the quality of elected politicians. They test the hypothesis that organized crime groups can lower the quality of politicians through bribery and coercion. To undertake this test, they rely on the assumption that the negative correlation between organized crime and quality of politicians is likely to be weaker when law enforcement is strengthened. The authors use data on the presence and activity of organized crime in Italian municipalities during the period 1985–2011. During this time, when there was the presumption of ties between local politicians and organized crime, the national government had the ability to dissolve the local government and replace it with a commission. The authors show that the dissolution of a local government as a result of Mafia infiltration induces a significant upward shift in the quality of local politicians, as measured by education. Similarly, Acemoglu, Robinson, and Santos (2013) use data from Colombia between 1991 and 2006 to show that paramilitary groups can have significant effects on elections for the legislature and the executive.

Other evidence from Germany on the rise of the Nazi party also shows how organized groups can reduce the quality of elected politicians. Satyanath, Voigtlaender, and Voth (2013) find that civil society organizations in Germany facilitated the rise of the Nazi party through democratic institutions, which ultimately led to the downfall of democracy in interwar Germany. The authors combine individual-level records of Nazi party membership from Falter and Brustein (2015) with more recently collected information on civic associations from a cross-section of 229 towns and cities from all over Germany in the 1920s. Their results show that the Nazi party grew more quickly where association density was higher. A diverse range of civil society groups, such as veterans' associations, animal breeders, chess clubs, and choirs, all positively predict the entry of the Nazi party. Party membership, in turn, is correlated with electoral success. Similar in essence to these results from Germany of the political capture of civil society, Acemoglu, Reed, and Robinson (2014) interpret evidence on the impact of traditional ruling families in Sierra Leone as suggesting that they can capture civil society to maintain their power.

Another strand of evidence provides indirect support to theoretical hypotheses that dishonest citizens may be more likely to seek public office because there are rents to be had. Leaders can use their time in office to find a variety of ingenious ways of enriching themselves that are difficult for voters to monitor. Voters are limited in their ability to monitor every action and enforce accountability. On the one hand, this points to the importance of other internal checks and balances, and the bluntness of elections as institutions of accountability, but on the other, it underscores the importance of understanding how political institutions can shape the intrinsic characteristics and behavioral norms among leaders.

Gehlbach, Sonin, and Zhuravskaya (2010) document the high share of businessmen who run for public office in the Russian Federation. Using data from Russian gubernatorial elections, they show that "businessman candidates" emerge in regions with low media freedom and government transparency. The authors suggest that this pattern may be indicative of candidates entering the political market with the objective of extracting private rents once in office.

Pande (2007) provides a review of evidence and case studies on the type of citizen who selects to become a politician. The pattern is consistent with the suggestion that political entrepreneurs can select into becoming politicians with rent-seeking motives. Her review further points out that business interests in politics in low-income countries is similar to the situation in the United States in the nineteenth century, when the business elite dominated urban politics and urban politics was associated with significant corruption.

Political engagement and behavioral norms

This section examines the available evidence that links political engagement to behavioral norms. Chapter 1 distinguished political norms as a subset of social norms, pertaining specifically to the behavior of citizens and public officials in the public sector. The theoretical literature reviewed in chapter 4 shows how unhealthy political engagement can be understood as behavioral norms to extract private benefits from public resources. Behavioral norms can vary within the same formal institutions and persist even when formal institutions change. The theory suggests that transitions between healthy and unhealthy behavioral norms happen through the experience of political engagement over time and through the role of leaders as prominent agents. There are no currently available direct empirical tests of the theory, or clear empirical strategies to measure political norms beyond qualitative descriptions. This section provides empirical support for the theoretical insights by connecting and interpreting a large literature on the impact of historical institutions on development and the role of leaders in shaping social norms.

Leaders influence norms

Significant evidence shows that political engagement and the leaders selected through it shape social norms related to gender and caste. Beaman et al. (2009) and Beaman et al. (2012) examine the impact of political reservations for women in the leadership of village governments in India on gender norms. The state of West Bengal began implementing the constitutional amendment in India that mandates political reservations for women leaders in 1998 and assigned the reservation to a random set of villages. These studies find that the experience of living under a woman leader reduces men's prejudice against women leaders by many measures. The experience of living under a woman leader also reduced the gender gap in parental aspirations for children. In villages that had had women leaders, parents' expectations for their daughters were higher and girls went to school longer and had somewhat fewer hours of housework. After the reservations ended in a village, women have run for free elections in higher percentages and in many cases won.

Several other papers exploit the variation in leader selection afforded by political reservations in India to examine the impact on behavioral norms. Deininger et al. (2015) examine the effect on individuals' political participation. The main outcome variables are individuals' levels of political participation, willingness to make a matching contribution to provide local public goods, and self-reported ability to hold leaders to account. The authors use data collected 15 years after the introduction of the policy to explore the persistence of reservation-induced effects and to distinguish short- from long-term effects. They find that reservations prompted a decline in the perceived quality of leaders and public goods provision, but an increase in the extent and nature of females' political participation. These effects persist over time, consistent with effects on long-lasting behavioral norms.

Iyer et al. (2011) use state-level variation in the timing of political reservations in India to find that an increase in female representation in local government induces a large and significant rise in documented crimes against women in India. Their evidence suggests that this increase is good news, driven primarily by greater reporting rather than greater incidence of such crimes. In contrast, they find no increase in crimes against men or gender-neutral crimes. They also examine the effectiveness of alternative forms of political representation: large-scale membership of women in local councils affects crime against them more than does their presence in higher-level leadership positions.

Contrasting results on the impact of mandated political participation comes from Afghanistan. Beath et al. (2014) examine a development program that mandated women's community participation. The community-driven development program (CDD) was part of a randomized controlled trial in 500 villages in Afghanistan. As part of the CDD, the village had to establish a development council with equal participation of men and women in the election of the council and in the selection of development projects. The study finds that increased female participation had an impact in various activities, both political and economic. However, no effects were found on the norms of intrafamily decision making or on attitudes toward the general role of women in society.

Another study shows how political parties with a particular social ideology can affect gender outcomes. Meyersson (2014) uses a regression discontinuity design to compare municipalities in Turkey, where the Islamic party barely won or lost the election and finds that in places where they won, Islamic rule increased female secular high school education. These effects persisted in the long run (17 years later), reduced adolescent marriages, and increased female political participation.

A history of inclusive political engagement influences norms

Research finds variation in outcomes across local places that are currently governed by the same set of formal institutions but vary in their experience with historical institutions. This evidence shows that the effects of historical institutions persist over time, long after those formal institutions have disappeared. Such persistence of effects of historical institutions is due to the importance of behavioral norms that have been variously defined as "informal institutions" or "culture," to distinguish them from formal institutions (Alesina and Giuliano 2015). This general interpretation is open to several different types of mechanisms through which behavioral norms could work, as follows:

• One, citizens could fail to make the local contributions that are needed for state-provided public services to work effectively, such as local maintenance (for example, village health committees gathering contributions from community members to maintain and equip the health clinics); local cooperation with public service providers, or conversely, local social sanctions on errant workers (for example, social pressure on nurses and doctors to show up to work at the health clinic); or local take-up of services (for example, mothers taking their young children for immunization).

- Two, citizens could fail to coordinate their *political* actions, such as voting, to demand the collective social welfare. This failure can lead to worse outcomes by reducing the incentives and quality of leaders to make the public sector perform better for citizens. Political beliefs and behavioral norms can be clientelist—with citizens likely to reward politicians who provide them with targeted private benefits, or who share their social identity, at the expense of broadly delivered public services. This course can shape both the incentives and the characteristics of those who select to become political leaders—the extent to which leaders have the incentives, the motivation, and the competence to use their positions of leadership in the public sphere to serve the public interest rather than to extract private rents.

Pandey (2010) provides direct evidence linking historical institutions of power concentration to subsequent political behavior and the delivery of public services. She takes advantage of historical variation across districts in India in colonial land revenue institutions that concentrated power among elite landlords. Landlord districts had more oppressive revenue systems that gave greater power to elite landlords rather than to peasants. In districts with nonlandlord control, village bodies that were more representative of peasants were responsible for collecting revenue. The results show that in ex-landlord control districts, elections are more likely to be won by leaders belonging to high-caste groups, who are the social elite. These high-caste groups are less likely to send their children to the public schools in the villages, as compared with low-caste groups. Lower-caste children are overrepresented and high- and middle-caste children underrepresented in enrollment rates in public schools relative to their respective populations. Teacher effort is significantly lower in villages in ex-landlord districts. When results are analyzed by teacher caste, the difference in teacher effort between ex-landlord and ex-nonlandlord districts is significant for high- or middle-caste teachers who would be considered elites (based on their caste status). For low-caste teachers, the difference in effort between ex-landlord and ex-nonlandlord areas is not significant.

This suggests that low-performing teachers may be protected by the local political leaders who often share common castes and class backgrounds because a large fraction of the teachers is upper caste and landed (Drèze and Saran 1995). Finally, student test scores and school infrastructure are significantly worse in villages belonging to ex-landlord districts.

The study by Acemoglu, Reed, and Robinson (2014) on the chieftaincy in Sierra Leone not only shows that chiefdoms with less political competition have significantly worse development outcomes today, but also suggests that the worse development outcomes are a function of weak political behavioral norms to hold leaders accountable. They find that despite worse performance of current political leaders in bringing public investments to their communities, chiefdoms with fewer ruling families are also associated with greater measures of citizen acceptance of the authority of chiefs and more "social capital" or cooperative behavior in communities (such as engaging in road brushing—a form of communal labor to maintain local assets). The authors interpret this pattern as suggesting elite capture of civil society, implicitly through the power of elites to exact obedience from civil society. Similar results and arguments are provided by Anderson, Francois, and Kotwal (2015) from India, that in villages dominated by landed, high-caste elites, there are greater reports of citizen satisfaction with leaders and willingness of citizens to contribute to local public goods, at the same time that public investments by the state to fight poverty are low.

This evidence from India and Sierra Leone suggests that political beliefs about the legitimacy of elite leaders and political behavioral norms to accept their authority can facilitate the persistence of power and influence of some groups, who have historically been in positions of power, despite changes in formal political institutions toward democracy and competitive elections. Local collective action to solve problems of local public goods can be a form of elite capture of civil society, contributing to the persistence of elite power and preventing citizens from organizing to demand political accountability from their leaders. Indonesia provides further suggestive evidence of this tension between local collective action to solve local problems versus holding leaders accountable for using their positions of leadership to service the community. Freire, Henderson, and Kuncoro (2011) provide evidence that the introduction of democratic elections at the village level in Indonesia led to a replacement of traditional village leaders drawn from the village elite, and a simultaneous reduction in volunteer labor that village elites previously mobilized for building local public infrastructure.

A strand of literature examining regional differences in the quality of government and social norms within Italy, between the center-north and the south, ultimately attributes better performance to earlier experience with participatory democracy, dating back to the twelfth century (Alesina and Giuliano 2015; Guiso, Sapienza, and Zingales 2006; Putnam, Leonardi, and Nanetti 1993). The inclusiveness of political institutions in "free cities"—a formal institution in the twelfth century—triggered a set of cultural traits (civic and cooperative behavior) whose effects persist today. Regions that were not free cities in the twelfth century but that currently have institutions of local political engagement are argued to suffer from "uncivic" voting, which allows corruption by political leaders to go unpunished (Nannicini et al. 2013). This series of arguments on variation in governance outcomes within Italy thus supports the notion of improvements in political norms coming about through the experience of political engagement over time. The earlier experience with democratic institutions and greater accumulation of such experience over time are the underlying source of differences in governance within Italy today.[4]

Nannicini et al. (2013) build on the previous work on variation in social capital across provinces within Italy. Social capital is defined as norms for cooperative behavior in society. The authors' main empirical measure of social capital is average per capita blood donations in the Italian provinces (following Guiso, Sapienza, and Zingales 2006). They link social norms to the notion of "civic" versus "uncivic" voting behavior, depending on whether voters assess politicians on the basis of general public interest and punish transgressions even when they have been the recipients of private favors from the politician. The authors use two indicators of transgression or misbehavior of incumbents in national elections: prosecutors' requests to proceed with a criminal investigation against a member of parliament; and the absenteeism rate in electronic votes by members of parliament over the legislative term. They find that both indicators are more frequent in electoral districts with less social capital. More important, the electoral punishment of the incumbent's misbehavior is stronger in districts with more social capital.

Finan and Schechter (2012) also show how social and political norms are linked, providing evidence from a field experiment in Paraguay. Politicians hire respected community leaders in each village to interact with voters to promote their candidacy and offer them money and other forms of aid in exchange for the promise of their vote. The authors conducted a survey with these community leaders who typically broker the vote-buying exchanges between voters and politicians. They combined survey information on vote buying experienced in a 2006 municipal election with experimental data on individual intrinsic reciprocity. They find that political brokers target vote-buying offers to individuals who have strong norms of reciprocity. It is interesting to note that a robust negative association between vote buying and public services in Khemani (2015), discussed earlier, is obtained from a country—the Philippines—that has been described as having cultural norms of reciprocity (*utang na loob,* or the obligation to appropriately repay a person who has done one a favor).

Historical inequality in the distribution of economic endowments can also explain unhealthy political behavioral norms. Sokoloff and Engerman (2000) argue that historically unequal economic institutions in Latin America, compared with those in the United States and Canada, were responsible for the delay in the adoption of inclusive political institutions, and this delay is associated with subsequent weak institutions and persistently worse economic outcomes. The authors provide evidence that exogenous variation in the climate to produce sugar led to variation across countries within the Americas in the timing of the adoption of egalitarian political institutions (democracy with universal adult suffrage) and social policies (education for universal literacy). Similarly, Acemoglu and Robinson (2012) argue that early experience with inclusive or egalitarian political institutions in the history of nations is the source of variation in subsequent paths of economic development.

However, although this body of work shows that early adoption of egalitarian institutions and social policies is important, the mechanisms behind why early adoption matters and has persistent effects is not clarified or made explicit. Why are countries not able to change outcomes within short time spans by instituting elections with universal adult suffrage and spending on public education? The answers in this report are that first, political behavioral norms are important in shaping the functioning of formal institutions; and second, political norms can vary within the same formal institutions, between healthy and unhealthy. Historical institutions of inequality can contribute to unhealthy political behavioral norms such as those that sustain clientelist forms of political competition where political support is won on the basis of providing targeted private benefits rather than broad public goods.[5]

Capacity building is not enough: Healthy political engagement is needed to change incentives and norms

Even when they function well, elections are designed only to hold elected officials accountable. But many of the functions of government are delegated to appointed officials rather than to elected politicians. Both elected and appointed officials exercise their powers through a myriad of working-level institutions of government, ranging from ministries and agencies all the way down to local public schools and clinics. Strong institutions of internal accountability within government, such as supreme audit institutions, and checks and balances, such as through independent judiciaries, therefore are important mechanisms to complement accountability through elections.

The problem is how to build such institutions when they are weak to begin with. A view that institutions and governance are central to development has influenced policy efforts to focus on deliberately investing in building institutions. One approach to better public sector institutions in places that lack them is to build the bricks-and-mortar infrastructure and provide human resources and training to staff, and equipment to bureaucracies and law and enforcement agencies. However, a wealth of experience with efforts to strengthen institutions has shown that programs to replicate successful rich country institutions in developing countries by providing equipment and training to bureaucracies often fail (Andrews, Pritchett, and Woolcock 2013; IDS 2010; Pritchett, Woolcock, and Andrews 2013).

When institutions are weak to begin with and political engagement is unhealthy, attempts to build better institutions by investing in capacity alone can run into problems of perverse incentives and behavioral norms in public bureaucracies. Nonelected public officials perform in the shadow of flawed elections that generate weak political incentives and perverse behavioral norms. For example, powerful leaders at both national and local levels might interfere with the recruitment and management of frontline public service providers by ensuring that their cronies are appointed or promoted to leadership positions in public facilities (Callen et al. 2014; La Forgia et al. 2014). Such use of government jobs as political patronage can dilute professional norms in the public sector. Although systematic empirical evidence on how elected political leaders shape the environment in which bureaucracies function is limited, the little that is available suggests that bureaucracies in poor countries are subject to pernicious political interference. Improving the management of public service providers within sectors, be they doctors, teachers, agriculture extension workers, or social safety net administrators, appears intimately linked to politics.

A growing body of empirical work finds evidence that elected leaders exert significant influence over public officials and frontline service providers (Brollo, Kaufmann, and La Ferrara 2015; Callen et al. 2014; Callen and Long 2015; Iyer and Mani 2012). Technical policy advice about how to improve the functioning of public bureaucracies may not be taken up or implemented seriously because of weak political incentives. Examples in the literature show how relatively obvious and easy-to-implement technocratic arrangements can be devised that work to control corruption and improve performance. Muralidharan, Niehaus, and Sukhtankar (2014) show how significant gains in performance can be achieved by using technology. The *World Development Report 2016* (World Bank 2016) further shows that the Internet and new technology afford ample opportunities to improve governance should leaders have the incentives and willingness to use them. Those incentives or "political will" are, in turn, shaped by the characteristics of political engagement.

Even when technological innovations are credibly adopted by higher-level decision makers, political incentives and behavioral norms can undermine their implementation. Banerjee, Duflo, and Glennerster (2008) and Callen et al. (2014) provide direct evidence that the use of technology to improve governance is influenced by political connections and political competition. Callen et al. (2014) find that the use of a smartphone technology that doubled inspection rates of health clinics in Pakistan was highly localized in competitive political constituencies where there are greater political incentives to monitor public providers. Banerjee, Duflo, and Glennerster (2008) provide evidence of the reversal of gains from an effective monitoring technology—timestamp machines—to reduce absenteeism among public health workers in India. The nurses sabotaged the machines and pressured local health administrators to deliberately undermine the incentive scheme. The authors suggest that the nurses were successful in doing so because of the lack of political will among leaders with power over the health system to enforce implementation.

Dhaliwal and Hanna (2014) evaluate the impact of another technological solution—using biometric scanning devices—to monitor the attendance of public sector health care workers in India, finding that it resulted in a 15 percent increase in medical staff attendance. Health outcomes improved, with a 16 percent increase in the delivery of infants by a doctor and a 26 percent reduction in the likelihood of infants born weighing less than 2,500 grams. However, the results also suggest that improvements in one aspect of service delivery performance (reduction in absenteeism) may have been replaced by other forms of corruption (for example, higher delivery costs, diversion of patients to private practice, and reductions in benefits to which patients are entitled).

At the same time, Dhaliwal and Hanna's (2014) discussion is occupied not so much with the success story of the technology but rather with the unwillingness and low motivation at every step in the public sector to take it up and implement it effectively. They report that:

> The idea for the original reform did not stem from the research team: the government identified the absence problem, conceived the program, developed the software, and piloted the equipment prior to the involvement of the researchers in the project ... Despite this "ownership," the project was plagued with both delays and inadequacies in implementation ... The implementation challenges stemmed from both the top–i.e., the state government—and the local bureaucrats and politicians who are responsible for further monitoring the PHC [primary health center] staff. At the top, the state government officials, the very office that conceived the project, did not always follow through with implementation ... lower level bureaucrats may have little incentive to enforce the rules: if they enforce them, the health officers would have to handle complaints by PHC staff and they get no personal return in terms of their careers. On the other hand, local elected politicians—in India, the Grand Pradhan, or GP—may have better incentives than bureaucrats to monitor PHC staff to be present: if service provision is low, they could be voted out of office. Yet, ... despite the high rates of absenteeism, GPs were generally satisfied with the doctor's attendance: 77 percent were either satisfied or very satisfied with their attendance. (Dhaliwal and Hanna 2014, 25–29).

A similar story comes from Kenya of impediments to implementing evidence-based policies that would improve provider performance. The research to inform policymakers about the impact of different policy options to improve education is summarized on the website of the Abdul Latif Jameel Poverty Action Lab. Standing out in this summary is a finding that public investment in hiring contract teachers in Kenya, rather than raising the salaries of regular civil service teachers, is highly cost-effective.

Contract teachers exert greater effort at a fraction of the cost of regular civil service teachers. Yet efforts by the government of Kenya to implement policies based on the implications of this research were strikingly unsuccessful. Bold et al. (2013) show that the contract teacher program could not be effectively implemented through the public sector. The authors provide anecdotal evidence consistent with the political power of the teachers' unions in thwarting program implementation.

Mungiu-Pippidi (2014) reports that the establishment of anticorruption agencies and several other formal policy measures for monitoring and enforcement are not robustly correlated with the control of corruption. Case studies of the experience with anticorruption agencies across countries point to the importance of political incentives in shaping the functioning of such agencies. Doig, Watt, and Williams (2006) and Meagher (2005) write that the success of some agencies, such as Singapore's Corrupt Practices Investigation Bureau founded in 1952, has provided models for other countries to emulate. They write that these agencies were established in contexts of rampant corruption that were threatening political stability and investor confidence. In response, single agencies were established that centralized information and facilitated coordination between institutions. However, these authors continue, the majority of anticorruption agencies (ACAs) established in other countries based on these models have been far less successful. Meagher (2005, 79) writes, "The majority of ACAs, which are most numerous in the developing world, probably serve no useful role in combating corruption. Some may indeed be actively harmful." These authors contend that ACAs do not address larger forces underlying systemic corruption in developing countries.

Maor (2004) considers the politics of anticorruption mechanisms, drawing on examples from the United States, the former Soviet Union, Italy, and Australia. He considers cases in which leaders establish ACAs and make other investments to reduce corruption, often in response to pressure from media or public outcry, but subsequently undermine those efforts when anticorruption investigations consider issues close to home, such as the actions of political executives. Maor (2004) considers five cases in which leaders have tried to thwart the credibility of anticorruption mechanisms and investigators' powers. Through comparative case study analysis, he finds that the outcome of such struggles depends largely on media accessibility and institutions. When the media have greater access to the government and institutions are not centralized, investigations are more difficult to derail.

Kaufmann, Mehrez, and Gurgur (2002) argue that in environments in which public institutions are captured to service the interests of economic and political elites, the path to improving governance lies not through traditional public sector reforms but rather through external institutions of accountability to citizens. Using in-depth micro surveys of 1,250 public officials working in 110 public institutions in Bolivia, the authors estimate a model of the determinants of corruption in and service delivery by government agencies. Their results show that internal indicators of public sector management, such as wages of civil servants and bureaucratic rules, are not significant, while measures of external accountability institutions, such as citizen voice and transparency, are significantly correlated with lower corruption and better quality of services provided.

An approach to fostering external accountability has been to build citizen organization, such as providing grants to civil society and establishing legal frameworks to allow citizen organization to flourish. However, laws that are abided by and organizations that are effective are more likely to emerge organically. The most systematic evidence in this regard comes from efforts to build the capacity of communities to undertake development projects. Mansuri and Rao (2013) argue that efforts to induce community participation run into large risks of failure because of inequality and socioeconomic barriers to participation. Yet there are examples of organic forms of participation that arise endogenously among communities, showing that citizens and communities *can* come together to address local problems. But getting them to do so through external interventions, when they are not ready, can fail.

One strand of thought on historical path dependency suggests strong limitations on the efficacy of any deliberate policy efforts to change institutions; critical junctures of institutional change involve a variety of forces that are likely outside the control of policy makers.[6] Some historical accounts of how effective state capacity and institutional change comes about is consistent with the role of healthy political engagement in creating the conditions for that change. Besley and Persson (2009) find that historical incidence of parliamentary democracy, and of shocks (external wars) that lead to demand for common-interest public goods, are stable predictors of state capacity. The common theme in Acemoglu and Robinson (2001, 2006b) and in Besley, Persson, and Reynal-Querol (2015) is that an incumbent leader's fear of losing power is critical for institutional change.

The research frontier is linking the development of effective public sector organizations and sound professional norms in bureaucracies to the "cleaning up" of politics.[7] A challenge for the public sector is how to strengthen providers' professional behavioral norms by using mechanisms other than incentives and accountability. When leaders are selected and sanctioned on the basis of good performance, they are more likely to have the incentives, capacity, and legitimacy to bring about institutional reforms such as the professionalization of bureaucracies. Conversely, when politics revolves around patronage and clientelism, providing jobs in the public sector becomes a currency of political competition, with pernicious consequences for professional behavioral norms among public employees.

This chapter has shown that political engagement, both its healthy and unhealthy forms, has profound consequences for governance, policy selection, and economic development. Healthy political engagement can be crucial for changing incentives and behaviors in the public sector and effectively building state capacity. The big question this raises is how to encourage healthy political engagement so that governments work better to support economic development. One way may be through transparency. The next chapter focuses on the evidence of transparency's impact in nourishing political engagement and working together with it to strengthen institutions for governance.

Notes

1. Casey (2015) is reviewed further in chapter 6. The paper shows that political information on local politicians provided through the radio improves voters' knowledge. Candidate information increases citizen willingness to cross ethnic-party lines. Complementary evidence shows that more information induces parties to distribute campaign spending in a more equitable way across districts.

2. These results need to be interpreted with caution because the diffusion rate of elections across villages is rapid, and some of the outcomes data are based on recall (which can involve measurement errors). There may also be an issue of external validity—or the extent to which the reported results are likely to be applicable outside the sample of villages used in this study. This point was raised in comments provided by John Giles to the authors of this report. The sample of villages on which data are available has been the focus of research for some time, which may impact the way in which respondents from these villages respond to surveys undertaken by researchers.

3. Directly elected municipal governments in the Philippines are responsible for delivering what can be characterized as a pro-poor public service: health programs for maternal and child well-being that are typically the only source for such services available to poor households. Municipalities hire and manage nurses, midwives, and community or village health workers, the key health personnel who are supposed to deliver basic maternal and child health services to the poor.

4. In chapter 6, the discussion turns to why several hundred years of experience, as in this example from Italy, may not be needed for societies today to improve political engagement. Changes can be far more rapid in this particular moment in time because of the confluence of current forces of political engagement and transparency.

5. Brixi, Lust, and Woolcock (2015) provide a study of government failures in the Middle East and North Africa region with a similar argument and interpretation of available evidence. They discuss how historical experience with colonial institutions and beliefs about the role of the state at the time of independence in the region led to political clientelism, elite capture of state resources, and citizen expectations that leaders would provide a broad range of private and public benefits (such as subsidies, health, and education). The coexistence of these three factors—that leaders organized to extract private rents from the economy, maintaining loyalty and political support through patronage, while providing subsidies and a broad range of public services to citizens to win their acquiescence—became untenable as economic inefficiencies mounted and citizens became dissatisfied with the social compact.

6. Banerjee and Duflo (2014) provide a view of this historical determinism literature. Dell, Lane, and Querubin (2015) and Dell (2012) provide direct evidence of path dependency in development. Acemoglu, Johnson, and Robinson (2005) describe "critical junctures" and North et al. (2007) describe "doorstep conditions" for institutional change.

7. As also discussed in chapter 4.

Bibliography

Acemoglu, Daron, Tarek A. Hassan, and Ahmed Tahoun. 2014. "The Power of the Street: Evidence from Egypt's Arab Spring." NBER Working Paper 20665, National Bureau of Economic Research, Cambridge, MA.

Acemoglu, Daron, Simon Johnson, and J. A. Robinson. 2005. "Institutions as a Fundamental Cause of Long-Run Growth." In *Handbook of Economic Growth*, 1, ed. Philippe Aghion and Steven Durlauf, 385–472.

Acemoglu, Daron, Suresh Naidu, Pascual Restrepo, and James A. Robinson. 2014. "Democracy Does Cause Growth." NBER Working Paper 20004, National Bureau of Economic Research, Cambridge, MA.

Acemoglu, Daron, Tristan Reed, and James A. Robinson. 2014. "Chiefs: Economic Development and Elite Control of Civil Society in Sierra Leone." *Journal of Political Economy* 122 (2): 319–68.

Acemoglu, Daron, and James A. Robinson. 2001. "Inefficient Redistribution." *American Political Science Review* 95 (3): 649–61.

———. 2006a. "De Facto Political Power and Institutional Persistence." *American Economic Association Papers and Proceedings* 96 (2): 325–30.

———. 2006b. *Economic Origins of Dictatorship and Democracy.* New York: Cambridge University Press.

———. 2012. *Why Nations Fail: The Origins of Power, Prosperity, and Poverty.* New York: Crown Publishing Group.

Acemoglu, Daron, James A. Robinson, and Rafael J. Santos. 2013. "The Monopoly of Violence: Evidence from Colombia." *Journal of the European Economic Association* 11 (S1): 5–44.

Aidt, Toke, Miriam Golden, and Devesh Tiwari. 2011. "Criminality in the Indian National Legislature." Unpublished.

Aidt, Toke, and Peter Jensen. 2014. "Workers of the World, Unite! Franchise Extensions and the Threat of Revolution in Europe, 1820–1938." *European Economic Review* 72 (November): 52–75.

Alesina, Alberto, and Paola Giuliano. 2015. "Culture and Institutions." *Journal of Economic Literature* 53 (4): 898–944.

Alesina, Alberto, Stelios Michalopoulos, and Elias Papaioannou. Forthcoming. "Ethnic Inequality." *Journal of Political Economy.*

Alt, James, Ethan Bueno de Mesquita, and Shanna Rose. 2011. "Disentangling Accountability and Competence in Elections: Evidence from U.S. Term Limits." *Journal of Politics* 73 (01): 171–86.

Andersen, Jørgen Juel, Niels Johannesen, David Dreyer Lassen, and Elena Paltseva. 2014. "Petro Rents, Political Institutions, and Hidden Wealth: Evidence from Bank Deposits in Tax Havens." Working Paper 0016, Center for Applied Macro and Petroleum Economics, Oslo.

Anderson, Siwan, Patrick Francois, and Ashok Kotwal. 2015. "Clientelism in Indian Villages." *American Economic Review* 105 (6): 1780–816.

Andrews, M., L. Pritchett, and M. Woolcock. 2013. "Escaping Capability Traps through Problem Driven Iterative Adaptation (PDIA)." *World Development* 51: 234–44.

Ashraf, Q., and O. Galor. 2013. "The Out of Africa Hypothesis, Human Genetic Diversity and Comparative Economic Development." *American Economic Review* 103 (1): 1–46.

Baland, Jean-Marie, and James A. Robinson. 2008. "Land and Power: Theory and Evidence from Chile." *American Economic Review* 98 (5): 1737–65.

Banerjee, Abhijit, and Esther Duflo. 2014. "Under the Thumb of History? Political Institutions and the Scope for Action." NBER Working Paper 19848, National Bureau of Economic Research, Cambridge, MA.

Banerjee, Abhijit, Esther Duflo, and Rachel Glennerster. 2008. "Putting a Band Aid on a Corpse: Incentives for Nurses in the Indian Public Health Care System." *Journal of the European Economic Association* 6 (2–3): 487–500.

Banerjee, Abhijit, and Lakshmi Iyer. 2005. "History, Institutions, and Economic Performance: The Legacy of Colonial Land Tenure Systems in India." *American Economic Review* 95 (4): 1190–213.

Banerjee, Abhijit, Lakshmi Iyer, and Rohini Somanathan. 2005. "History, Social Divisions, and Public Goods in Rural India." *Journal of the European Economic Association* 3 (2–3): 639–47.

Banerjee, Abhijit, and Rohini Pande. 2009. "Parochial Politics: Ethnic Preferences and Politician Corruption." Faculty Research Working Papers Series, John F. Kennedy School of Government, Harvard University, Cambridge, MA.

Banuri, S., and P. Keefer. 2013. "Intrinsic Motivation, Effort and the Call to Public Service." World Bank Policy Research Working Paper 6729, World Bank, Washington, DC.

Beaman, Lori, Raghabendra Chattopadhyay, Esther Duflo, Rohini Pande, and Petia Topalova. 2009. "Powerful Women: Does Exposure Reduce Bias?" *Quarterly Journal of Economics* 124 (4): 1497–540.

Beaman, Lori, Esther Duflo, Rohini Pande, and Petia Topalova. 2012. "Female Leadership Raises Aspirations and Educational Attainment for Girls: A Policy Experiment in India." *Science* 335 (6068): 582–86.

Beath, Andrew, Fotini Christia, Georgy Egorov, and Ruben Enikolopov. 2014. "Electoral Rules and Political Selection: Theory and Evidence from a Field Experiment in Afghanistan." NBER Working Paper 20082, National Bureau of Economic Research, Cambridge, MA.

Bernheim, D., and N. Kartik. 2014. "Candidates, Character, and Corruption." *American Economic Journal: Microeconomics* 6 (2): 205–46.

Besley, Timothy. 2005. "Political Selection." *Journal of Economic Perspectives* 19 (3): 43–60.

Besley, Timothy, and Anne Case. 1995. "Does Electoral Accountability Affect Economic Policy Choices? Evidence from Gubernatorial Term Limits." *Quarterly Journal of Economics* 110 (3): 769–98.

Besley, Timothy, and Masayuki Kudamatsu. 2008. "Making Autocracy Work." In *Institutions and Economic Performance*, edited by E. Helpman. Cambridge, MA: Harvard University Press.

Besley, Timothy, Jose G. Montalvo, and Marta Reynal-Querol. 2011. "Do Educated Leaders Matter?" *Economic Journal* 121 (554): F205–27.

Besley, Timothy, Rohini Pande, Lupin Rahman, and Vijayendra Rao. 2004. "The Politics of Public Good Provision: Evidence from Indian Local Governments." *Journal of the European Economic Association* 2 (2–3): 416–26.

Besley, Timothy, and Torsten Persson. 2009. "The Origins of State Capacity: Property Rights, Taxation, and Politics." *American Economic Review* 99 (4): 1218–44.

Besley, Timothy, Tortsen Persson, and Marta Reynal-Querol. 2015. "Resilient Leaders and Institutional Reform: Theory and Evidence." Unpublished working paper. http://perseus.iies.su.se/~tpers/papers/BPR160409.pdf.

Besley, Timothy, Torsten Persson, and Daniel Sturm. 2005. "Political Competition and Economic Performance: Theory and Evidence from the United States." NBER Working Paper 11484, National Bureau of Economic Research, Cambridge, MA.

———. 2010. "Political Competition and Economic Performance: Theory and Evidence from the United States." *Review of Economic Studies* 77 (3): 1329–52.

Besley, Timothy, and Marta Reynal-Querol. 2011. "Do Democracies Select More Educated Leaders?" *American Political Science Review* 105 (03): 552–66.

Bhalotra, Sonia, and Irma Clots-Figueras. 2014. "Health and the Political Agency of Women." *American Economic Journal: Economic Policy* 6 (2): 164–97.

Bold, Tessa, Mwangi Kimenyi, Germano Mwabu, Alice Ng'ang'a, and Justin Sandefur. 2013. "Scaling Up What Works: Experimental Evidence on External Validity in Kenyan Education." Center for Global Development Working Paper 321, Center for Global Development, Washington, DC.

Brender, Adi, and Allan Drazen. 2009. "Do Leaders Affect Government Spending Priorities?" NBER Working Paper 15368, National Bureau of Economic Research, Cambridge, MA.

Brixi, Hana Polackova, Ellen Marie Lust, and Michael Woolcock. 2015. *Trust, Voice, and Incentives: Learning from Local Success Stories in Service Delivery in the Middle East and North Africa.* Washington, DC: World Bank. http://documents.worldbank.org/curated/en/2015/04/24367276/trust-voice-incentives-learning-local-success-stories-service-delivery-middle-east-north-africa.

Brollo, Fernanda, Katja Kaufmann, and Eliana La Ferrara. 2015. "The Political Economy of Enforcing Conditional Welfare Programs: Evidence from Brazil." Unpublished.

Burgess, Robin, Remi Jedwab, Edward Miguel, Ameet Morjaria, and Gerard Padró i Miquel. 2015. "The Value of Democracy: Evidence from Road Building in Kenya." *American Economic Review* 105 (6): 1817–51.

Callen, Michael, Saad Gulzar, Ali Hasanain, and Yasir Khan. 2014. "The Political Economy of Public Employee Absence: Experimental Evidence from Pakistan: Do Local Politics Determine the Effectiveness of Development Interventions? Why Are Service Providers Commonly Absent in Developing Countries?" Unpublished, Harvard Kennedy School, Cambridge, MA.

Callen, Michael, and James D. Long. 2015. "Institutional Corruption and Election Fraud: Evidence from a Field Experiment in Afghanistan." *American Economic Review* 105 (1): 354–81.

Carruthers, Celeste, and Marianne Wanamaker. 2015. "Municipal Housekeeping: The Impact of Women's Suffrage on Public Education." NBER Working Paper 20864, National Bureau of Economic Research, Cambridge, MA.

Caselli, Francesco, and Massimo Morelli. 2004. "Bad Politicians." *Journal of Public Economics* 88 (3–4): 759–82.

Casey, Katherine. 2015. "Crossing Party Lines: The Effects of Information on Redistributive Politics." *American Economic Review* 105 (8): 2410–48.

Chattopadhyay, Raghabendra, and Esther Duflo. 2004. "Women as Policy Makers: Evidence from a Randomized Policy Experiment in India." *Econometrica* 72 (5): 1409–43.

Chin, Aimee, and Nishith Prakash. 2011. "The Redistributive Effects of Political Reservation for Minorities: Evidence from India." *Journal of Development Economics* 96 (2): 265–77.

Clots-Figueras, Irma. 2011. "Women in Politics: Evidence from the Indian States." *Journal of Public Economics* 95 (7–8): 664–90.

Collier, Paul. 2009. *Wars, Guns, and Votes: Democracy in Dangerous Places.* New York, NY: Harper Collins.

Dal Bó, Ernesto, Pedro Dal Bó, and Jason Snyder. 2009. "Political Dynasties." *Review of Economic Studies* 76 (1): 115–42.

Dal Bó, Ernesto, Frederico Finan, and Martin A. Rossi. 2013. "Strengthening State Capabilities: The Role of Financial Incentives in the Call to Public Service." *Quarterly Journal of Economics* 128 (3): 1169–218.

Daniele, Gianmarco, and Benny Geys. 2015. "Organised Crime, Institutions and Political Quality: Empirical Evidence from Italian Municipalities." *Economic Journal* 125 (586): F233–F255.

Deininger, Klaus, Songqing Jin, Hari Nagarajan, and Fang Xia. 2015. "Does Female Reservation Affect Long-Term Political Outcomes? Evidence from Rural India." *Journal of Development Studies* 51 (1): 32–49.

De Janvry, Alain, Frederico Finan, and Elisabeth Sadoulet. 2012. "Local Electoral Incentives and Decentralized Program Performance." *Review of Economics and Statistics* 94 (3): 672–85.

Dell, Melissa. 2012. "Path Dependence in Development: Evidence from the Mexican Revolution." Working Paper, Department of Economics, Harvard University.

Dell, Melissa, Nathan Lane, and Pablo Querubin. 2015. "State Capacity, Local Governance, and Economic Development in Vietnam." Working Paper, Department of Economics, Harvard University.

Dhaliwal, Iqbal, and Rema Hanna. 2014. "Deal with the Devil: The Successes and Limitations of Bureaucratic Reform in India." NBER Working Paper 20482, National Bureau of Economic Research, Cambridge, MA.

Doig, Alan, David Watt, and Robert Williams. 2006. "Hands-On or Hands-Off? Anti-Corruption Agencies in Action, Donor Expectations, and a Good Enough Reality." *Public Administration and Development* 26 (2): 163–72.

Drèze, Jean, and Mrinalini Saran. 1995. "Primary Education and Economic Development in China and India: Overview and Two Case Studies." In *Choice, Welfare and Development: A Festschrift in Honor of Amartya Sen*, edited by K. Basu, P. Pattanaik, and K. Suzumura, 182–241. Oxford: Clarendon Press.

Easterly, William. 2011. "Benevolent Autocrats." Unpublished working paper. https://williameasterly.files.wordpress.com/2011/05/benevolent-autocrats-easterly-2nd-draft.pdf.

Enikolopov, Ruben, and Ekaterina Zhuravskaya. 2007. "Decentralization and Political Institutions." *Journal of Public Economics* 91 (11–12): 2261–90.

Falter, Jürgen W., and William Brustein. 2015. "Die Mitglieder der NSDAP 1925-1945." Arbeitsbereich Vergleichende Faschismusforschung, FU Berlin; Department of Sociology, University of Minnesota; Forschungsprofessur des Instituts für Politikwissenschaft, JGU Mainz. Datenfile Version 2.0 (unpublished data file).

Ferraz, Claudio, and Frederico Finan. 2011. "Electoral Accountability and Corruption: Evidence from the Audits of Local Governments." *American Economic Review* 101 (4): 1274–311.

Ferreira, Fernando, and Joseph Gyourko. 2011. "Does Gender Matter for Political Leadership? The Case of U.S. Mayors." NBER Working Paper 17671, National Bureau of Economic Research, Cambridge, MA.

Finan, Frederico, and Laura Schechter. 2012. "Vote-Buying and Reciprocity." *Econometrica* 80 (2): 863–81.

Freire, Tiago, Vernon Henderson, and Ari Kuncoro. 2011. "Volunteerism after the Tsunami: Democratization and Aid." Working Paper, Department of Economics, Brown University. http://www.econstor.eu/handle/10419/62664.

Fujiwara, Thomas. 2015. "Voting Technology, Political Responsiveness, and Infant Health: Evidence from Brazil." *Econometrica* 83 (2): 423–64.

Galasso, Vincenzo, and Tommaso Nannicini. 2011. "Competing on Good Politicians." *American Political Science Review* 105 (1): 79–99.

Gehlbach, Scott, Konstantin Sonin, and Ekaterina Zhuravskaya. 2010. "Businessman Candidates." *American Journal of Political Science* 54 (3): 718–36.

Guiso, L., P. Sapienza, and L. Zingales. 2006. "Does Culture Affect Economic Outcomes?" *Journal of Economic Perspectives* 20 (2): 23–48.

Hanna, Rema, and Shing-Yi Wang. 2013. "Dishonesty and Selection into Public Service: Evidence from India." NBER Working Paper 19649, National Bureau of Economic Research, Cambridge, MA.

Humphreys, Macartan, William Masters, and Martin Sandu. 2007. "The Role of Leaders in Democratic Deliberations: Results from a Field Experiment in São Tomé and Príncipe." *World Politics* 58: 583–622.

IDS (Institute of Development Studies). 2010. *An Upside-Down View of Governance.* Institute of Development Studies, University of Sussex, Brighton.

Iyer, Lakshmi, and Anandi Mani. 2012. "Traveling Agents: Political Change and Bureaucratic Turnover in India." *Review of Economics and Statistics* 94 (3): 723–39.

Iyer, Lakshmi, Anandi Mani, Prachi Mishra, and Petia Topalova. 2011. "The Power of Political Voice: Women's Political Representation and Crime in India." *American Economic Journal: Applied Economics* 4 (4): 165–93.

Jones, Benjamin, and Benjamin Olken. 2005. "Do Leaders Matter? National Leadership and Growth Since World War II." *Quarterly Journal of Economics* 120 (3): 835–64.

Kaufmann, Daniel, Gil Mehrez, and Tugrul Gurgur. 2002. "Voice or Public Sector Management? An Empirical Investigation of Determinants of Public Sector Performance Based on a Survey of Public Officials." World Bank Research Working Paper, World Bank, Washington, DC.

Keefer, Philip. 2007. "Clientelism, Credibility, and the Policy Choices of Young Democracies." *American Journal of Political Science* 51 (4): 804–21.

———. 2011. "Collective Action, Political Parties, and Pro-Development Public Policy." *Asian Development Review* 28 (1): 94–118.

Khemani, Stuti. 2015. "Buying Votes versus Supplying Public Services: Political Incentives to Under-Invest in Pro-Poor Policies." *Journal of Development Economics* 177: 84–93.

Kitschelt, Herbert, and Steven I. Wilkinson. 2008. *Patrons, Clients and Policies. Patterns of Democratic Accountability and Political Competition.* Cambridge and New York: Cambridge University Press.

Ksoll, Christopher, Rocco Macchiavello, and Ameet Morjaria. 2014. "Guns and Roses: Flower Exports and Electoral Violence in Kenya." CSAE Working Paper 2009-06, Center for the Study of African Economies, Oxford, U.K.

Kudamatsu, Masayuki. 2012. "Has Democratization Reduced Infant Mortality in Sub-Saharan Africa? Evidence from Micro Data." *Journal of the European Economic Association* 10 (6): 1294–317.

La Forgia, Gerard, Shomikho Raha, Shabbeer Shaik, Sunil Kumar Maheshwari, and Rabia Ali. 2014. "Parallel Systems and Human Resource Management in India's Public Health Services: A View from the Front Lines." World Bank Working Paper 6953, World Bank, Washington, DC.

Lee, David, Enrico Moretti, and Matthew J. Butler. 2004. "Do Voters Affect or Elect Policies? Evidence from the U.S. House." *Quarterly Journal of Economics* 119 (3): 807–60.

List, John, and Daniel M. Sturm. 2006. "How Elections Matter: Theory and Evidence from Environmental Policy." *Quarterly Journal of Economics* 121 (4): 1249–81.

Madestam, Andreas, Daniel Shoag, Stan Veuger, and David Yanagizawa-Drott. 2013. "Do Political Protests Matter? Evidence from the Tea Party Movement." *Quarterly Journal of Economics* 128 (4): 1633–85.

Mansuri, Ghazala, and Vijayendra Rao. 2013. *Localizing Development: Does Participation Work?* World Bank Policy Research Report. Washington, DC: World Bank. https://openknowledge.worldbank.org/handle/10986/11859.

Maor, Moshe. 2004. "Feeling the Heat? Anticorruption Mechanisms in Comparative Perspective." *Governance* 17 (1): 1–28.

Martínez-Bravo, Monica. 2014. "The Role of Local Officials in New Democracies: Evidence from Indonesia." *American Economic Review* 104 (4): 1–45.

Martínez-Bravo, Monica, Gerard Padró-i-Miquel, Nancy Qian, and Yang Yao. 2011. "Do Local Elections Increase Accountability in Non-Democracies? Evidence from Rural China." NBER Working Paper 16948, National Bureau of Economic Research, Cambridge, MA.

———. 2014. "The Effects of Democratization on Public Goods and Redistribution." NBER Working Paper 18101, National Bureau of Economic Research, Cambridge, MA.

Meagher, Patrick. 2005. "Anti-Corruption Agencies: Rhetoric Versus Reality." *Journal of Policy Reform* 8 (1): 69–103.

Meyersson, Erik. 2014. "Islamic Rule and the Empowerment of the Poor and Pious." *Econometrica* 82 (1): 229–69.

Miller, Grant. 2008. "Women's Suffrage, Political Responsiveness, and Child Survival in American History." *Quarterly Journal of Economics* 123 (3): 1287–327.

Mobarak, A. M. 2005. "Democracy, Volatility, and Economic Development." *Review of Economics and Statistics* 87 (2): 348–61.

Mungiu-Pippidi, Alina. 2014. "Quantitative Report on Causes of Performance and Stagnation in the Global Fight against Corruption." Anti-Corruption Policies Revisited. ANTICORRP. Pillar 4, WP3.

Muralidharan, Karthik, Paul Niehaus, and Sandip Sukhtankar. 2014. "Building State Capacity: Evidence from Biometric Smartcards in India." NBER Working Paper 19999, National Bureau of Economic Research, Cambridge, MA.

Nannicini, Tommaso, Andrea Stella, Guido Tabellini, and Ugo Troiano. 2013. "Social Capital and Political Accountability." *American Economic Journal: Economic Policy* 5 (2): 222–50.

North, Douglass, John Joseph Wallis, Steven Webb, and Barry Weingast. 2007. "Limited Access Orders in the Developing World: A New Approach to the Problems of Development." World Bank Policy Research Working Paper 4359, World Bank, Washington, DC.

Pande, Rohini. 2003. "Can Mandated Political Representation Increase Policy Influence for Disadvantaged Minorities?" *American Economic Review* 93 (4): 1132–51.

———. 2007. "Understanding Political Corruption in Low-Income Countries." Working Paper Series rwp07-020, Harvard University, John F. Kennedy School of Government, Cambridge, MA.

Pandey, Priyanka. 2010. "Service Delivery and Corruption in Public Services: How Does History Matter?" *American Economic Journal: Applied Economics* 2 (3): 190–204.

Papaioannou, Elias, and Gregorios Siourounis. 2008. "Democratisation and Growth." *Economic Journal* 118 (532): 1520–51.

Prakash, Nishith, Marc Rockmore, and Yogesh Uppal. 2014. "Do Criminal Representatives Hinder or Improve Constituency Outcomes? Evidence from India." IZA Discussion Paper 8452, Institute for Labor Studies, Bonn.

Pritchett, Lant, Michael Woolcock, and Matt Andrews. 2013. "Looking Like a State: Techniques for Persistent Failure in State Capability for Implementation." *Journal of Development Studies* 49 (1): 1–18.

Putnam, R., R. Leonardi, and R. Y. Nanetti. 1993. *Making Democracy Work.* Princeton, NJ: Princeton University Press.

Rehavi, M. Marit. 2007. "Sex and Politics: Do Female Legislators Affect State Spending?" Unpublished, University of California, Berkeley.

Rodrik, Dani. 2000. "Institutions for High-Quality Growth: What They Are and How to Acquire Them." *Studies in Comparative International Development* 35 (3): 3–31.

Rodrik, Dani, and Romain Wacziarg. 2005. "Do Democratic Transitions Produce Bad Economic Outcomes?" *American Economic Review* 95 (2): 50–55.

Satyanath, Shanker, Nico Voigtlaender, and Hans-Joachim Voth. 2013. "Bowling for Fascism: Social Capital and the Rise of the Nazi Party." NBER Working Paper 19201, National Bureau of Economic Research, Cambridge, MA.

Schaffer, Frederic C., ed. 2007. *Elections for Sale: The Causes and Consequences of Vote Buying.* Boulder, CO: Lynne Rienner Publishers.

Sokoloff, Kenneth L., and Stanley L. Engerman. 2000. "History Lessons: Institutions, Factors Endowments, and Paths of Development in the New World." *Journal of Economic Perspectives* 14 (3): 217–32.

Stokes, S. 2005. "Perverse Accountability: A Formal Model of Machine Politics with Evidence from Argentina." *American Political Science Review* 99 (3): 315–25.

———. 2007. "Is Vote Buying Undemocratic?" In *Elections for Sale: The Causes and Consequences of Vote Buying,* edited by Frederic C. Schaffer. Boulder, CO: Lynne Rienner Publishers.

Vicente, Pedro, and Leonard Wantchekon. 2009. "Clientelism and Vote Buying: Lessons from Field Experiments in African Elections." *Oxford Review of Economic Policy* 25 (2): 292–305.

Washington, Ebonya L. 2008. "Female Socialization: How Daughters Affect Their Legislator Fathers." *American Economic Review* 98 (1): 311–32.

World Bank. 2016. *World Development Report 2016: Digital Dividends.* Washington, DC: World Bank.

CHAPTER SIX

Evidence on the Impact of Transparency

Overview

This chapter reviews research on the impact of transparency, defined as citizen access to publicly available information about the actions of those in government and the consequences of these actions. It examines how citizens and leaders respond to transparency. The first part reports substantial evidence that political engagement responds to transparency within and across a variety of institutional contexts. Citizens and leaders change their actions in response to new information. Citizens are influenced by the framing of issues and messages broadcast by mass media. However, the details of transparency are important—the types of information, the credibility of sources, and the media of communication all matter.

The following section examines research on transparency's impact on governance outcomes. This research has focused on the role of mass media in particular and its mechanisms of impact on governance through political engagement. Leaders respond to mass media because it amplifies the role of political engagement to hold them accountable. Historical accounts of institutional transition in developed countries such as the United States and the United Kingdom suggest that the spread of independent mass media can work together with political engagement to create the conditions that lead to the establishment of effective public sector institutions.

In contrast to the potentially transformative role of transparency when working together with political engagement, the following section shows that the impact of transparency initiatives outside the political realm is not enough to improve governance. The impact of transparency initiatives targeted at engaging citizens to take actions to improve service delivery depends upon political incentives. The last section of this chapter examines a role for transparency in improving behavioral norms in the public sector. It highlights this as a particularly important area for future work.

Political engagement responds to transparency

The bulk of the available research on transparency's impact shows that it can play a powerful role through its effects on political engagement. A substantial strand of the literature provides evidence that political engagement by voters responds to transparency. Transparency can increase voter turnout or shift the distribution of vote shares in a variety of institutional contexts. A smaller but growing strand of work uncovers the impact of information on which policy issues voters consider; for example, whether citizens are more likely to vote against corrupt candidates or on the basis of the performance record of the incumbent, and are less likely to vote on the basis of ethnic identity or the receipt of targeted benefits in direct exchange for their vote.

Independent media, such as radio, television, newspapers, and the Internet, are important in bringing about changes in voting behavior. Yet the type of information, its source, and its "fit" with the institutional context are important. Examples have been found in which information had the opposite effect of discouraging voter turnout or increasing vote buying. The direction of impact depends upon the nature of the media market and the extent to which it provides credible information or reflects political biases and polarization. The same type of information can have different effects depending on the credibility of the source that generated the information. Furthermore, in contexts in which political engagement is unhealthy, there is no clear evidence on whether the transparency's impact is sufficient to get leaders to respond with sustainable or long-term improvements in outcomes, by using the powers of their office to strengthen institutions.

These differences in the available evidence on the impact of transparency on political engagement are linked to the design of specific interventions. The pattern of evidence does not suggest that lack of impact or detrimental impact of transparency is limited to weak institutional settings or that successful impacts occur only in strong institutional settings.

Evidence of impact on voter behavior

A growing number of randomized controlled trials have been implemented in developing countries to try to encourage poor voters to participate in the democratic process. Most of these interventions are based on information campaigns that make voters more knowledgeable about the electoral system and aware of the importance of voting.

Information interventions implemented in countries as diverse as India, China, Mozambique, and Pakistan have found that more informed voters are more likely to participate in elections (Aker et al. 2013; Banerjee et al. 2011; Giné and Mansuri 2011; Guan and Green 2006). However, some studies show the opposite effect, where the availability of new information and media can reduce voter turnout (Chong et al. 2015; Gentzkow 2006). These contrasting results are echoed in other research in which the outcome variable of interest is different (such as corruption or responsiveness of leaders). The discussion below shows how all of the evidence is consistent with the sensitivity of voting behavior to information, even though the direction of impact depends upon a variety of conditions. Some of these conditions may pertain to the formal institutional environment, which is beyond the scope of this report. However, as discussed in the previous two chapters, these conditions also pertain to characteristics of political engagement that can vary within the same formal institutional and country context. Finally, some of the variation comes from the nature of the information itself. For example, Gentzkow (2006) shows that the negative effect of the penetration of television on voter turnout in the United States is driven by the crowding-out of other media (such as newspapers) that carry more information about public affairs and political leaders.

Complementary evidence comes from studies that focus on information that improves voters' knowledge about the quality of politicians and their actions. Ferraz and Finan (2008) use exogenous variation in the timing of disclosure of information on corruption in Brazil and find that voters change their choices when audit reports disclose information about corrupt practices. Corrupt mayors are punished at the polls while mayors with no irregularities are rewarded. These effects are stronger in municipalities in which local radio is present to diffuse this information. Similar results are found by Bobonis, Cámara Fuertes, and Schwabe (forthcoming) using information disclosed in audit reports in Puerto Rico, and by Larreguy, Marshall, and Snyder (2015), who use audit information from Mexico. They find that voters punish the party of malfeasant mayors, but only in precincts covered by local media stations.

Although the availability of information can have significant effects on political engagement, the impact might depend on the source and the credibility of the information being provided. Alt, Lassen, Marshall (forthcoming) examine the credibility of the source of information within the same (strong) institutional context (Denmark). They focus on how information may affect belief updating: the effect of the source of the message depends upon the source's objective and subjective credibility, while the ideological content of the message may update beliefs by reinforcing previously existing beliefs or persuading voters with different ideological predispositions. Based on their survey experiment in Denmark, they find that objective credibility of the information source matters: an unemployment projection from the Danish Central Bank, which is highly credible among citizens, causes voters to update their beliefs more than does information received from government or opposition political parties.

Another example of the importance of the credibility of the source comes from contrasting results across different studies that examine how voters react to information about corruption of incumbent politicians. When information comes from a credible source (such as audits implemented by an independent agency) and is distributed through existing media, it generates significant changes in voting patterns. In contrast, Chong et al. (2015) do not find significant effects when the information is provided by nongovernmental organizations (NGOs) through a door-to-door campaign in Mexico. An important difference between this study and the work based on audit reports is the type of information being provided. The authors report "spending according to rules (*gasto que cumple con normas*)," which is very different from the type of audit reports used by Ferraz and Finan (2008) in Brazil; by Bobonis, Cámara Fuertes, and Schwabe (forthcoming) in Puerto Rico; and by Larreguy, Marshall, and Snyder (2015) in Mexico. In experiments such as Chong et al. (2015), the information NGOs provided in flyers could have been interpreted in an ambiguous way, given that it is not necessarily a measure of corruption. These differences suggest that information and its credibility based on technical quality, with a clear connection to the well-being of voters, is more likely to have an impact.[1]

Positive information about the quality of politicians can also affect political selection, as shown in the work of Kendall, Nannicini, and Trebbi (2015). The authors implemented a field experiment on the provision of information in an Italian city where the mayor was running for reelection. However, instead of negative information, they provided information on the fact that the mayor of Arezzo developed an urban development plan that was highly ranked by the regional government and received extra funding because of its quality. The extra funding was used to rebuild monuments, roads, and parking lots in the city center. They show how voters update their beliefs and change their voting patterns when provided with this information on the competence, effort, or performance of leaders. Much weaker effects were estimated when information was provided only on ideological policy positions.

Transparency interventions—in this case providing more information on the quality of politicians—lead voters to change their behavior across myriad contexts. In what follows, evidence from Sierra Leone, India, Benin, Mali, Indonesia, and São Tomé and Principe is reviewed.

- In Sierra Leone, Bidwell, Casey, and Glennerster (2015) used political debates to provide information to voters. Large groups of voters were exposed to films of the debates via a mobile cinema that visited 112 of 224 randomly selected polling centers in the five weeks before the election. The authors find strong positive impacts of watching the debates on voter knowledge and changes in votes cast, especially in favor of candidates who performed best during the debates.

- In the slums of Delhi in India, Banerjee et al. (2011) distributed newspapers containing report cards on the quality of legislators. On average, they find small increases in turnout and no change in incumbent vote share in treatment slums. However, they find larger effects on turnout and vote shares in localities where the incumbent's performance was worse and where the challengers were better qualified. For the best-performing legislators, incumbent vote share increased by 6.9 percent with the information treatment. They also find a significant decline in vote buying through cash.

- In Benin, Fujiwara and Wantchekon (2013) implemented a field experiment in collaboration with leading candidates in the 2006 presidential election. In randomly selected villages, the candidates adopted a nonclientelist campaign strategy, while pursuing the standard clientelist strategies in control villages. The treatment also included public deliberation; voters were invited to debate the platforms in town hall meetings. The combined treatment increased voters' perception that the campaign informed voters about candidate qualifications, but had no effects on reported vote buying, voter turnout, and vote shares of candidates running the town meetings. However, the treatment reduced the votes of the dominant candidate in the treatment villages. One important aspect of this study is that the authors cannot distinguish the effects of information provided by candidates about their policy positions during these town halls from the effects of public deliberation.

- In Mali, Gottlieb (2016) examined the impact of providing different types of information. She implemented a randomized intervention in which she provided civic education about budget size and mandated responsibilities of government officials. A second treatment arm provided additional information on the local government's performance relative to neighboring governments to improve voter ability to benchmark politician performance. She finds that the randomly assigned civics course successfully increased voter expectations of local government performance, as measured by survey questions about local government capacity and responsibility to provide public goods. She also finds that people in treated communes were more likely to challenge their local leadership at community meetings. The effects were stronger when civic education was combined with information on politicians' relative performance.

- In Indonesia, Paler (2013) used a laboratory experiment to show that citizens are more willing to take actions to monitor the performance of local leaders when they have more information. The experiment is designed to examine the role of information in comparison with the role that taxation is supposed to play as a source of accountability. The hypothesis is that when governments finance their spending through taxation, they are more likely to be accountable to citizens because citizens will have greater incentives to monitor performance. In contrast, when government revenues are windfalls from fiscal transfers, donors, or natural resources, citizens would have lower incentives to monitor. The author finds that citizens are indeed more likely to monitor governments and take political action when revenues come from taxes rather than windfalls. However, when provided with information on spending performance, citizens care as much about monitoring governments when revenues come from windfalls as from taxes.[2]

- In São Tomé and Principe, Vicente (2014) implemented a randomized door-to-door campaign against vote buying during the presidential election. The campaign was sponsored by the country's National Electoral Commission (instead of by an independent NGO) and had a strong emphasis on voting according to one's judgment about the quality of the politicians and not according to whoever had bought one's vote. The campaign decreased the reported perception that voting decisions were affected by the money offered by candidates, and increased the reported perception that voters cast their votes in good conscience. It also decreased turnout (consistent with the idea of turnout buying) and favored the incumbent politician, whose vote share increased by close to 4 percentage points. The author interprets the results as implying that challengers rely more heavily on vote buying as a means of campaigning. This type of study is not designed to assess the overall impact on governance, but rather to examine whether vote-selling behavior is responsive to information and persuasion. Other work, discussed below, shows contrasting effects of transparency on vote buying by politicians.

Evidence of the role of different types of mass media

Another set of evidence comes from studies that examine the role of media as a source of information to voters. This growing literature suggests that the type of media and the source of the information disclosed matters for voter behavior. This review of the literature draws upon surveys by Strömberg (2015) and Prat and Strömberg (2011).

The presence of news media that provide political information leads to increases in voter turnout. Strömberg (2004) shows that the introduction of radio across U.S. counties during the period 1920–40 increased political participation. Similar results emerge from Gentzkow, Shapiro, and Sinkinson (2011), who show that the entry of newspapers in U.S. cities increases turnout in both congressional and presidential elections. Drago, Nannicini, and Sobbrio (2014) show that newspapers increase turnout in Italian municipal elections. Also, Oberholzer-Gee and Waldfogel (2009) and Prat and Strömberg (2005) find that television increases voter turnout in the United States and Sweden, respectively.

These effects are expected if voters become more informed about politics and if more-informed voters are more likely to participate in the political process. Prat and Strömberg (2005) provide evidence that the entry of commercial television in Sweden increased political knowledge. Snyder and Strömberg (2010) use variation in the access to political information through newspapers and find that media are a key provider of political information to citizens. They find that voters in areas where newspapers have greater coverage of politicians are better informed about their representatives.

There is evidence, however, that new media outlets can reduce political knowledge and participation when political information competes with entertainment programs or when competition in the media market reduces the quantity and quality of news provided (Cagé 2014). Gentzkow (2006) shows that increases in television penetration in the United States had a small negative effect on political participation, consistent with Putnam's (1995) hypothesis that media can also act as a source of reduction in political information for citizens as a result of its entertainment value. Similarly, Olken (2009) shows that access to television in Indonesia is associated with reduced participation in social groups, fewer organizations in the village, and lower levels of reported trust in the community.

A growing number of studies show that the introduction of new media outlets affects not only political participation, but also how citizens vote. A series of papers use the rich data available from mostly developed countries to show how coverage of political information in different types of media can shift voters' views on parties' policy positions or ideology. DellaVigna and Kaplan (2007) show that the entry of Fox News across U.S. cities increased the presidential vote share of Republicans. Using a similar strategy, Enikolopov, Petrova, and Zhuravskaya (2011) find that citizens who have access to the independent television station in Russia (NTV) were more likely to vote for anti-Putin parties. Knight and Chiang (2011) show that newspaper endorsements change voting intentions in the United States, while Gentzkow, Shapiro, and Sinkinson (2011) use variation in entry and exit from newspapers in cities across the United States and find effects on political participation, but do not find significant effects on vote shares or incumbency advantage. Drago, Nannicini, and Sobbrio (2014) use variation in entry and exit of newspapers in Italian cities and find that incumbents are more likely to be reelected where there is greater entry by newspapers. They interpret their results as suggesting that newspapers increase the visibility of politicians in office and may make it easier for the good-quality politicians to signal their quality.

The entry of the Internet in developing countries is likely to affect the provision of information to voters and politicians and the citizens' capacity for coordination, and therefore might have significant effects on policy outcomes and governance. Although the Internet is a relatively new phenomenon, an emerging literature is looking at its political effects. The main question is whether information available through the Internet increases or crowds out political knowledge and interest and whether it helps individuals solve the collective action problem of coordinating expectations and actions.

The penetration of the Internet can reduce political participation if it crowds out other media that carry political information. Falck, Gold, and Heblich (2014) provide evidence from Germany showing that the emergence of the Internet crowded out traditional media such as newspapers and television, and reduced voters' political information and voter turnout. Campante, Durante, and Sobbrio (2013) find that broadband penetration also decreased turnout in the Italian parliamentary elections, but the effect was temporary. In the longer run, they find broadband access to be positively associated with political participation and facilitation of the emergence of new political entrepreneurs. Miner (2015) looks at the effects of Internet penetration in Malaysia and finds that the growth of the Internet is associated with an increase in turnout and a reduction of support for the dominant incumbent party. He suggests that the information available on the Internet undermined the incumbent party's ability to suppress negative information about candidates.

A different effect of the proliferation of the Internet, and especially social media, is the possibility of coordination and peer effects in political behavior. Moreover, as suggested by Halberstam and Knight (2015), social media are different from other forms of communication because they allow users to produce information, and access to information depends upon self-chosen links. Bond et al. (2012) implemented a randomized controlled trial of political mobilization messages delivered to 61 million Facebook users during the 2010 U.S. congressional elections and found that messages affected information-seeking and voting behavior. The messages influenced both the users who received them and their friends, suggesting that social media can be a powerful source of political influence.

Although little evidence is available on how social media influence electoral outcomes and governance in developing countries, it might be expected to act as an important coordinating device for changes and an alternative form of independent provision of information, as documented by Enikopolov, Petrova, and Sonin (2016) in Russia. Evidence presented by Grossman, Humphreys, and Sacramone-Lutz (2014) suggests that new technologies can increase the communication between marginalized citizens and politicians. Of course, media can also act as a negative coordinating device when it allows coordination for such actions as the Rwandan genocide (Yanagizawa-Drott 2014) or the rise of the Nazi party (Adena et al. 2015).

Casey (2015) and Keefer and Khemani (2014a, 2014b, 2015) examine the impact of a type of media that is particularly salient for poor citizens and in one of the poorest regions of the world: community radio in Africa. Casey (2015) examines whether information available through radio helps relax ethnic and partisan loyalties in Sierra Leone. She shows that political information provided through radio on local politicians improves voters' knowledge. She finds that candidate information increases citizen willingness to cross ethnic-party lines. Complementary evidence shows that more information induces parties to distribute campaign spending in a more equitable way across districts. Although she interprets this as evidence of more equitable distribution of public goods spending, it could also be that parties respond to the presence of more-informed voters with targeted vote buying together with campaign spending. Unfortunately, she does not have data to test this.

In related work in Sierra Leone, Bidwell, Casey, and Glennerster (2015) document that politicians who participated in debates, videotapes of which were shown to a random selection of localities, increased their campaigning effort, as measured by gift giving, the monetary value of gifts, and the number of in-person visits. They find little evidence for treatment effects on the activity level of elected members during sittings of Parliament, but they find that using debates to increase the information voters have affects politicians' engagement with their constituencies, as measured by public meetings and higher spending on development projects. Because infrastructure spending can be captured by local elites and can be a source of corruption,[3] more data on welfare measures would be needed to understand whether information obtained through debates actually improves governance.

Keefer and Khemani (2014a, 2014b) use a natural experiment in radio markets in Benin to examine the impact of broadcasts of public interest programming aimed at increasing household demand for health and education services. They find evidence suggesting that although such programming indeed affected household attitudes toward health and education, the changes were not sufficient to change politicians' incentives to respond by providing greater services. Households living in villages with access to signals from a larger number of community radio stations are more exposed to public-interest programming and are more likely to invest their private resources in health and the education of their children, but they are not likely to receive more or better public services.

At the same time, Keefer and Khemani (2015) uncover some media effects in shifting preferences or beliefs about the appropriate roles of public policies that could be important for the transition to better-quality political engagement, even if no impact on public service delivery outcomes is discerned in the short term. The authors use survey vignettes to impose an explicit trade-off between political promises of jobs for a few versus health or education for all. They achieve this through the device of a budget constraint, emphasizing to respondents that politicians who allocate resources to government jobs for some members of the community have fewer resources available to finance inputs into broadly delivered health or education services for all of the community. Respondents then choose whether to support the candidate who would allocate resources to jobs for a few rather than to greater inputs for health and education for all. Consistent with Wantchekon's (2003) pioneering work in Benin, responses to these surveys reflect widespread citizen support for clientelist candidates who offer jobs. Yet, respondents living in villages with greater access to community radio are significantly less likely to support these candidates who offer jobs at the expense of broad public services.

Additional results in Keefer and Khemani (2015) highlight the importance of programming content and issue framing on mass media. Despite reductions in support for clientelist candidates who offer jobs at the expense of health and education, radio access does not reduce support for candidates who offer gifts at the time of elections, a practice that is regarded as indicative of vote buying. However, from the vignette designed to measure attitudes toward gift-giving candidates, as in actual practice, citizens have no information to infer whether gift-giving candidates have any impact on the provision of health and education. In fact, greater information conveyed through radio about established public programs in health and education might lead citizens to believe that gift-giving candidates have little influence, one way or another, on those programs. Keefer and Khemani (2015) show how this pattern of results is consistent with a particular mechanism for radio's impact: it increases citizens' demand for public health and education services, thereby reducing their support for candidates who make clientelist offers at the expense of public health and education spending.

Evidence of impact on politicians' response to transparency

Politicians can strategically respond to the disclosure of information and expected changes in voting behavior by increasing their campaigning efforts, increasing vote buying, using coercion, or affecting other types of information to counteract the information about their quality. Although less evidence on this mechanism is available, Humphreys and Weinstein (2012) suggest that it was at play in Uganda, where they implemented a large field experiment to evaluate the impact of providing information to voters based on a detailed scorecard on the performance of members of Parliament. They find that voters are sensitive to the information provided in the scorecard and update their beliefs. However, the information ultimately had no impact on politicians' vote shares. The results suggest that politicians can more easily obfuscate information and deflect scrutiny away from themselves when the information does not clearly specify the consequences of their actions for the services voters care about.

Gottlieb (2016) finds that leaders appear to be less transparent when voters are part of an information treatment about local government performance. Casey (2015) shows that political information provided through radio induces parties to distribute campaign spending in a more equitable way across districts. Similar effects are found by Bidwell, Casey, and Glennerster (2015), as discussed above, who document that politicians whose debates were videotaped and shown in communities increased their campaign efforts, as measured by gift giving, the monetary value of gifts, and the number of in-person visits.

Evidence that politicians respond to information disclosure through vote buying is provided by Cruz, Keefer, and Labonne (2015). They implemented a field experiment in which they provided information to voters in the Philippines about the existence and importance of a large infrastructure public spending program one week before a municipal election. The authors show that the intervention led to changes in voter knowledge about the program and about incumbent politicians, and that incumbent politicians responded by increasing resources targeted at voters through vote buying. But Cruz, Keefer, and Labonne (2015) find no significant effects on turnout or voting patterns. Because the information interventions undertaken by Cruz, Keefer, and Labonne (2015) were restricted to just before elections, the authors cannot show how voters and politicians would react if information campaigns against vote buying and information on availability of resources to politicians was disseminated in the beginning of their electoral term and repeated throughout the term. Indeed, the authors argue that their results could be different if the intervention were implemented earlier in the electoral cycle, when incumbents have greater opportunity to react by increasing the provision of public goods.

These results on vote buying in the Philippines are consistent with Khemani (2015), who argues that politicians tradeoff vote buying against the provision of broad public services in the Philippines and elsewhere. An increase in competitive pressure that was induced by the information campaigns studied by Cruz, Keefer, and Labonne (2015) in a clientelist setting led to politicians increasing vote buying, especially when they could not respond by improving the quality of public services. The results of increases in vote buying by politicians in response to transparency in the Philippines are also consistent with the results from Benin of the (lack of) radio's effects on citizen support for gift-giving candidates (Keefer and Khemani 2015). In the absence of information about the effects of electing vote-buying candidates on service delivery, transparency about other areas can lead to greater vote buying by politicians to woo voters.

A final piece of evidence suggesting that political leaders might respond to the disclosure of information comes from Malesky, Schuler, and Tran (2012). They examine the impact of a randomized broadcast of information through an online newspaper in Vietnam, which is an environment in which a centralized political party controls the nomination of candidates who are exposed to greater transparency. The results suggest that the transparency intervention induced significant changes in the central political party's decisions to nominate and allocate candidates across districts.[4]

Summarizing lessons by making connections between the literature

In sum, the existing evidence on transparency's impact on political engagement suggests that information from trustworthy sources (for example, independent agencies, backed by credible technical capacity) can increase political participation and allow voters to punish badly performing politicians at the polls. However, the extent to which incumbent politicians and party elites can undo the positive effects of information on voters is not clear. In addition, more research is necessary to develop an understanding of both the long-term effects of information provision as well as the general equilibrium effects taking into account public officials', politicians', and parties' responses.

The evidence of impact on incumbent vote shares suggests that if the interventions primarily strengthen the hands of incumbent politicians (by reducing the efficacy of vote-buying tactics used by political challengers), they may be further protected from losing office and able to continue rent-extraction policies. On the other hand, if the interventions have a strong anti-incumbent bias, the incentives of incumbents to try to remain in office by improving performance may be reduced.

Furthermore, there is an important distinction between information about performance versus information about specific policy actions, as emphasized in the theory covered in chapter 4, and which also emerges in the empirical evidence. The evidence suggests that information on "valence issues," which most voters find desirable, such as the competence and effort of politicians and their performance in service delivery, has greater impact than information about ideological policy positions that divide voters (Kendall, Nannicini, and Trebbi 2015). Studies of interventions that provide information about politicians' specific actions, such as in legislative debate, also find little impact, and suggest that politicians can obfuscate information to prevent voters from using it to assess their performance (Humphreys and Weinstein 2012).

Transparency's impact on governance outcomes occurs through political engagement

Transparency affects governance outcomes through political engagement, and ultimate impact on governance depends upon the characteristics of political engagement. A growing number of studies examine whether governments respond to voters who have access to more information. These studies explain the impact of transparency on government actions as resulting from changes in voting behavior that then change the political incentives of government leaders to respond to voters by improving governance.

Media's impact on government performance occurs through media's impact on political engagement

A body of research on the impact of media on public spending and government performance shows how media's impact occurs through changes in political engagement. Strömberg (2004) measures the effects on public spending of the introduction of radio across U.S. counties during the period 1920–40. He finds that radio increased federal spending, such as social assistance funds in the New Deal programs, particularly in rural counties. He shows that increases in voter turnout in counties with greater radio ownership is the mechanism behind this impact of radio on public spending.

Lim, Snyder, and Strömberg (2015) study the effect of newspaper coverage of state trial court judges in the United States, and find that it significantly increases average sentence length awarded by those judges. It is specifically trial judges who are elected who are more likely than appointed judges to increase sentence length when there is greater newspaper coverage.

Snyder and Strömberg (2010) exploit mismatches between the geography of congressional districts and the geography of media markets in the United States to trace the entire process by which more or less media coverage leads to more or less responsiveness to reelection concerns. The theory is that in places where the media market and the congressional district overlap to a greater extent, voters will be more informed about politicians and politicians will respond accordingly. The authors show that more congruence leads to more coverage of the incumbent. This increase is consequential: more congruence is associated with greater knowledge about the incumbent congress members. However, more congruence does not lead to more knowledge about senators, suggesting that congruence is not just serving as a proxy for political knowledge in general. Congruence also leads citizens to be more likely to turn out to vote. Turning to incumbent behavior, the authors find that incumbents in more congruent districts are more active in committee hearings and vote on roll calls in a less partisan way. Finally, congruence feeds through to policy: federal spending in a district is greater when there is more congruence. These results constitute a powerful case that media's effects in making governments accountable operate through electoral institutions.

Campante and Do (2014) provide further evidence from the United States for how the interaction between media markets and political markets influences government performance. First, they provide the reduced-form result that states in the United States whose capital cities are more isolated, as defined relative to the spatial distribution of the state's population, have greater levels of corruption. They then provide direct evidence of the mechanism underlying the association between isolation and corruption: newspapers cover state politics more when readers are closer to the capital. Voters who live far from the capital are less knowledgeable and interested in state politics, and they turn out less in state elections (but not in presidential elections). The authors report additional supporting results that isolated capitals are associated with more money in state-level campaigns and worse public goods provision. This evidence shows how even in a context with strong internal checks and balances, external accountability through the interaction of media and elections is important for governance.

Some results in Nannicini et al. (2013), discussed in chapter 5 on the role of historical institutions within Italy in shaping "civic voting," or healthy political engagement to punish corrupt leaders, can be interpreted as supporting the notion that transparency can help bring about changes in political engagement in the short run (without waiting for history to run its course). The authors find that newspaper circulation is significantly correlated with lower corruption. When newspaper circulation is included in the analysis, the estimated impact of historical institutions shrinks and loses statistical significance. That is, the historically rooted differences in institutions within Italy are not significant in explaining "civic" voting behavior to punish transgressions once newspaper circulation is taken into account. When using measures of political engagement (average turnout in national elections, European elections, and referenda during the 1990s) instead of historical social capital, the negative correlation between corruption and the political engagement measures of social capital is strongly robust to the inclusion of newspapers' diffusion as an explanatory variable.[5] That is, political engagement and transparency together explain civic voting to punish transgressions by political leaders and thereby strengthen incentives for lower corruption, even in an environment in which there are historical differences in social norms.

The role of transparency in improving governance in developing countries

Because most of the evidence on the interaction between media and political markets comes from rich countries with well-functioning institutions, whether politicians in developing countries respond the same way to media-informed citizens is unclear. One of the first studies to examine this proposition was Besley and Burgess (2002) in India. They study how governments respond to natural disasters such as droughts and floods with relief to local populations and whether these responses vary according to the presence of local media (that is, newspapers). They find that higher newspaper circulation is associated with greater government responsiveness to declines in food production and flood damage. They argue that this association is driven by greater political engagement of more informed citizens.

The work by Ferraz and Finan (2011) evaluating the role of electoral accountability in reducing corruption in Brazil also extends to examining the complementary role of mass media. They find that the presence of local radio enhances the incentives of mayors who face reelection to reduce corruption compared with the incentives of mayors who face term limits. They also find a smaller difference in corruption between term-limited and other mayors in municipalities that have local radio stations, which they interpret as evidence that even term-limited mayors might suffer other types of punishment and therefore have incentives to reduce corruption in the presence of the media.

Bobonis, Cámara Fuertes, and Schwabe (forthcoming) show that the impact of the public disclosure of audit reports on municipal corruption in Puerto Rico is concentrated in municipalities that experience greater political competition. Furthermore, they provide evidence that transparency's effects are short-lived and occur only when audit disclosure happens close to an election. They also provide suggestive evidence that voters use the information to select more competent leaders who may perform better in office. Their study makes a case for timely, regular, and sustained long-term commitments to audit disclosure to improve governance.

A case study from Peru shows that media can play a powerful role in holding leaders accountable. Using data from bribery records maintained by Vladimiro Montesinos, the security chief in Peru under President Fujimori, McMillan and Zoido (2004) show how political support and acquiescence were purchased from media owners as well as from opposition politicians and judges. The importance of media is reflected in the fact that the bribe price of media owners was an order of magnitude greater than what was paid to politicians and judges. On the one hand, this case shows how politicians can manipulate and capture accountability institutions. On the other, the case also highlights the special properties media markets have that would improve accountability, given that plurality (dispersed ownership) can be an effective defense against capture. It takes just one media outlet to make information public. McMillan and Zoido (2004) discuss how Montesinos was unable to purchase the support of one television channel, which remained resolute and continued to criticize the political regime in Peru. It was this channel that ultimately contributed to the demise of the regime by broadcasting taped evidence of Montesinos's corrupt practices. Prat and Strömberg (2011) argue that commercial media can be a strong force for achieving such plurality and dispersion because of the commercial motive to win an audience and maintain a reputation for credibility.

In places where political engagement is flawed, even when some voters are sensitive to transparency, the net impact on governance depends upon how selected politicians behave during their tenure in office. Politicians'

187

behavior, in turn, depends upon the larger institutional context and what might informally be referred to as the "size" of the impact on political engagement—whether sufficient voters have changed their behavior to make it politically unprofitable for leaders to continue with corruption or clientelism. In work in Sierra Leone, although Bidwell, Casey, and Glennerster (2015) and Casey (2015) show that information available through radio helps relax ethnic and partisan loyalties, neither study clearly shows whether information helped improve the performance of public spending and public service delivery versus inducing politicians to deliver more clientelist transfers. In Benin, Keefer and Khemani (2014a, 2014b) find that radio did not lead to greater public accountability and argue that it did not because it did not have a sufficient impact on political engagement. Schools located in villages with greater radio access enjoyed no greater government inputs (such as teachers or books), nor more responsive service providers (lower teacher absenteeism), nor more active parent-teacher associations. Households in villages with better community radio access were also less likely to receive free bed nets from the government.

In sum, although the previous section finds consistent evidence across a large literature and in a variety of institutional contexts that political engagement is sensitive to transparency, the research on the ultimate impact on governance is more limited. Little existing empirical research in developing countries is designed to address the question of how transparency shapes governance by leaders during their tenure in office. The available evidence comes from the United States and a few countries in Latin America, taking advantage of rich time series data on media and political markets as well as on governance outcomes. The available empirical work in poorer countries, such as in Africa and South Asia, has so far been designed to focus on short-term changes in voters' and politicians' behavior at the time of elections. This situation points to a fertile agenda for future work to examine how transparency, especially through media markets that intersect with political markets, can bring about governance transitions in developing countries.

Media's effects on political polarization

Additional evidence from the United States on how citizens change their beliefs and political behavioral norms that constrain policies from being pursued on the basis of technical merit highlights the interaction between the forces of transparency and political engagement. Examples of such problems were provided in chapter 1, including popular demand for energy subsidies without due regard to the cost of these subsidies. Another example is ideological polarization that leads to policy gridlock. Glaeser and Sunstein (2013) show that in the presence of preexisting beliefs that polarize citizens, transparency alone is not only unlikely to shift beliefs but might in fact cause previous beliefs to become even more entrenched. The same information can activate completely different memories of personal experiences and associated convictions, thus producing polarized responses to that information.

Glaeser and Sunstein (2013) further show that leaders can play a role in credible communication that can persuade citizens to shift their beliefs. They provide the following example from the United States in this regard:

> When liberals and conservatives are asked for their private views about a generous welfare policy and a more stringent one, they react in the predictable ways, with liberals favoring the former and conservatives the latter. But things change dramatically when they are informed of the distribution of views within the House of Representatives. More specifically, conservatives end up disapproving of the more stringent policy, and favor the generous one, when they are told that 90 percent of House Republicans favor the generous policy. Liberals show the same willingness to abandon their private opinions, and thus end up favoring the stringent policy, when told that this is the position of 90 percent of House Democrats. Notably, the effect of learning about party views is as strong among those who are knowledgeable about welfare policy as it is among people who were not. Also notably, both conservatives and liberals believe that their judgments are driven largely by the merits, and not by what they learn about the views of their preferred party—but in that belief, they are wrong. (Glaeser and Sunstein 2013, 23)

However, whether leaders have incentives to support policies on technical merit, and the credibility to signal that they are doing so to their constituents (as in the example above), rather than to reflect polarization among the electorate, links back to the role of transparency in shaping political engagement. The congruence between media markets and political markets is significant in determining the degree of polarized voting in the American legislature (Campante and Hojman 2013; Snyder and Strömberg 2010).

Campante and Hojman (2013) show how the intersection of media and political markets influences another source of political impediments to good public policies—ideological polarization among politicians and citizens. They provide robust evidence that the introduction of broadcast television decreased the ideological polarization of the U.S. Congress. Information provided by television acted as an important force for bringing members of Congress toward the political center. They also find similar effects for the expansion of radio in the 1930s. Their framework can be extended to suggest how different types of media play a role in the steady increase in polarization in the United States since the 1970s. This increase in polarization has coincided with significant structural changes in the American media environment—the rise of talk radio, the expansion of cable television, and the growth of the Internet, all of which are associated with content differentiation and market segmentation that may have contributed to increased polarization.

Gentzkow and Shapiro (2011) use data on the ideological composition of news website visitors (Democrat or Republican) to compare ideological segregation online and offline. They examine whether new sources of information (that is, the Internet) expose individuals to a more diverse set of news or cause consumers to self-segregate in consuming news that is closer to their initial beliefs. The authors measure segregation in online news compared with other forms of more traditional news and face-to-face interactions. They find that ideological segregation on the Internet is higher than in most offline media, but significantly lower than segregation in face-to-face interactions. They find no evidence that users of or audiences on the Internet are becoming more segregated over time.

This body of evidence from U.S. experience has implications for how to generate ideas about harnessing transparency to address similar problems of entrenched ideological beliefs among citizens in developing countries, such as the government's role in controlling prices by subsidizing essential commodities. The insights from the United States can explain developing countries' experience with subsidy reforms—informing citizens about the cost of subsidies is not sufficient to solve the problem (Clements et al. 2013). Leaders who emerge from healthy political processes, with popular mandates for public service delivery, may be key to shifting general beliefs and norms in the public sector among public officials, frontline service providers, and citizens, as argued in the theoretical work covered in chapter 4. This conclusion completes the feedback circle between transparency and political engagement in selecting better-quality and motivated leaders who are able to govern well through their own actions and policy decisions as well as through the role they play in shifting behavioral norms in the public sector.

The role of media in controlling corruption

A number of studies report that the presence of competitive media markets is significantly associated with greater control of corruption across countries. Besley and Prat (2006), using data from 90 countries in 1999, find that a high degree of state ownership of newspapers (market share of more than 30 percent) is associated with greater corruption and political longevity. Adsera, Boix, and Payne (2003) and Brunetti and Weder (2003) provide similar cross-country evidence that the presence of independent media is associated with better indicators of governance.

In contrast to the robust correlation with media markets, results on the correlation between public disclosure policies and governance outcomes are both fewer and more ambiguous. Escaleras, Lin, and Register (2009) examine whether recently implemented freedom of information (FOI) laws are correlated with changes in public sector corruption. They analyze data from 128 countries between 1984 and 2003, and use propensity score matching methods to address the problem of endogenous selection of FOI laws. Considering all 128 countries, they find no significant effect of FOI on reducing public sector corruption. However, in subdividing the sample between developed and developing countries, the authors find that the existence of FOI acts is positively and significantly related to public sector corruption in developing countries, with no correlation in developed countries. The surprising result is that FOI acts are associated with *greater* levels of public sector corruption in developing countries. The authors cannot rule out that part of this correlation might arise from greater revelation of instances of corruption, or greater measured corruption after the enactment of FOI. That is, the study is not able to discern whether actual corruption or incentives for corruption changed as a result of the FOI act.

Mungiu-Pippidi (2014) reports press freedom as being among the robust correlates of the control of corruption. In an equilibrium cross-sectional model explaining the control of corruption for the period 1996–2011 for a sample of 148 countries, variables that are positively correlated with the control of corruption are an independent judiciary system, controls on executive power, robust civil society, and press freedom. In separate analysis, she also finds that legislation of FOI acts (FOIAs) is positively correlated with the control of corruption. However, there are fewer tests of the robustness of the correlation between corruption and FOIA compared with what is obtained within her study and from the larger literature reviewed above on the role of independent media.

Mass media can work together with political engagement to strengthen institutions: Lessons from history

Thus far this chapter has reviewed the accumulating empirical evidence that transparency influences political engagement, and joins previous chapters showing that political engagement, in turn, has profound consequences for governance. Yet the available empirical tests do not extend to rigorously examining whether these forces together bring about changes in the myriad institutions of government through which services are delivered and internal accountability is maintained. The literature on institutional change is either theoretical or descriptive, using historical accounts to bolster theoretical explanations. It is also limited. Most writers acknowledge that little is known about how societies that begin with weak institutions move toward strengthening them. This section reviews arguments available in this literature that transparency can play a role in institutional transition, working together with broad-based political engagement.

Accounts of historical transitions from weak to stronger institutions in the public sector in the United States and United Kingdom suggest that independent mass media played a role in that transition by working together with political engagement (Camp, Dixit, and Stokes 2014; Glaeser and Goldin 2006; Lizzeri and Persico 2004). Political institutions in both the United States and in the United Kingdom in the nineteenth century have been described as exhibiting instances of vote buying similar to those in currently poor countries. Bensel (2004) writes that for many men in the mid-nineteenth century in the United States, "the act of voting was a social transaction in which they handed in a party ticket in return for a shot of whiskey, a pair of boots, or a small amount of money" (Bensel 2004, ix). In the United Kingdom, Seymour (1970 [1915], 184) writes that party agents carried ledgers with "a space for special circumstances which might give an opportunity for political blackmail, such as debts, mortgages, need of money in trade, commercial relations, and even the most private domestic matters."

Camp, Dixit, and Stokes (2014) document historical accounts of how the efficacy of vote buying through agents declined in the

United Kingdom and thereby precipitated legislation such as the 1883 Corrupt and Illegal Practices Act, which was upheld and enforced with bipartisan political support. Cox (1987) and Phillips and Wetherell (1995) argue that the expansion of the franchise with the Reform Act of 1832 in the United Kingdom led to dramatic changes in voting patterns. Elite support for extending the franchise, in turn, is explained in this literature by the rise in demand for broad public health goods in British cities around the industrial revolution (Lizzeri and Persico 2004). The expanding electorate began to have access to cheaper newspapers, which enabled politicians to directly reach voters with their messages rather than having to rely on agents (Camp, Dixit, and Stokes 2014). Leaders of both the Liberal and Conservative parties have been quoted as becoming aware of the reduced effectiveness of vote buying because "the new mass electorate, through increased education and a cheap press, would become politically free and independent in a sense that their predecessors would not have thought possible" (O'Leary 1962, 231).

Accounts of the Progressive Era in the United States are even more explicit about the role of newspapers and mass media along with the demise of machine politics in bringing about institutional change. Glaeser and Goldin (2006) review this literature and suggest that voter dissatisfaction with machine politics and the rise of independent media contributed to the conditions for institutional reform that created professional bureaucracies. Rauch (1995) describes the reforms in this era that resulted in the professionalization of the bureaucracy in American cities and the ensuing reduction in the political power to intervene in city management.

Transparency initiatives targeted only at improving local service delivery are not enough

A variety of transparency policy initiatives have focused on citizen engagement outside the political realm to solve service delivery problems. One prominent initiative involves the generation of information as a tool for mobilizing citizens to monitor and demand accountability from frontline public service providers. These types of "citizen report card" initiatives emphasize the "social" accountability of public providers, without relying on changes in the political incentives of leaders in government, who ultimately are responsible for managing these providers.

Social accountability

Social accountability initiatives are more likely to be successful when they influence political incentives. Evidence shows that low motivation and effort by public providers can be linked to political incentives that reward leaders for providing jobs in the public sector as political patronage or in exchange for bribes rather than for holding providers accountable for service delivery.[6] In contexts in which political incentives encourage patronage and clientelism, citizen report cards may have no effect on public service delivery. Among the mixed evidence of the impact of citizen report cards, those studies that find no effect are more likely to be situated in unhealthy political contexts.[7] Even among successful cases, little evidence indicates that transparency alone spurred communities to organize to solve local public goods problems. Instead, committees instituted for citizen engagement in a community are frequently defunct and require intensive mobilization efforts by civil society to take any action.

A study by Björkman and Svensson (2009) finds that a social accountability intervention led to a significant improvement in the performance of health workers and a reduction in child mortality. The intervention consisted of mobilizing community-based monitoring, whereby citizens and local health workers met to discuss the quality of health and put together a plan to monitor and improve the quality of services at local health facilities. The authors' preferred explanation of the mechanisms of impact is that citizens were able to engage in local collective action to hold providers accountable for what they were supposed to do, as well as to generate new resources to collaboratively solve local delivery problems. Disentangling these two very different mechanisms through which local collective action could work is important to gaining an understanding of how to make governments perform better for citizens. Although improving service delivery outcomes through greater citizen contributions is valuable in its own right, it can nevertheless leave intact governance impediments that prevent public officials from performing better with existing resources. This distinction is particularly important in the case of the poorest and most vulnerable segments of society for whom citizen contributions can be an undue burden and who rely on state-provided services. If the poor need to spend their resources—their money or their voluntary labor—to maintain public services, this may be at odds with the goals of other public programs for poverty eradication.

Furthermore, the results are also consistent with the political engagement mechanism. Provider behavior may have improved because directly elected local leaders managed them better once information about health service delivery made communities demand better performance. The Health Users Management Committee (HUMC) system in Uganda was described as dysfunctional to begin with at the time this work was undertaken. After the intervention, more than one-third of the HUMCs were dissolved in the communities receiving the intervention, and new members were elected, with no such turnover in the comparator communities that did not receive the intervention. This suggests that the information and mobilization around health services might have affected how people voted and how locally elected leaders exerted pressure on local providers to improve the quality of health provision.

In more recent work, Björkman, De Walque, and Svensson (2014) try to disentangle the effects of information provision from the effects of collective mobilization through community participation in meetings. They designed an intervention that focused on mobilization alone. Their original intervention (Björkman and Svensson 2009) included community meetings and a report card on the community's health clinic's performance compared with that of other communities and benchmarked against the national standard for primary health care provision. The new intervention also provided information through a report card on the community's health clinic, but did not include information relative to other health facilities. The authors conclude that without information on relative performance, participation in community meetings had little impact on health workers' performance or on health outcomes. Their interpretation of the results is that relative performance information enables users to distinguish between health workers' effort and factors outside health workers' control.

However, Björkman, De Walque, and Svensson (2014) are not able to test whether information alone could have generated the results in the absence of the mobilization efforts. Results from very similar social accountability interventions in other work suggest that information is unlikely to make a difference in the absence of mobilization. Banerjee et al. (2010) evaluate a similar initiative in the education sector in India that was aimed at improving the functioning of citizen participation in village education committees (VECs). Just like the HUMCs in Uganda, the VECs in India were found to be inactive at baseline. Fewer than 8 percent of community respondents were aware of the existence of the VEC. Furthermore, among those community respondents who local officials indicated were VEC members, as many as 22 percent were not aware of the VEC or their own role in it.

In the face of such widespread ignorance of the VEC, a civil society organization designed an initiative to raise awareness about the VEC's intended role that was expected to spark local action. However, the results show that information did not activate the defunct VECs. But when community members were given, in addition to information, the opportunity to be trained in a teaching tool that gave them the ability to directly improve educational outcomes, it was taken up by community volunteers and resulted in a large impact on learning. The mechanism, however, completely bypassed the public school system. Private reading classes were led by community volunteers who received no support from the elected village head or the public school teachers.

Transparency's impact on private actions, bypassing the public sector

Some of the cases show that transparency can affect private actions that bypass governance problems in the public sector. Outcomes, such as in health and education, can improve because transparency plays a role in changing private household behaviors and the functioning of private markets that are independent of or bypass governance problems in the public sector. However, bypassing these problems means that they are then left intact as impediments to fulfilling the role of the public sector in promoting those outcomes. For example, Banerjee et al.'s (2010) study of the intervention in India that targeted transparency at community mobilization finds improved education outcomes among children because community volunteers held remedial classes outside the public school system. However, transparency had no impact on the performance of school teachers on the public payroll who are frequently absent and do not teach even when present in school (Banerjee et al. 2010).[8] It, therefore, did not address the governance problem of teacher absence, which has been estimated to cost about $1.5 billion per year (Muralidharan et al. 2014). Therefore, even though outcomes can improve if transparency is used outside the political realm, those improvements depend on citizens taking on the burden of providing public goods themselves, such as by contributing their labor and material resources, rather than on holding government officials accountable for what they are paid from public resources.

An older strand of literature (among others, Stigler 1961; Stiglitz and Weiss 1981) examines transparency's role in solving problems of asymmetric information in economic and financial markets. The East Asian financial crisis of the 1990s, for example, was later partially explained by the lack of transparent accounting standards and financial reporting (Kaufmann and Bellver 2005).[9] Analysis of the role of information in improving the functioning of markets has been extended beyond the financial sector to that of education. Andrabi, Das, and Khwaja (2015) provide evidence that information about local education markets led to improvements in the functioning of those markets and to better education outcomes.

However, as discussed at the outset of this report, bypassing problems in the public sector means, logically, that they are then left intact as impediments to development goals. Keefer and Khemani (2014a, 2015a) provide evidence and review the literature showing that information can improve private household behaviors that contribute to health and education outcomes, but with no impact on public sector governance or public accountability.

Other evidence is consistent with information's effects on private actions and contrasts with the lack of effect on organized group action. Lieberman, Posner, and Tsai (2014) evaluate an intervention in Kenya that provided parents with information about children's performance in schools and guidelines for actions parents could take to improve school quality. They find that the informational intervention did not improve parents' participation in education groups or meetings, or the number of actions taken by officials to improve schooling. However, they do report large point estimates, although not statistically significant, for the information's impact on parent efforts at home to improve their children's learning.

Using transparency to improve "last-mile" service delivery problems

Information revealed to citizens by higher-tier government authorities can potentially elicit their help in holding frontline officials accountable for service delivery at the last mile. Reinikka and Svensson (2005, 2011) undertook a pioneering study of such an intervention by the Ministry of Education in Uganda to publicize information about grants that were supposed to flow to schools. Before this campaign was undertaken by the ministry, the researchers gathered data that revealed that more than 90 percent of the funds were not reaching the schools. After the ministry's information campaign, the researchers found that schools located closer to newspaper outlets received more government funds from the capitation grants. Although the authors provide evidence that information reduced corruption, the campaign had many components, and it is difficult to determine what caused the reduction in leakages. The authors' preferred interpretation is that information published in the newspaper empowered the school community to bargain with local officials to provide the school's entitlement. However, several other interpretations are possible, including that the information campaign served as a signal from higher-tier ministries to lower-level officials that they were being monitored and would be held accountable for leakages.[10]

The results of the interventions documented in Banerjee et al. (2010) contrast with those of another information intervention undertaken by Pandey et al. (2009) in similar villages in the same part of northern India. Pandey et al. (2009) find that information campaigns resulted in reduced absenteeism among village public school teachers, but with modest effects on improvements in learning. A key difference between the information interventions across these two studies was the mode of communication. Banerjee et al. (2010) relied on participatory activities undertaken by civil society with the aim of promoting local collective action. In contrast, the central plank of the information intervention in Pandey et al. (2009) was a sophisticated video that was played at village gatherings, produced by the researchers and carrying the endorsement of the state Department of Education rather than being owned and implemented by civil society. This Department of Education imprimatur suggests that one reason for the difference in results may be the signal from higher-tier authorities that they are monitoring local providers and will back up citizen complaints. This interpretation resonates with the Uganda example discussed above and another result from Indonesia, discussed below.

Banerjee et al. (2015) provide evidence from a context in which transparency is used by credible political leaders to encourage citizen engagement to hold local officials accountable. They examine the impact of letters mailed to citizens in Indonesia from the central government informing them about the rules and functioning of a subsidized rice program implemented by local governments. They find that the information increased the subsidy received by eligible households. Fewer ineligible households received subsidized rice in treatment villages, but those that continued to purchase subsidized rice received more in quantity. The fact that the eligible households received more, while ineligible households in total received no less, implies that the information reduced leakage, increasing the total amount of rice distributed in the villages by 17 percent.

Banerjee et al. (2015) provide further evidence on the mechanisms of impact that show how political engagement by citizens, in the form of protests and pressure upon locally elected officials, played a role in improving governance in this rice subsidy program. In one set of villages, information was provided in a more "public" way, through public announcements and posters in addition to the mailing of private letters that could lower the costs of coordinated citizen action. Citizens were more likely to organize protests in these villages to hold the village head accountable. Although the authors do not focus on political accountability mechanisms, furthering instead a story of bargaining that can occur between election cycles, political engagement is at the center of their theoretical model. For example, they state, "Complaints have a political cost: the higher the number of complaints, the more likely the leader will be replaced" (Banerjee et al. 2015, 12). Both their theory and their empirical results are consistent with village heads improving governance because of the disciplining feature of local electoral institutions. Whether similar results would be obtained had the central government provided information about a program administered by nonelected officials remains an open question in this study.

Other work examines the role of information in enabling citizens to hold appointed public officials, not elected leaders, accountable. Peisakhin (2012) and Peisakhin and Pinto (2010) examine the impact of information on the performance of appointed public officials in the context of the FOIA in India. They find that citizens can use the act to spur local public officials to process their applications for benefits under government programs, reducing the number of days it takes to receive their benefits. Submission of an information request under the act is a close substitute for paying a bribe to the official to speed up the receipt of benefits. As modeled in Banerjee et al. (2015) and framed in chapter 4, the impact mechanisms in this channel depend on the functioning of political engagement, because public officials risk complaints and punishment from higher-level leaders should they fail to respond. That is, transparency can effectively engage citizens to improve governance within public bureaucracies when leaders' political incentives are aligned appropriately.

The examples above suggest that a key condition for successful local action is the signal by higher-tier government departments that local citizen action would be taken seriously and used by leaders with power over formal mechanisms within government to hold local officials accountable. This supposition is consistent with the conceptual framework in chapter 4 on how citizen engagement initiatives to improve the performance of local officials will succeed to the extent that higher-tier officials have the incentives to use that local engagement to improve accountability. The incentives of higher-tier officials, in turn, depend upon the larger principal-agent problem (see chapter 4) in which citizens hold government leaders accountable. That is, the success of citizen engagement initiatives to improve last-mile service delivery problems depends on whether higher-level leaders' political incentives are aligned with those initiatives.

Research on the impact of transparency initiatives that aim to engage citizens in solving last-mile service delivery problems further show that transparency is more likely to be effective when it targets citizen engagement methods that do not depend upon organized, group-based collective action.

Comparing the above results from Banerjee et al. (2015) in Indonesia and Peisakhin (2012) in India with another study from India of a public program that provides more broadly distributed benefits sheds light on what citizens are likely to do when they have more information. Ravallion et al. (2015) provided information to households in Bihar about procedural rules and citizen entitlements under India's flagship anti-poverty program, the Mahatma Gandhi National Rural Employment Guarantee Act (MGNREGA), which is administered by elected village governments. The use of information to improve program delivery is similar in essence to the Indonesia situation in which elected village governments distribute subsidized rice and citizens are provided information about the program rules. The contexts differ in the nature of the public program being studied—citizens would have to organize collectively to demand a public works program for employment under the MGNREGA program in India, rather than simply pressure local leaders at an individual level to give them the rice to which they are entitled as in Indonesia. Similarly, in the study on the facilitating environment provided by the FOIA (Peisakhin 2012), citizens were able to use information to individually demand private benefits.

In contrast to the results in Banerjee et al. (2015) and in Peisakhin (2012), Ravallion et al. (2015) find that although the information intervention improved knowledge of entitlements, it did not affect actual outcomes in the program governance. There was no effect on work programs executed, wage rates, or days worked. They conclude that although households learned their rights, they did not use the information to demand greater performance.

Results in another study in Indonesia are also consistent with citizens more easily using information to take individual-level action rather than organized group action. Olken (2007) reports differential impacts of a community mobilization and information campaign on leakage in wages versus in materials expenses in the implementation of local construction projects. This pattern is consistent with informed community members being able to individually bargain for the right wages to be paid to them, but not to organize collective action to reduce corruption in other places, where the costs are diffused throughout the community.

This pattern is consistent with a large literature on collective action by groups (pioneered by Olson [1965]) and bears resemblance to the Lowi-Wilson Matrix, which provides an understanding of the conditions under which groups organize (Lowi 1972; Wilson 1973). In that literature, information does not play a significant role in explaining whether citizens are organized in groups. Incentives to organize are linked to concentrated benefits and dispersed costs of policies, with small groups being more likely to sustain collective action for concentrated group benefits. An exception may be cases of larger political organization when citizens take to the streets to overthrow an oppressive and corrupt regime. Anecdotal evidence and ongoing research suggest that such large-group action can be facilitated by new information and communications technologies (Acemoglu, Hassan, and Tahoun 2014; Manacorda and Tesei 2016).

The importance of local political engagement comes to the fore when contrasting the results of Banerjee et al. (2010) and Lieberman, Posner, and Tsai (2014) on the lack of transparency's impact on local public schools with those found by Pradhan et al. (2014) in the context of a more politically relevant intervention to improve schools in Indonesia. Pradhan et al. (2014) implement a randomized evaluation of alternative approaches to strengthening school committees in public schools in Indonesia. They find that interventions that increase the engagement of members of the village council, who are elected by citizens, had the highest impact in improving school outcomes. They attribute the effects to the mechanisms of increased electoral accountability of politicians on the basis of education improvements. Their results support the idea that political engagement and political accountability are important factors in inducing change in the quality of public services. Moreover, the Indonesia school interventions also changed the institutional rules through which representatives of education committees were chosen so that new representatives were brought into power. This result is similar to the evidence in Uganda of turnover in the elected members of the HUMCs, and again highlights the critical role of selection and sanctioning of leaders (that is, political engagement).

Transparency and behavioral norms in the public sector

The research discussed so far has focused on how transparency can encourage political engagement to reduce corruption, and enable public providers to be held to account. Another channel through which transparency might improve public sector performance is by strengthening professional behavioral norms among public officials and service providers. This channel may be especially important for sectors such as health and education, in which professional expertise and pride in work can have a role. Excessive reliance on the incentive mechanism of accountability to citizens via monitoring and feedback runs the risk of spreading canards and can weaken the role of professional norms. For example, powerful parents who are local elites might demand preferential treatment for their own children and make it difficult for teachers to effectively serve all the children in their classroom by adhering to the norms of the professional training they have received. Instead, powerful parents might extract favorable treatment for their own children by unduly influencing teachers to deviate from professional behavior. The available research on the use of transparency to spur social accountability pays little attention to these issues.

A growing body of research examines the role of intrinsic behavioral norms in shaping the performance of public service providers.[11] Although analysis of sector-specific human resource behavior and management is outside the scope of this report, the general insight provided through the research covered in chapters 4 and 5 is that political engagement and the leaders selected through it shape behavioral norms in the public sector. Transparency can play a role by improving the basis upon which leaders are selected and sanctioned. Box 6.1 provides an example from Brazil of how transparency was combined with political engagement to improve the management and professional behavior of public health workers.

Transparency might also contribute to increasing competition among public officials and increasing peer pressure to improve performance. Experiential evidence from the success of initiatives such as the Doing Business project demonstrates that publicizing performance indicators can bring about governance reforms by spurring competition among countries to attract private investment. However, there is as yet no theoretical or empirical research available on the impact of such a channel of transparency.

Finally, transparency could play a direct role in shifting political beliefs and behavioral norms in society. It could potentially address the problem

Box 6.1   How the "Big I" institutions of transparency and elections matter for the functioning of the "small i" institutions of public sector management

A case study from the state of Ceara, one of the poorest states in Brazil, shows how reform leaders used local media (radio) and forces of municipal political competition to complement reforms in the recruitment and management of health workers (Tendler and Freedheim 1994). The reforms were targeted at depoliticizing the management of public health workers and making them more performance oriented. It involved the direct recruitment by the governor's office of a large cadre of public health workers on performance contracts, circumventing the formal authority of municipal mayors. The study describes how before the reforms, health workers were recruited and managed by municipal mayors as political patronage, with weak incentives and motivation for service delivery. However, this is not a story of bypassing mayoral politics, because in fact that would likely have been ineffective. The new cadre of health workers would only be able to work in communities if the mayors signed up for the program. Furthermore, the mayors were responsible for managing the technically qualified nurses who would supervise the new health workers.

Instead, the story is one in which the public management reforms were able to work by going hand-in-hand with a strategic transparency initiative to address the political problem head on, and in the process shift the culture of performance in the state's health sector. The governor's office flooded the airwaves with messages about what the new health workers were expected to deliver. Tendler and Freedheim (1994, 1775) write that the radio messages "regaled citizens with promises of dramatic improvements in the health of their babies and, on the other hand, instructed them as to what they would have to do in order to bring that about: namely, they were to urge their mayors to hire a competent nurse, pay her salary, and run the program cleanly. 'Simply don't vote for your mayor,' some of the program's managers advised or implied on their trips to the interior, 'if he doesn't provide you access to our health program.'" The overall package of reforms—combining improved technical management of health workers with transparency interventions specifically targeted at overcoming political impediments—has been credited with dramatically improving child health outcomes in the state within the span of a few years.

of a "culture of corruption" that was discussed in chapter 1 that stems from rational beliefs about how others are behaving. For example, one prominent initiative pioneered by civil society actors in India (that has spread beyond to other countries) is directed toward inducing changes in the culture of bribery through an information and communication campaign. The organization Janaagraha in India has developed and supports a website, www.ipaidabribe.com, that invites citizens to submit reports of bribes paid, bribes requested but not paid, and encounters with honest officers who did their job without asking for a bribe. While much of the discussion around this initiative focuses on how it might reveal information about the extent of bribery and the market price of bribes for different public services,[12] another way in which it may work is by signaling a shift in public demands for receiving high-quality and corruption-free public services.

Dixit (2015) describes a similar initiative undertaken by another civil society group in India—the "Zero Rupee Note" campaign of the Fifth Pillar group. This group distributed specially printed zero-rupee notes to citizens to exhort them to use these as symbolic payments to bribe-demanding public officials. The thinking behind such campaigns is that they can help persuade people to shift their actions and refrain from supplying bribes. The publicizing of these initiatives might work as forces for coordinating changes in individual actions, thereby creating the collective action needed to root out corruption.

However, these examples are not yet backed by hard research on how transparency in the form of persuasion campaigns might change behavioral norms in the public sector. The little research that can be found highlights the role of mass media as a force for persuasion and as an institution that can address coordination problems among citizens going beyond information alone. Some evidence from developing countries indicates that mass media plays a significant role in shifting social norms, particularly those related to the role of women. La Ferrara, Chong, and Duryea (2012) show that access to the TV Globo network in Brazil, which carried soap operas with independent female characters with few, or even no, children, reduced fertility in the population. Viewing the soap operas had an effect equal to 1.6 years of additional education. In India, access to similar soap operas carried on cable television reduced fertility and son preference and increased women's autonomy (Jensen and Oster 2009). The *World Development Report 2015: Mind, Society, and Behavior* (World Bank 2015) reviews the literature on how programs on mass media that are both entertaining and educational—infotainment—can be designed to shift social and gender norms.

This finding suggests that the role of infotainment might extend to influencing political beliefs and strengthening political behavioral norms—what policies to demand, what issues to consider when evaluating leaders, and whether to become a contender for leadership. However, there is relatively little evidence available on this role for transparency.[13] Problems of political beliefs are likely to be harder to address with transparency than cases of information asymmetries that might be solved through the provision of new information. The role of persuasion through different means of communication—including through credible leaders who emerge from processes of political engagement—is likely to be key.

****

The research reviewed in this chapter suggests that citizens even in the poorest countries are ready to use transparency to hold leaders accountable. Transparency's impact in one area—on voting behavior—is significant across all regions and in a variety of institutional contexts. Whether this responsiveness of voting behavior to transparency will bring about sustained changes in the institutions of governance in poor countries, where these institutions are weak to begin with, is more of an open question. Evidence from the historical experience of rich and middle-income countries shows that transparency works hand-in-hand with political engagement to gradually build better institutions to serve the goals of economic development.

Conditions in several countries that are home to the vast majority of the poor resemble the conditions described in historical accounts of institutional transition. However, there are several risks to worry about, such as perverse responses of leaders to obfuscate information and repress attempts to hold them accountable. The next and final chapter draws lessons for various policy actors for ways in which to manage the risks and channel these forces toward the goals of sustained and equitable economic development. Policy actors can harness transparency to nourish the growing forces of political engagement and thereby complement other capacity-building efforts to establish effective public sector institutions. Research on the attributes of transparency that work to bring about positive change suggests a comparative advantage of external actors—the technical capacity for generating new data and credible information through politically independent expert analysis.

Notes

1. Another possible reason behind the different results in Chong et al. (2015) in Mexico and the results from Brazil and Puerto Rico may be the different institutional context in Mexico wherein individual mayors are not allowed to stand for reelection. Political parties field a new candidate after a mayor completes a term. However, the similarity of other results from Mexico (Larreguy, Marshall, and Snyder 2015) to the evidence from other countries casts doubt on the role of differences in formal electoral rules as explaining the different results in Chong et al. (2015).
2. Banerjee et al.'s (2015) study of the impact of transparency on the governance of a subsidized rice program in Indonesia (discussed in more detail later in this chapter) is one of the few pieces of evidence on how information can trigger political engagement (in the form of public protests) between elections.

3. As documented by Olken (2007), for example.

4. A replication analysis and critique by Anderson (2013) of the original results reported in Malesky, Schuler, and Tran (2012) has been helpful. We thank James Anderson for providing valuable feedback on this.

5. The results of including newspaper circulation are presented in table 5 of the working paper version. The robustness of alternate measures of social capital, which equate it with political engagement, when newspaper circulation is included are discussed on page 15: http://didattica.unibocconi.it/mypage /upload/92884_20130406_031702_ACCOUNTABILITY_AEJ_FINAL _JULY2012.PDF.

6. Callen et al. (2014) find in Pakistan that doctors are present at 42 percent of clinics in political constituencies that are competitive, as opposed to only 13 percent of clinics in uncompetitive constituencies. Doctors who know their local parliamentarian personally are present at an average of 0.727 of three unannounced visits, while doctors without this connection are present at 1.309 of the three visits. About 40 percent of inspectors and health administrators report interference by politicians when they try to sanction doctors. Finally, the effect of a smartphone monitoring technology, which almost doubled inspection rates, is highly localized to competitive constituencies.

7. Grandvoinnet, Aslam, and Raha (2015) review the evidence and conclude that political context matters.

8. Separate case studies have shown that teachers in this state, Uttar Pradesh, are politically connected and a powerful force in mobilizing political support (Beteille 2009; Chhibber and Nooruddin 2004; Kingdon and Muzammil 2001). Beteille (2009) further finds that politically connected teachers are more likely to be absent.

9. The current report does not examine the role of transparency in addressing governance problems in private transactions in economic and financial markets.

10. Despite the highly celebrated initial success of the transparency effort in Uganda to improve the flow of funds to schools, subsequent reports by the Ministry of Finance, Planning, and Economic Development indicate that diversion of funds in education is a continuing problem. That is, the problem of leakage appears to be recurring or persistent, despite efforts toward greater budget transparency.

11. Ashraf, Bandiera, and Jack (2014) and Dal Bo, Finan, and Rossi (2013) provide reviews.

12. *Economist*, March 10, 2011, "Corruption in India: A Million Rupees Now" (http:// www.economist.com/node/18338852?story_id=18338852&fsrc=rss).

13. The few pieces of available evidence discussed in previous sections are from Campante, Durante, and Sobbrio (2013); Glaeser and Sunstein (2013); Gottlieb (2016); and Keefer and Khemani (2014b).

Bibliography

Acemoglu, Daron, Tarek A. Hassan, and Ahmed Tahoun. 2014. "The Power of the Street: Evidence from Egypt's Arab Spring." NBER Working Paper 20665, National Bureau of Economic Research, Cambridge, MA.

Adena, Maja, Ruben Enikolopov, Maria Petrova, Veronica Santarosa, and Ekaterina Zhuravskaya. 2015. "Radio and the Rise of the Nazis in Interwar Germany." Working paper, June 3. http://ssrn.com/abstract=2242446.

Adsera, Alicia, Carles Boix, and Mark Payne. 2003. "Are You Being Served? Political Accountability and Quality of Government." *Journal of Law, Economics and Organization* 19 (2): 445–49.

Aker, Jenny C., Paul Collier, and Pedro C. Vicente. 2013. "Is Information Power? Using Mobile Phones and Free Newspapers during an Election in Mozambique." Center for Global Development Working Paper 328, Center for Global Development, Washington, DC.

Alt, James E., David D. Lassen, and John Marshall. Forthcoming. "Information Sources, Belief Updating, and the Politics of Economic Expectations: Evidence from a Danish Survey Experiment." *Journal of Politics.*

Anderson, James. 2013. "Sunshine Works: Comment on 'The Adverse Effects of Sunshine.'" Policy Research Working Paper No. 6602, World Bank, Washington, DC.

Andrabi, Tahir, Jishnu Das, and Asim Khwaja. 2015. "Report Cards: The Impact of Providing School and Child Test-Scores on Educational Markets." Policy Research Working Paper 7226, World Bank, Washington, DC.

Ashraf, N., O. Bandiera, and B. K. Jack. 2014. "No Margin, No Mission? A Field Experiment on Incentives for Public Service Delivery." *Journal of Public Economics* 120: 1–17.

Banerjee, Abhijit V., Rukmini Banerji, Esther Duflo, Rachel Glennerster, and Stuti Khemani. 2010. "Pitfalls of Participatory Programs: Evidence from a Randomized Evaluation in Education in India." *American Economic Journal: Economic Policy* 2 (1): 1–30.

Banerjee, Abhijit, Rema Hanna, Jordan C. Kyle, Benjamin A. Olken, and Sudarno Sumarto. 2015. "The Power of Transparency: Information, Identification Cards and Food Subsidy Programs in Indonesia." NBER Working Paper 20923, National Bureau of Economic Research, Cambridge, MA.

Banerjee, Abhijit V., Selvan Kumar, Rohini Pande, and Felix Su. 2011. "Do Informed Voters Make Better Choices? Experimental Evidence from Urban India." Working paper. https://www.hks.harvard.edu/fs/rpande/papers/DoInformedVoters_Nov11.pdf.

Bensel, Richard F. 2004. *The American Ballot Box in the Mid-Nineteenth Century.* Cambridge, UK: Cambridge University Press.

Besley, Timothy, and Robin Burgess. 2002. "The Political Economy of Government Responsiveness: Theory and Evidence from India." *Quarterly Journal of Economics* 117 (4): 1415–51.

Besley, Timothy, and Andrea Prat. 2006. "Handcuffs for the Grabbing Hand? Media Capture and Political Government Accountability." *American Economic Review* 96 (3): 720–36.

Beteille, Tara. 2009. "Absenteeism, Transfers and Patronage: The Political Economy of Teacher Labor Markets in India." PhD dissertation, Stanford University, Palo Alto, CA.

Bidwell, Kelly, Katherine Casey, and Rachel Glennerster. 2015. "Debates: Voter and Politician Response to Political Communication in Sierra Leone." Unpublished.

Björkman, Martina, Damien De Walque, and Jakob Svensson. 2014. "Information Is Power: Experimental Evidence on the Long-Run Impact of Community-Based Monitoring." World Bank Policy Research Working Paper 7015, World Bank, Washington, DC.

Björkman, Martina, and Jakob Svensson. 2009. "Power to the People: Evidence from a Randomized Field Experiment on Community-Based Monitoring in Uganda." *Quarterly Journal of Economics* 124 (2): 735–69.

Bobonis, Gustavo J., Luis R. Cámara Fuertes, and Rainer Schwabe. Forthcoming. "Monitoring Corruptible Politicians." *American Economic Review.*

Bond, Robert M., Christopher J. Fariss, Jason J. Jones, Adam D. I. Kramer, Cameron Marlow, Jaime E. Settle, and James H. Fowler. 2012. "A 61-Million-Person Experiment in Social Influence and Political Mobilization." *Nature* 489: 295–98.

Brunetti, Aymo, and Beatrice Weder. 2003. "A Free Press Is Bad News for Corruption." *Journal of Public Economics* 87 (7–8): 1801–24.

Cagé, Julia, 2014. "Media Competition, Information Provision and Political Participation." Working Paper, Department of Economics, Harvard University, Cambridge, MA.

Callen, Michael, Saad Gulzar, Ali Hasanain, and Yasir Khan. 2014. "The Political Economy of Public Employee Absence: Experimental Evidence from Pakistan: Do Local Politics Determine the Effectiveness of Development Interventions? Why Are Service Providers Commonly Absent in Developing Countries?" Unpublished, Harvard Kennedy School, Cambridge, MA.

Camp, Edwin, Avinash Dixit, and Susan Stokes. 2014. "Catalyst or Cause? Legislation and the Demise of Machine Politics in Britain and the United States." *Legislative Studies Quarterly* 39 (4): 559–92.

Campante, Filipe, and Quoc-Anh Do. 2014. "Isolated Capital Cities, Accountability and Corruption: Evidence from US States." *American Economic Review* 104 (8): 2456–81.

Campante, Filipe, Ruben Durante, and Francesco Sobbrio. 2013. "Politics 2.0: The Multifaceted Effect of Broadband Internet on Political Participation." NBER Working Paper 19029, National Bureau of Economic Research, Cambridge, MA.

Campante, Filipe, and Daniel Hojman. 2013. "Media and Polarization: Evidence from the Introduction of Broadcast TV in the US." *Journal of Public Economics* 100: 79–92.

Casey, Katherine. 2015. "Crossing Party Lines: The Effects of Information on Redistributive Politics." *American Economic Review* 105 (8): 2410–48.

Chhibber, Pradeep, and Irfan Nooruddin. 2004. "Do Party Systems Matter? The Number of Parties and Government Performance in the Indian States." *Comparative Political Studies* 37 (2): 152–87.

Chong, A., A. L. De La O, D. Karlan, and L. Wantchekon. 2015. "Does Corruption Information Inspire the Fight or Quash the Hope? A Field Experiment in Mexico on Voter Turnout, Choice, and Party Identification." *The Journal of Politics* 77 (1), 55–71.

Clements, Benedict J., David Coady, Stefania Fabrizio, Sanjeev Gupta, Trevor Alleyne, and Carlo Sdralevich, eds. 2013. *Energy Subsidy Reform: Lessons and Implications.* Washington, DC: International Monetary Fund.

Cox, Gary. 1987. *The Efficient Secret.* Cambridge, UK: Cambridge University Press.

Cruz, Cesi, Philip Keefer, and Julien Labonne. 2015. "Incumbent Advantage, Voter Information and Vote Buying." Unpublished.

Dal Bó, Ernesto, Frederico Finan, and Martin A. Rossi. 2013. "Strengthening State Capabilities: The Role of Financial Incentives in the Call to Public Service." *Quarterly Journal of Economics* 128 (3): 1169–218.

DellaVigna, Stefano, and Ethan Kaplan. 2007. "The Fox News Effect: Media Bias and Voting." *Quarterly Journal of Economics* 122 (3): 1187–234.

Dixit, Avinash. 2015. "How Business Community Institutions Can Help Fight Corruption." *World Bank Economic Review* 29 (suppl 1): S25–S47.

Drago, Francesco, Tommaso Nannicini, and Francesco Sobbrio. 2014. "Meet the Press: How Voters and Politicians Respond to Newspaper Entry and Exit." *American Economic Journal: Applied Economics* 6 (3): 159–88.

Enikolopov, Ruben, Maria Petrova, and Konstantin Sonin. 2016. "Social Media and Corruption." CEPR Discussion Paper No. DP11263 (May).

Enikolopov, Ruben, Maria Petrova, and Ekaterina Zhuravskaya. 2011. "Media and Political Persuasion: Evidence from Russia." *American Economic Review* 101 (7): 3253–85.

Escaleras, Monica, Shu Lin, and Charles Register. 2009. "Freedom of Information Acts and Public Sector Corruption." *Public Choice* 145 (3–4): 435–60.

Falck, Oliver, Robert Gold, and Stephan Heblich. 2014. "E-lections: Voting Behavior and the Internet." *American Economic Review* 104 (7): 2238–65.

Ferraz, Claudio, and Frederico Finan. 2008. "Exposing Corrupt Politicians: The Effect of Brazil's Publicly Released Audits on Electoral Outcomes." *Quarterly Journal of Economics* 123 (2): 703–45.

———. 2011. "Electoral Accountability and Corruption: Evidence from the Audits of Local Governments." *American Economic Review* 101 (4): 1274–311.

Fujiwara, Thomas, and Leonard Wantchekon. 2013. "Can Informed Public Deliberation Overcome Clientelism? Experimental Evidence from Benin." *American Economic Journal: Applied Economics* 5 (4): 241–55.

Gentzkow, Matthew. 2006. "Television and Voter Turnout." *Quarterly Journal of Economics* 121 (3): 931–72.

Gentzkow, Matthew, and Jesse M. Shapiro. 2011. "Ideological Segregation Online and Offline." *Quarterly Journal of Economics* 126 (4): 1799–839.

Gentzkow, Matthew, Jesse M. Shapiro, and Michael Sinkinson. 2011. "The Effect of Newspaper Entry and Exit on Electoral Politics." *American Economic Review* 101 (7): 2980–3018.

Giné, Xavier, and Ghazala Mansuri. 2011. "Together We Will: Evidence from a Field Experiment on Female Voter Turnout in Pakistan." World Bank Policy Research Working Paper 5692, World Bank, Washington, DC.

Glaeser, Edward, and Claudia Goldin, eds. 2006. *Corruption and Reform: Lessons from America's Economic History.* Chicago, IL: University of Chicago Press.

Glaeser, Edward, and Cass Sunstein. 2013. "Why Does Balanced News Produce Unbalanced Views?" NBER Working Paper 18975, National Bureau of Economic Research, Washington, DC.

Gottlieb, Jessica. 2016. "Greater Expectations: A Field Experiment to Improve Accountability in Mali." *American Journal of Political Science* 60 (1): 143–57.

Grandvoinnet, Helene, Ghazia Aslam, and Shomikho Raha. 2015. *Opening the Black Box: The Contextual Drivers of Social Accountability.* Washington, DC: World Bank.

Grossman, Guy, Macartan Humphreys, and Gabriella Sacramone-Lutz. 2014. "'I wld like u WMP to extend electricity 2 our village': On Information Technology and Interest Articulation." *American Political Science Review* 108 (3): 688–705.

Guan, Mei, and Donald P. Green. 2006. "Noncoercive Mobilization in State-Controlled Elections: An Experimental Study in Beijing." *Comparative Political Studies* 39 (10): 1175–93.

Halberstam, Yosh, and Brian Knight. 2015. "Homophily, Group Size, and the Diffusion of Political Information in Social Networks: Evidence from Twitter." Working Paper, Department of Economics, University of Toronto.

Humphreys, Macartan, and Jeremy Weinstein. 2012. "Policing Politicians: Citizen Empowerment and Political Accountability in Uganda—Preliminary Analysis." Working Paper, International Growth Centre, London.

Jensen, Robert, and Emily Oster. 2009. "The Power of TV: Cable Television and Women's Status in India." *Quarterly Journal of Economics* 124 (3): 1057–94.

Kaufmann, Daniel, and Ana Bellver. 2005. "Transparenting Transparency: Initial Empirics and Policy Applications." World Bank Policy Research Working Paper, World Bank, Washington, DC.

Keefer, Philip, and Stuti Khemani. 2014a. "Mass Media and Public Education: The Effects of Access to Community Radio in Benin." *Journal of Development Economics* 109 (C): 57–72.

———. 2014b. "Radio's Impact on Preferences for Patronage Benefits." Policy Research Working Paper 6932, World Bank, Washington, DC.

———. 2015. "The Government Response to Informed Citizens: New Evidence on Media Access and the Distribution of Public Health Benefits in Africa." *World Bank Economic Review*, published online August 6. doi: 10.1093/wber/lhv040.

Kendall, Chad, Tommaso Nannicini, and Francesco Trebbi. 2015. "How Do Voters Respond to Information? Evidence from a Randomized Campaign." *American Economic Review* 105 (1): 322–53.

Khemani, Stuti. 2015. "Buying Votes versus Supplying Public Services: Political Incentives to Under-Invest in Pro-Poor Policies." *Journal of Development Economics* 177: 84–93.

Kingdon, Geeta, and Mohammed Muzammil. 2001. "A Political Economy of Education in India: The Case of UP." *Economic and Political Weekly* 36 (32): 3052–63.

Knight, Brian, and Chun-Fang Chiang. 2011. "Media Bias and Influence: Evidence from Newspaper Endorsements." *Review of Economic Studies* 78: 795–820.

La Ferrara, Eliana, Alberto Chong, and Suzanne Duryea. 2012. "Soap Operas and Fertility: Evidence from Brazil." *American Economic Journal* 4 (4): 1–31.

Larreguy, Horacio A., John Marshall, and James M. Snyder, Jr. 2015. "Revealing Malfeasance: How Local Media Facilitates Electoral Sanctioning of Mayors in Mexico." NBER Working Paper 20697, National Bureau of Economic Research, Cambridge, MA.

Lieberman, Evan, Daniel Posner, and Lily Tsai. 2014. "Does Information Lead to More Active Citizenship? Evidence from an Education Intervention in Rural Kenya." *World Development* 60: 69–83.

Lim, Claire, James Snyder, and David Strömberg. 2015. "The Judge, the Politician, and the Press: Newspaper Coverage and Criminal Sentencing across Electoral Systems." *American Economic Journal: Applied Economics* 7 (4): 103–35.

Lizzeri, Alessandro, and Nicola Persico. 2004. "Why Did the Elites Extend the Suffrage? Democracy and the Scope of Government, With an Application to Britain's 'Age of Reform.'" *Quarterly Journal of Economics* 119 (2): 707–65.

Lowi, Theodore J. 1972. "Four Systems of Policy, Politics and Choice." *Public Administration Review* 32 (4): 298–310.

Malesky, Edmund, Paul Schuler, and Anh Tran. 2012. "The Adverse Effects of Sunshine: Evidence from a Field Experiment on Legislative Transparency in an Authoritarian Assembly." *American Political Science Review* 106 (4): 762–86.

Manacorda, Marco, and Andrea Tesei. 2016. "Liberation Technology: Mobile Phones and Political Mobilization in Africa." Working Paper, Queen Mary University of London.

McMillan, John, and Pablo Zoido. 2004. "How to Subvert Democracy: Montesinos in Peru." *Journal of Economic Perspectives* 18 (4): 69–92.

Miner, Luke. 2015. "The Unintended Consequences of Internet Diffusion: Evidence from Malaysia." *Journal of Public Economics* 132 (December): 66–78.

Mungiu-Pippidi, Alina. 2014. "Quantitative Report on Causes of Performance and Stagnation in the Global Fight against Corruption." Anti-Corruption Policies Revisited. ANTICORRP. Pillar 4, WP3.

Muralidharan, Karthik, Jishu Das, Alaka Holla, and Aakash Mohpal. 2014. "The Fiscal Cost of Weak Governance: Evidence from Teacher Absence in India." NBER Working Paper 20299, National Bureau of Economic Research, Cambridge, MA.

Nannicini, Tommaso, Andrea Stella, Guido Tabellini, and Ugo Troiano. 2013. "Social Capital and Political Accountability." *American Economic Journal: Economic Policy* 5 (2): 222–50.

Oberholzer-Gee, Felix, and Joel Waldfogel. 2009. "Media Markets and Localism: Does Local News en Español Boost Hispanic Voter Turnout?" *American Economic Review* 99 (5): 2120–28.

O'Leary, Cornelius. 1962. *The Elimination of Corrupt Practices in British Elections, 1868–1911.* Oxford: Oxford University Press.

Olken, Benjamin. 2007. "Monitoring Corruption: Evidence from a Field Experiment in Indonesia." *Journal of Political Economy* 115 (2): 200–49.

———. 2009. "Do Television and Radio Destroy Social Capital? Evidence from Indonesian Villages." *American Economic Journal: Applied Economics* 1 (4): 1–33.

Olson, Mancur. 1965. *The Logic of Collective Action.* Cambridge, MA: Harvard University Press.

Paler, Laura. 2013. "Keeping the Public Purse: An Experiment in Windfalls, Taxes, and the Incentives to Restrain Government." *American Political Science Review* 107 (04): 706–25.

Pandey, Priyanka, Sangeeta Goyal, and Venkatesh Sundararaman. 2009. "Community Participation in Public Schools: Impact of Information Campaigns in Three Indian States." *Education Economics* 17 (3): 355–75.

Peisakhin, Leonid. 2012. "Transparency and Corruption: Evidence from India." *Journal of Law and Economics* 55 (1): 129–49.

Peisakhin, Leonid, and Paul Pinto. 2010. "Is Transparency an Effective Anti-Corruption Strategy? Evidence from a Field Experiment in India." *Regulation and Governance* 4 (3): 261–80.

Phillips, John A., and Charles Wetherell. 1995. "The Great Reform Act of 1832 and the Political Modernization of England." *American Historical Review* 100 (2): 411–36.

Pradhan, Menno, Daniel Suryadarma, Amanda Beatty, Maisy Wong, Arya Gaduh, Armida Alisjahbana, and Rima Prama Artha. 2014. "Improving Educational Quality through Enhancing Community Participation: Results from a Randomized Field Experiment in Indonesia." *American Economic Journal: Applied Economics* 6 (2): 105–26.

Prat, Andrea, and David Strömberg. 2005. "Commercial Television and Voter Information." CEPR Discussion Paper 4989, Centre for Economic Policy Research, London.

———. 2011. "The Political Economy of Mass Media." CEPR Discussion Paper 8246, Centre for Economic Policy Research, London.

Putnam, Robert. 1995. "Bowling Alone: America's Declining Social Capital." *Journal of Democracy* 6 (1): 65–78.

Rauch, James. 1995. "Bureaucracy, Infrastructure, and Economic Growth: Evidence from US Cities during the Progressive Era." *American Economic Review* 85 (4): 968–79.

Ravallion, Martin, Dominique van de Walle, Puja Dutta, and Rinku Murgai. 2015. "Empowering Poor People through Public Information? Lessons from a Movie in Rural India." *Journal of Public Economics* 132: 13–22.

Reinikka, Ritva, and Jakob Svensson. 2005. "Fighting Corruption to Improve Schooling: Evidence from a Newspaper Campaign in Uganda." *Journal of the European Economic Association* 3 (2–3): 259–67.

———. 2011. "The Power of Information in Public Services: Evidence from Education in Uganda." *Journal of Public Economics* 95 (7–8): 956–66.

Seymour, Charles. 1970 [1915]. *Electoral Reform in England and Wales: The Development and Operation of the Parliamentary Franchise.* Devon, UK: David/Charles Reprints.

Snyder, James M., and David Strömberg. 2010. "Press Coverage and Political Accountability." *Journal of Political Economy* 118 (2): 355–408.

Stigler, George J. 1961. "The Economics of Information." *Journal of Political Economy* 69 (3): 213–25.

Stiglitz, Joseph, and Andrew Weiss. 1981. "Credit Rationing in Markets with Imperfect Information." *American Economic Review* 71 (3): 393–410.

Strömberg, David. 2004. "Radio's Impact on Public Spending." *Quarterly Journal of Economics* 119 (1): 189–221.

———. 2015. "Media and Politics." *Annual Review of Economics* 7 (1): 173–205.

Tendler, Judith, and Sara Freedheim. 1994. "Trust in a Rent-Seeking World: Health and Government Transformed in Northeast Brazil." *World Development* 22 (12): 1771–91.

Vicente, P. C. 2014. "Is Vote Buying Effective? Evidence from a Field Experiment in West Africa." *The Economic Journal* 124 (574): F356–87.

Wantchekon, Leonard. 2003. "Clientelism and Voting Behavior: Evidence from a Field Experiment in Benin." *World Politics* 55: 399–422.

Wilson, James Q. 1973. *Political Organizations.* New York: Basic Books.

World Bank. 2015. *World Development Report 2015: Mind, Society, and Behavior.* Washington, DC: World Bank.

Yanagizawa-Drott, David. 2014. "Propaganda and Conflict: Evidence from the Rwandan Genocide." *Quarterly Journal of Economics* 129 (4): 1947–94.

CHAPTER SEVEN

Implications for Policy Actors

Overview

This report confronts the problem that leaders with the power to pursue policies that are good for economic development are often constrained from doing so because of politics. Treating such perverse political incentives as fixed constraints that have to be navigated rather than relaxed often leads to second-best solutions that do little to solve the fundamental problems of development. This chapter recommends a shift in approach toward tackling political constraints head-on, using transparency and citizen engagement to try to change political incentives so that these are aligned with development objectives.

The bulk of development work occurs in imperfect governance environments where things need to get done and get done quickly. The majority of practitioners may have little patience with political economy analysis, finding it a luxury or a distraction.[1] When politics impedes development, the easy response is to treat it as a largely insurmountable constraint. Perhaps more important than providing ideas for specific policy action, the report aims to shift how development practitioners think about politics. Practitioners may then be able to make greater contributions to incremental change by more effectively using the levers available to them to overcome political impediments to good policy. This approach includes not just getting governments to adopt good policies, but designing implementation arrangements that are more likely to succeed because they are based on a better understanding of political incentives and behavioral norms in the public sector.

The *World Development Report 2004, Making Services Work for Poor People* (WDR 2004) was one of the first major World Bank reports to include an analysis of political incentives. It spawned policy innovations and a rich research agenda on accountability and governance, going beyond capacity building alone. Yet the bulk of the operational work on governance that followed chose to bypass the so-called "long route" of accountability, which goes through political institutions, in favor of a so-called "short-route" by which citizens might directly solve local problems of service delivery (figure 7.1). That is, at the same time as making the discussion of political incentives and accountability more prominent, the WDR 2004 appears to have inadvertently contributed to popularizing the idea that politics can be bypassed when it is a problem.[2] The idea of the short route continues to be popular as one of *social* accountability—whereby citizens can solve delivery problems in the public sector through local collective action to influence frontline providers directly—in contrast to *political* accountability—whereby citizens demand accountability from political leaders and public officials who lead government agencies.

Figure 7.1   How this report builds on the *World Development Report 2004*

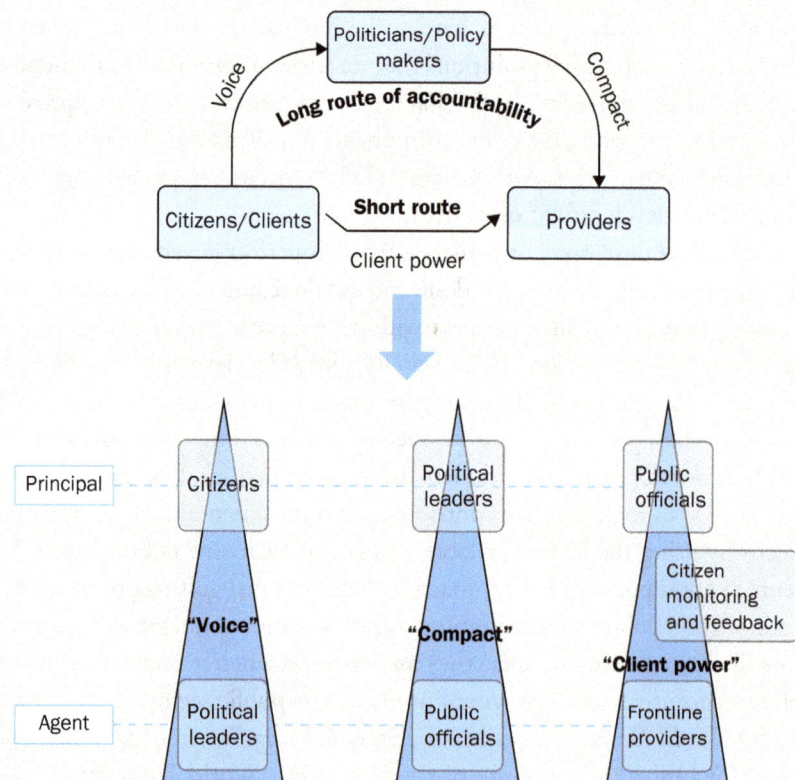

The evidence in this report shows that effective citizen participation in the short route depends upon citizens' political incentives to act and providers' incentives to respond. Previous reports have shown that for community participation to be effective, institutions must be specifically designed to facilitate it, by giving communities "teeth" to hold providers accountable (Grandvoinnet, Aslam, and Raha 2015; Mansuri and Rao 2013). Whether leaders select institutional arrangements that give communities this power depends upon their political incentives.

This report is about the fundamental importance of the "voice" or "politics" leg of the WDR 2004 triangle of accountability relations. Figure 7.1 depicts how this report builds on the WDR 2004. This report uses the advances in research since then to show how political engagement shapes each of the following three principal-agent relationships of government: (i) between citizens as the principals of political leaders; (ii) between political leaders as the principals of public officials who lead government agencies; and (iii) between public officials who manage frontline public providers. Non-political citizen engagement—to monitor frontline providers and public officials and provide feedback on their performance—can be used by leaders to enlist the help of citizens to address their principal-agent problems within government agencies.[3] Unhealthy political engagement can "invert" these relationships leading to perverse accountability, such as when political leaders buy votes and hold citizens accountable for providing political support in exchange for targeted benefits.[4]

Citizens' political engagement shapes the incentives and characteristics of leaders who, in turn, determine the "compact" with public officials and providers and whether to provide citizens with any effective institutional arrangements for "client power" to exert direct pressure on providers. How citizens behave in the political realm is intertwined with the beliefs and behavioral norms that shape the functioning of the compact and client power in the public sector. For example, if political norms allow vote buying and patronage to flourish in elections, those same norms can impede effective organization outside of elections to hold teachers accountable in public schools. Leaders who can get away with poor service delivery during their term in office by purchasing votes at election time also tend to provide jobs to teachers as political patronage and not hold them accountable for teaching. This insight into the inseparable links between political behavior at election time and behavior in the public sector in between elections has implications for the design of governance arrangements for managing a range of nonelected public sector officials—teachers, doctors, administrators, and so on—who perform in the shadow of flawed elections that generate weak political incentives and perverse behavioral norms.

It is also important to acknowledge examples of committed providers and galvanized communities that maintain high-quality public schools and health centers even within contexts of weak institutions and rent-seeking political leaders. The study by Brixi, Lust, and Woolcock (2015) is replete with shining examples of successful local delivery in a region of the world where political engagement by citizens is restricted and where elite capture of state institutions has been blamed for poor economic performance and mismanagement by public bureaucracies.

The diversity of successful experiences within and between countries tempts practitioners to find ways to bypass politics rather than improve it. At the macro level, this translates into a search for benevolent elite institutions such as technocratic bureaucracies that are insulated from political pressures. At the micro level, it translates into a search for local collective action between citizens and public providers, working together to improve outcomes in their communities. This approach runs into the problem of replicating successful experiences in places where local collective action and benevolent elites have not emerged naturally. Even successful communities can grapple with problems of sustaining their success in the face of poverty, lack of resources, and demoralization if the systems around them continue to be weak and captured. Furthermore, relying on communities to help themselves can let the corrupt leaders of government get away with capturing and wasting larger public resources, providing little to the communities who need services the most.

Efforts toward enhancing social accountability and citizen participation that provide powers to citizens to manage public funds (such as in community-driven development projects) may also have an impact on the principal-agent relationships in the larger public systems by shaping how citizens view the state and how they act toward powerful leaders. However, research reports few indications that public sector governance is changed by programs designed to induce participation in communities, even when participation improves service delivery and development outcomes (Casey et al. 2012; Mansuri and Rao 2013). Yet this may be an area in which evidence gathering is methodologically constrained. Qualitative studies suggest that participatory programs might contribute to strengthening citizen capacity for collective action for the public good (Ananthpur et al. 2014; Grandvoinnet et al. 2014).

The evidence uncovered in this report points to existing forms of political engagement by citizens that can be supported with transparency instruments, particularly mass media. The recommendations in this report are therefore complementary to efforts that seek to promote social accountability. The two approaches—social accountability and political accountability—share the goal of promoting norms of cooperative behavior in society to solve collective action problems for the greater public good.

Political engagement is a blunt accountability instrument. Various other institutions of checks and balances and internal accountability within government are needed to hold public officials accountable in between elections and across multiple dimensions of performance. The conundrum is how to foster such institutions in environments in which leaders are able to gain and remain in power by keeping institutions weak. Research suggests that transparency can work together with political engagement to improve political incentives and behavioral norms such that citizens and leaders gradually build those larger institutions that are crucial for good governance.

The typology of political incentives and behavior presented in the Overview is useful here to distill messages from the research (table 7.1). The typology can be used to craft a variety of policy options using available entry points and situational analyses in specific country and institutional contexts. When facing government failures and seeking to solve them, the types of questions that policy actors might ask are summarized in the top panel of table 7.1. The main answers to these questions—of what to do when politics impedes development—that the report offers as options for policy actors to consider are in the bottom panel of table 7.1. These policy options all involve strengthening transparency and citizen engagement to solve government failures.

The next section distills lessons for policies to strengthen transparency. These lessons take existing political institutions as given, and involve leveraging the instruments of transparency to improve the quality of political engagement. The following section distills lessons for policies to strengthen citizen engagement. It shows how citizen engagement policies can be designed to be more effective when they explicitly take citizens' and leaders' political behavior into account. In pursuing the engagement of citizens to hold local officials accountable, higher-tier policy makers may consider local elections to be the mechanism through which citizens are empowered to do so. Without such power of selecting and sanctioning local leaders, citizens are unlikely to have the capacity to exact accountability.

217

Table 7.1 Applying the typology of political behavior for policy lessons

Assessing the context to find entry points for solving government failures

	Individual action	Organized group action
***Actions for Private Benefits at the Expense of Public Goods* (Unhealthy Actions)**	• Does political competition and voting revolve around the provision of targeted benefits (for example, vote buying and ethnic politics)? • Is there popular demand for costly policies, such as subsidies, without regard to the costs of those policies? • Is noncooperative behavior, such as asking for and giving bribes to avoid public interest rules and regulations, widely prevalent?	• Are political parties organized around particularistic benefits, such as targeting using ethnic identity? • Is the state captured by a powerful elite who have weak incentives to provide public goods and who restrict political engagement by citizens at large? • Have special interest groups captured policies for their group benefit, at the expense of the larger public interest?
***Actions for Public Goods* (Healthy Actions)**	**Policy questions:** **How can reform leaders within government and civil society and external partners use transparency to shift political behavior toward the broader public interest?** • By generating information on performance of leaders in delivering public goods • By strengthening media markets to serve the public interest • By tailoring information and support to media markets in those jurisdictions where citizens are active in selecting and sanctioning leaders **How can reform leaders within government design citizen engagement to solve service delivery problems?** • By designing beneficiary feedback to be credible and protected from elite capture • By complementing capacity building and new technologies for delivery with institutions for political engagement that enable leaders to be selected and sanctioned on the basis of performance • By designing local political jurisdictions whose leaders have clear responsibility for delivering public goods and that overlap with local media markets	

The final section addresses the fundamental dilemma that motivates the report. The same problem—that leaders with the power to choose technically sound policies are constrained by politics—applies to the recommendations here aimed at harnessing transparency and citizen engagement. Nevertheless, different policy messages considered in the report may be feasible for a range of diverse policy actors—reform leaders within government, civil society, and international development partners. External agents can play potentially transformative roles in contexts in which they are most needed to address political impediments to development. For example, research findings emphasize the importance of relevance, credibility, and impartiality of information about the performance of leaders and their policy actions. External agents might offer these attributes when they have technical capacity to generate meaningful information from large data and when they are regarded as politically independent and non-partisan.

Policies to strengthen transparency

The research in this report suggests that transparency has far-reaching impacts on institutions and implementation of policies across sectors. Transparency can help to build effective homegrown institutions that are capable of pursuing technically sound policies, through its interaction with forces of political engagement. Transparency can enable coordination among citizens in actions that they are already taking (voting, competing in elections, engaging politically) in ways that improve the selection of leaders and strengthen behavioral norms in the public sector. Mass media's role as a force for persuasion and as a coordinating device for solving collective action problems is likely to be important beyond information content alone.

Desirable attributes of transparency policies are described below, pertaining to the nature of data, evidence, and the characteristics of media markets that can be supported, and to the tailoring of this information and its communication to existing institutions of political engagement. Although the research conclusively shows that political engagement is responsive to transparency, it also shows that final impact on governance and development outcomes vary greatly within any institutional context and depend on the specific details of transparency. Powerful leaders and elites can also undo positive effects of transparency on citizens' political action. This suggests that experimentation and iterative adaptation are needed to exploit the potential of transparency (Andrews, Pritchett, and Woolcock 2013).

Information about leaders' performance and the consequences of their actions

Transparency is most effective when it supports the generation of specific, reliable, and impartial evidence on the performance of leaders tasked

219

with the delivery of public policies. The information provided through transparency must be specific about both policy actions and the resulting outcomes so that citizens can use this information to select and sanction leaders. For example, information only on budget allocations is of limited use without information on how these allocations were spent, what that spending accomplished, and what that means about the performance of leaders. In the absence of information about performance that is clearly attributable to leaders, there is more scope for leaders to deflect scrutiny away from themselves and blame other factors outside their control for poor outcomes.

Research on how voters and leaders respond to the availability of specific information about performance rather than to information about policy actions alone supports this recommendation.[5] For example, regularized disclosure of audit reports on the financial management performance of elected governments has been shown to improve both voting behavior and leaders' responsiveness, resulting in the removal of corrupt leaders from office and a reduction in corruption among incumbents (Bobonis, Cámara Fuertes, and Schwabe forthcoming; Ferraz and Finan 2008).

Information on budget allocations without corresponding information on spending performance in providing public goods also runs the risk of fueling political incentives to pander to inefficient demands from citizens without considering the trade-offs between different allocations. Performance information about public goods is more likely to feed constructive public debate about how to allocate scarce resources. The data revolution (WDR 2016, 244) can be leveraged to provide more specific information about performance. Different government ministries and practices related to service delivery, such as health, education, agriculture, infrastructure, business regulation, and so on, can contribute to such performance measurement. Data from across sectors can be combined to assess the performance of leaders and of public policies in making appropriate intersectoral trade-offs in allocating scarce resources for public interest goals.

The research evidence also supports the importance of the credibility of the sources of data about and analysis of government performance.[6] This need for credibility has implications for creating statistical agencies that are independent of political control and for leveraging data from any existing government agencies that have a reputation for independence, such as central banks and audit departments. Apart from any existing, credibly independent institutions within countries, there is also a particular role for external development partners and civil society organizations that are nonpartisan and have the technical capacity to ensure the quality of the data and the analysis. Box 7.1 illustrates this point using the example of

Box 7.1 The experience of benchmark indicators of government performance and options for future directions

International development partners have used their technical capacity in data production and analysis to develop cross-country indicators that benchmark the performance of governments. The Doing Business project is a good example. Such indicators are useful first and foremost because they provide data and peer-learning platforms about development problems, and they contribute to evidence about what policies are technically sound and have merit. Even governments that are captured by political interests and exhibit failures in some dimensions can use such indicators to pursue policy reforms in other dimensions. This is consistent with the arguments of this report about the coexistence of healthy and unhealthy political incentives within the same country and institutional environment.

Global indicators can also be used to address accountability problems and government failures. Disaggregation of Doing Business to subnational levels, such as is being undertaken in Mexico, may allow these indicators to foster political competition at local levels on platforms of good governance. Improvements in local political competition may account for the observed growth of reforms in Mexican states, which outpaces the average performance of Latin American economies and many high-income Organisation for Economic Co-operation and Development countries.

A new World Bank initiative, Citizen Engagement in Rulemaking, tracks citizens' experience in learning about new regulations and engaging with the government on their content. Such citizen engagement can help governments to make better rules and formulate better regulations. These indicators of regulatory quality can also be used to address a more fundamental problem of government incentives to pursue public interest regulation in the first place. Indicators of government performance can be further developed and more purposefully disseminated to make it more likely that citizens use them to demand healthy regulations and a level playing field. The Citizen Engagement in Rulemaking indicators show that outcomes are worse in low-income countries, and worse outcomes of citizen engagement in rulemaking are correlated with lower government effectiveness. Publicizing these indicators through local, pro-poor media, such as radio, that are used by smaller businesses and household enterprises run by poor people in large parts of the developing world, can play a crucial role in improving outcomes. This approach can be used to shift political engagement to demand public interest regulations. Household enterprises, for example, as has been documented in Africa (Fox and Sohnesen 2012), tend to involve poor people who are unlikely to be politically connected or organized into business groups for collective action, and who fall prey to rent-seeking local officials responsible for enforcing regulations. The trends uncovered in this report suggest that the owners of these enterprises may nevertheless be politically engaged through local electoral institutions that overlap with radio stations. Information provided through such pro-poor media is more likely to promote healthy political engagement and effectively empower citizens to hold leaders accountable.

Sources: Citizen Engagement in Rulemaking database (http://rulemaking.worldbank.org); Doing Business, World Bank Group.

benchmark indicators of government performance that are produced by the World Bank.

While policy advisors and technical experts are already aware of the importance of producing reliable and credible evidence, the new consideration here from the political economy perspective is even more focused investments in scientific methods to assess the performance of government leaders in providing *public goods*. Scientific credibility is needed to defend information about public goods against allegations of ideological and partisan bias. Investments in understanding how current public policies and spending programs are performing can bring down to earth the grand debates between the left and the right on the role of government, to find solutions to those problems the public sector may be uniquely positioned to address. Generating information that can attribute performance to leaders is needed to help citizens select and sanction leaders on the basis of performance.

Strengthening public interest programming in media markets to effectively communicate performance information

Policies to strengthen the functioning of media markets so that information about government policies and performance are effectively communicated can be a crucial part of governance strategies to foster healthy political engagement.[7] Policies in this area can promote healthy competition in media markets and can be complemented by interventions to support public interest programming that provides impartial information to cultivate citizens' political engagement. Even when media are independent from state control and markets are competitive, citizens can choose to access primarily entertaining programs that do not sufficiently inform them about public interest issues. Sponsorship of appealing programs, or "infotainment," to communicate evidence on the actions of leaders and the effects of public policies, has the potential to persuade citizens to shift political beliefs in ways that strengthen demand for good leaders and good policies. This recommendation is supported by a body of research on characteristics of political engagement and the role of media that is discussed in chapters 4, 5, and 6.

By influencing political engagement, media markets have been shown to matter significantly for governance.[8] Market forces and the diffusion of technology are resulting in the proliferation of different media outlets, contributing to plurality and independence of media. The strengthening of these markets, including by increasing the access of media outlets and journalists to credible sources of data and information, is a key policy instrument. Media markets can be assessed on the basis of whether they provide sufficient coverage of public interest programming and effective access by citizens to such programming. This means targeting policies to the type of media and the type of programming to which citizens actually pay attention.

Following are some key issues to contend with:

- *Access:* Access to media by all citizens in all regions is often a major challenge. Access can be an infrastructure challenge, for instance, where technology-dependent media cannot reach remote regions. It can also be a question of media content and pluralism, where the interests, needs, and specific issues of certain sections of a national community are not served by the media. This last issue is often one of the justifications for community broadcasting in remote rural areas. Leading global technology companies are experimenting with ways of providing Internet access in remote regions. Wu (2010) shows how information technologies have historically had a democratizing effect—by being cheap and easily accessible—but have usually ended up being dominated by monopolies.

- *Media ownership and pluralism:* The question of who owns the media is a challenging one everywhere because of the strong link between media and power. If the government or a few firms control the preponderance of the media, the possibility of transparency to nourish political engagement becomes severely curtailed. One major issue is market censorship or the pressures on media independence emanating from powerful forces in society. These pressures take many forms, including bribery; the use of advertising to control media content; unreasonably harsh defamation and sedition laws; harassment, even murder, of journalists; and the general absence of the rule of law.

- *Broadcast regulation under digital convergence designed to create an informed citizenry:* Most countries have agreed to switch from analog to digital TV in 2015, while others will wait a few years more. The switch should, under many circumstances, lead to greater pluralism on the airwaves because digital technology makes more channels possible. However, the switch can also be used as an opportunity for governments to dominate the airwaves.

  The trend toward technological convergence leads to regulatory powers being combined over both telecommunications and broadcasting. These regulators often have the difficult challenge of attempting to make sure that the emerging system contains enough news and current affairs programming to meet the citizenship needs of consumers of media fare. In addition, these regulators themselves need to be protected from regulatory capture.

- *Public service and public interest content in the media:* Plural and independent media systems do not automatically generate good public interest or public service content. The media do not always prioritize the provision of information needed to educate citizens on the great issues of the day or encourage debate and discussion and the emergence of informed public opinion. The preponderance of donor interventions in media markets focus on this challenge. Policy responses include the promotion of public service broadcasting on the BBC model; training of journalists on specific issues, including mastery of data; the funding of popular entertainment-education programs around the world; and so on.

Untargeted, general availability of greater information in the public domain, without support to media markets to communicate that information, is unlikely to get information to citizens in a form that enhances their capacity to hold leaders accountable for delivery of public goods.[9] Citizens can ignore information, especially in environments in which there is a lot of it, without persuasive and appealing media programming that brings it to their attention. Even when media are independent and competitive, citizens might choose to access only entertaining programming that does not inform them about public interest issues.

Media markets can be supported not only to ensure plurality and independence from state capture, but also to increase citizens' access to public interest information that competitive markets might not deliver without such support (Keefer and Khemani 2014; Prat and Strömberg 2011; Strömberg 2015). Sponsorship of appealing programs, or infotainment, that persuade citizens to shift their beliefs about public policies on the basis of technical evidence can potentially serve as a complement to competitive media markets. The design of such programming and its targeting through outlets that citizens access and find persuasive, requires investments in rigorous impact evaluation similar to that undertaken for other policy interventions. The research reviewed in this report shows that communication of scientific evidence to shift the beliefs of citizens also requires investment in scientific investigation.

The credibility of the sponsors of public interest programming is critical for such policy interventions to have the intended impact. Technical government agencies—such as audit departments or research departments within sector ministries—can be the source for such programming when they can back up the messages with rigorous data and analysis. International research organizations and development partners often work with government ministries to sponsor such programs. For example, the international Roll Back Malaria program sponsors community radio stations' broadcasts of information in Africa about the value of public health policies. There is evidence that such programming affects citizens' political attitudes, shifting them away from patronage politics toward increased demands for health and education services (Keefer and Khemani 2014).

Relevance and timeliness of information to the political process

Policies can encourage the provision of information and the access to media to be more relevant and timely to the political process. A key dimension of relevance is jurisdictional: information on the performance of public policies needs to be targeted to the jurisdictions in which citizens select leaders. Information on public goods provision at the local level is more relevant to voters' decisions in local elections than is information at the national level. Chapter 2 has reported trends of increasing political engagement across and within countries through the spread of electoral institutions at multiple levels of government. It also reports evidence consistent with voting being regarded by citizens as a relatively low-cost action to influence governance. Chapter 6 reports evidence that the act of voting, compared with other forms of citizen engagement, is particularly sensitive to information. These findings suggest that the data and media policies described above can be tailored to the multiple levels of government where citizens engage through elections. Performance assessments of both current incumbents and challengers in these multiple jurisdictions can enable citizens to take more informed actions in selecting leaders.

Regular compilation and generation of such information, spanning times when different political parties or leaders are in office, is not only a nonpartisan approach but can also avoid a potential incumbency bias in transparency policies. Such information could enable citizens to assess the relative potential of political contenders, not just incumbents, to prevent an incumbency bias. If information only enables assessment of the incumbent, citizens could use it to punish incumbents despite their best efforts under overly optimistic expectations of better performance from alternative candidates. This effect could reduce the incentives of all incoming leaders to exert greater effort—"why bother if people are not going to reward you for trying?" Another way of providing information about contenders, especially those who may not have previously held office, is through economic analysis of their proposed policy promises. Such an intervention was evaluated (Fujiwara and Wantchekon 2013) and found to reduce unhealthy forms of clientelist politics. Economic analysis of the performance of public policies at the level of disaggregated political jurisdictions can enable citizens to select leaders on the basis of technical evidence on performance. Such economic analysis is already being under-taken by multilateral development agencies. The recommendation here is to shape that analysis to the level of existing geographic and administrative units at which citizens are politically engaged.

Data and media policies can be combined to lower barriers to entry for contenders to compete on platforms of improving public policies and government performance. For example, policies that allow contenders access to mass media to debate the merits of public policies can improve the quality of political engagement (Fujiwara and Wantchekon 2013). Regulation that allows local media, such as radio or cellphone-based services, to thrive can enable communication between leaders and citizens and among citizens about public policy performance in spe-cific jurisdictions. This intersection of media and political markets has been shown to be significant in explaining better governance outcomes (Campante and Do 2014; Campante and Hojman 2013; Snyder and Strömberg 2010).

Timeliness matters as well: the availability of performance assessments of incumbents and challengers is most relevant at the time of elections. Research has shown that information is more likely to have an impact when there is competition from political opponents and when the informa-tion is available at election time.[10]

The potential impact of more information at the time of elections extends beyond election season by shaping what leaders choose to do dur-ing their terms in office and the legitimacy of leaders to manage complex public bureaucracies. Legitimacy of leaders is at the frontier of theoretical developments that attempt to provide an understanding of how to improve the performance of public bureaucracies. Leaders that emerge from healthy political competition on the basis of good public performance could have greater legitimacy to effectively manage public bureaucracies.

This approach to the importance of leaders is different from having the "right people" as leaders, such as those who are regarded as reform champions and who have the personal will or personal commitment to reforms. Reform champions can lose public office if they try to implement reforms without political support for doing so. Furthermore, the "wrong people," such as those with lower personal integrity, can try to masquerade as the "right people" by pandering to citizens' ideological beliefs or by opportunistically exploiting divisions among citizens, without building common ground for public goods. Strengthening incentives for both the "right" and the "wrong" people is key by persuading citizens to be attentive to leaders' performance in delivering public goods. At the same time, research suggests that improving the selection of better-quality leaders has consequences for economic development. That is, transparency is most likely to solve government failures when it improves both incentives and the selection of high-quality leaders. The attributes of transparency discussed here are geared toward accomplishing these goals.

Once again, credibility of information sources about incumbents and challengers is important. Government agencies, even those that are supposed to be independent of political control, are likely to be subject to conflicts of interest in providing objective assessments of the performance of political opponents. Other external policy actors, such as civil society organizations, the media, and international development partners, are also likely to be constrained by perceptions of their ideological biases. Agencies can be more effective in implementing the transparency policy strategies recommended here if they establish greater credibility for being nonpartisan, nonideological, and politically independent, by investing in the technical quality of the information they produce.

To highlight the overall message of the importance of targeting transparency policies to enable political markets to function better, box 7.2 contrasts case studies from Brazil and India.

Sensitivity to existing political institutions

What is different about the recommendation here is the importance of communicating to citizens and in ways that effectively shift citizens' beliefs about public policies on the basis of technical evidence. The traditional policy approach has treated leaders as the only primary audience of expert analysis, and has treated communication to citizens as a matter not requiring scientific investigation. Communicating information to influence

Box 7.2   How the impact of transparency depends on political engagement: Contrast between Brazil and India

Brazil instituted a transparency policy that lent itself to nurturing political engagement in local jurisdictions. The national audit agency publicly discloses audit reports for directly elected municipal governments. Evidence shows that this policy works through competitive elections and media markets to improve governance. Local radio stations publicize information in the audit reports. Citizens use this information as voters in local elections to remove corrupt mayors from office. Citizens also use this information in conjunction with media platforms when they contend for public office to check incumbents and to provide alternative choices of leaders. Leaders, in turn, are in a position to implement far-reaching changes in governance through the powers they wield over state resources and institutions. For example, other evidence from this same context in Brazil shows that lower municipal corruption can lead to improvements in student learning outcomes through better management and greater resource availability in public schools.

India instituted a landmark Right to Information (RTI) Act for general transparency, but does not specifically generate information applicable to local jurisdictions where political engagement occurs. Several civil society organizations have used the RTI Act to uncover cases of corruption and then organized public protests that led to the successful recovery of stolen public resources. Related research shows that civil society organizations can assist citizens in using the RTI Act to get speedier responses from government bureaucracies to their requests for personal entitlements as a close substitute for bribes.

The unfolding experience in India shows that some civil society leaders who championed the cause of transparency and *social* accountability, outside the realm of elections, have now come to embrace elections. They have turned their civil society organization into a political party to contest and win elections on anticorruption platforms. The research covered in this report suggests that these developments should be interpreted as reflective of changing political behaviors in India as in Brazil. These new political behaviors can improve governance by strengthening the incentives of *all* political parties to demonstrate competence in controlling corruption, regardless of the performance of any particular party in any particular election, that is, by making good governance the platform upon which citizens select and sanction leaders.

At the same time, even as leaders become more accountable and corruption falls, leaders will need to contend with populist beliefs that could bankrupt public utilities and impede the appropriate allocation of scarce public resources. For example, prominent among the policy promises of the new political party (and erstwhile civil society organization) in India are free electricity and free water. Reforms to professionalize bureaucracies may also face similar populist impediments when public sector workers' unions find common cause with citizens who think that governments should be providing secure jobs in the public sector. The potential for such beliefs and their consequences is why the report flags the targeting of transparency to shift not only incentives but also political beliefs and political behavioral norms, such that public sector institutions allow leaders to seek and implement effective technical solutions for public goods.

Sources: Ferraz and Finan 2008; Ferraz, Finan, and Moreira 2012; Peisakhin 2012; Roberts 2010; *Economist* December 14, 2013, "India's Left-Leaning, Anti-Graft Party Made a Stunning Debut" (http://www.businessinsider.in/Indias-Left-Leaning-Anti-Graft-Party-Made-A-Stunning-Debut/articleshow/27328073.cms); *Hindu*, February 11, 2015, "Highlights of AAP's Manifesto" (http://www.thehindu.com/elections/delhi2015/aam-aadmi-party-manifesto-for-delhi-2015-polls/article6842252.ece).

beliefs and political behavioral norms requires an understanding of the institutions within and through which citizens form these beliefs. This report has offered a better understanding of how political engagement, and the leaders selected through it, shapes beliefs and behavior in the public sector. Transparency can be targeted at these political institutions to try to improve beliefs and behavior toward solving shared problems of public goods for economic development.

Applying these policy lessons for transparency depends on the characteristics of existing government jurisdictions: which tasks are assigned to which leaders, and who are the citizens who select and sanction them. If government jurisdictions have clearly assigned responsibilities for public goods, then it is easier to generate performance data that can be attributed to the leaders of those jurisdictions and to communicate that information to enable citizens to hold those leaders accountable for public goods. Most places will have a complex set of political and bureaucratic institutions that share responsibilities for the provision of public goods. Higher-order transparency, such as civic education about the roles of different government jurisdictions and officials, can play a role in strengthening governance.

However, when citizens are not empowered to select and sanction leaders of government jurisdictions, then citizens are unlikely to have the capacity to use information to exact accountability. In environments that restrict or repress political engagement, both the scope for implementing these recommendations and expectations of impact will be more limited.

Policies to strengthen citizen engagement

The evidence in the report of how politics shapes the incentives and norms of public providers and of citizens can be used by policy actors when approaching governance reforms to engage citizens to improve outcomes.

Policies to strengthen non-political forms of citizen engagement

Policies have sought to engage citizens to solve local service delivery problems in non-political ways, such as by providing beneficiary feedback, monitoring local officials, directly managing public funds, and contributing to the maintenance of local public goods. These policies can be designed to be more effective based on a better understanding of citizens' and leaders' political behavior. Their success depends on the political characteristics of the environment in which services are delivered.

When higher-tier policy makers with oversight powers over local public officials seek to hold these officials more accountable by enlisting the help of citizens in monitoring them, they would need to design policy initiatives to assure citizens that their feedback would be taken seriously and that citizens would be protected from retaliation. For example, if beneficiary feedback is solicited through local elites who are the ones capturing public resources, then citizens are unlikely to respond by providing reliable feedback to reduce local capture. Olken (2007) shows the impact of such attention to design, finding that anonymous comment forms distributed independently of village government leaders in Indonesia made a significant difference. Another example from Indonesia shows that when beneficiaries are informed with the purpose of strengthening their bargaining power vis-à-vis local elites, such as when they are provided with official letters from higher-tier authorities about their entitlement to subsidized rice, then they are more likely to demand their entitlements and complain about poor performance (Banerjee et al. 2015).

The research on these examples from Indonesia further shows that the success of policy initiatives depends on the incentives of higher-level leaders to get the design right and send credible signals that complaints about local officials will be taken seriously (Banerjee et al. 2015). This insight is consistent with the conclusions of Mansuri and Rao (2013) in their review of programs for local citizen engagement: success depends on effective design and local institutions of accountability that are established by higher-tier leaders. In the absence of healthy political engagement, both higher-tier and local leaders are unlikely to have the incentives or the credibility to engage citizens effectively to solve delivery problems. Non-political citizen engagement to solve last-mile delivery problems is embedded within political engagement, which shapes the incentives of leaders.

The effectiveness of other forms of non-political citizen engagement, such as getting citizens to contribute their time, labor, effort, and money to produce local public goods, also depends on political incentives and behavior. Prior reports have documented the risk of elite capture of public resources that are devolved to the local level (Mansuri and Rao 2013). Recent research suggests that in addition to the risk of capturing the benefits of resources coming from higher levels, elites may also capture local civil society (Acemoglu, Reed, and Robinson 2014; Anderson, Francois, and Kotwal 2015). This situation can result in citizens providing public services for themselves while the leaders do little to fulfill their responsibilities and yet maintain their grip on power.

The design issues are likely to be technically detailed and to vary depending upon the type of service that is being delivered. For example, the type of citizen engagement that is likely to reduce corruption in local roads construction or distribution of private entitlements may be very different from what is needed in sectors like health and education. While sector-specific technical design issues are outside the scope of the report, the insights above may help to strengthen citizen engagement policies.

Policies to strengthen local political engagement within countries of different national political systems

Growing devolution of public resources in developing countries for local implementation of public programs has to deal with the lack of capacity for monitoring and enforcement at both local and national levels (Mansuri and Rao 2013). The exigencies of development have led to disbursement of public spending across millions of villages where poor people live but where there are few formal enforcement institutions. In one such environment in Indonesia, Sacks, Ensminger, and Clark (2014) document high rates of corruption among local officials. Widespread beliefs of and actual experience with corruption can contribute to a culture of poor performance in the public sector, stemming not from values or norms but rather from rational beliefs about how others are behaving and about the probability of detection and punishment in environments with scarce resources to combat corruption.

Innovative technologies for monitoring and managing funds, so that opportunities for graft are reduced and corruption is easier to detect, are being explored to address this problem (for example, Muralidharan, Niehaus, and Sukhtankar 2014; Sacks, Ensminger, and Clark 2014; World Bank 2016). Locally targeted transparency for healthy political engagement at the local level can complement innovative technological solutions and may together contribute to shifting the political beliefs that support a culture of poor performance in the public sector. Pursuit of this direction requires collaboration between policy actors and researchers to identify what specifically works, or does not work, in different contexts.

Higher-tier leaders who are pursuing citizen engagement to hold local officials accountable may find themselves in a position of considering local elections as the mechanism through which citizens are empowered to do so. The research findings of the impact of local political engagement on local accountability and the responsiveness of political engagement to transparency, suggest that policy makers across different national political systems can craft policies for local political engagement suited to their contexts and make it healthy through transparency. Research shows how local audit disclosure interacts with local electoral competition to reduce corruption (Bobonis et al. Forthcoming; Ferraz and Finan 2011).

A number of social accountability initiatives that seek to work outside the political realm rely on catalyzing group action by citizens. They use transparency campaigns to trigger action by citizen committees charged with monitoring public schools, health clinics, or other public spending programs. However, there is little evidence that transparency alone encourages group action through such committees. Survey evidence that these committees are typically inactive suggests that organized group action of this type can be costly for citizens (reviewed in chapter 6). Theory suggests that this is because groups rarely organize to pursue broadly shared public goods. In contrast, individual actions of political engagement, such as voting, respond to transparency. More amorphous group-based political engagement, such as protests, are also facilitated by transparency and social media in particular. In local political markets, higher-tier authorities can use transparency to enable citizens to hold local leaders accountable by coordinating their individual actions as people who vote on the basis of performance.

Who will take up these recommendations?

This report confronts a fundamental challenge: the political incentives of those who have the power to implement technically sound policies may not be aligned with development objectives. An integral part of the policy recommendations of this report is highlighting how the relative comparative advantages, incentives, and goals of different policy actors matter in implementing these recommendations.

Sovereign governments

Governments have the power to adopt or facilitate all of the policy recommendations in this report, but might not have the incentives to do so. However, even in governments with significant political problems and concomitantly weak incentives, leaders might nevertheless find it in their self-interest to use the lessons of this report. They might feel the need to respond to growing forces of citizen political engagement and disaffection with government performance, or to find ways to constructively channel these forces. Using transparency and political engagement along the lines recommended in this report can help governments build legitimacy in the eyes of citizens. In contrast, policy efforts that focus exclusively on direct citizen engagement to bypass governance problems, so that citizens step in to help themselves where the government fails, can leave these problems intact.

Furthermore, governments are not monolithic entities but exhibit substantial differences among leaders across multiple agencies and jurisdictions. Reform leaders within government who are struggling to overcome political constraints may be able to use instruments of transparency that are at their disposal and that are more tractable compared with other types of policies. Other policies may be outside their control—depending on the actions of more powerful colleagues—or encumbered by prevailing political beliefs among citizens. Transparency may be more easily pursued by these reform leaders than policy reforms that could cause them to lose office should they try to implement them. For example, it may be too politically costly to reform electricity subsidies, but leaders may nevertheless facilitate and support the types of transparency measures outlined here on the costs and benefits of these policies and target the information to the jurisdictions where political engagement occurs. This process can improve the selection of local leaders who build support for reforms, by making the case for reforms to citizens rather than to fan protests and exploit the issue for political gain.

Technical institutions within countries often function as islands of good governance in environments in which the executive and legislative branches of government might be plagued by perverse political incentives. For example, supreme audit institutions and supreme courts are prominent in many examples for curbing political transgressions and enabling citizens and civil society to demand accountability. The historical trajectory of when and how developing countries were born as nation-states may explain the simultaneous emergence of political incentives that were inimical to the adoption of good public policies in some countries (because the conditions were ripe for clientelist politics)[11] but nevertheless allowed certain technical institutions to flourish, build a reputation over time, and attract technically competent and public-spirited leaders to serve on them.

The research covered in this report suggests that such technically reputed institutions, where they exist, can be systematically leveraged to improve political incentives and political behaviors by bringing credible information to the forefront.

The existence of multiple layers of government within a country can provide an opportunity to implement some recommendations of the report. Even if there is no space for political engagement by citizens at the national level and if policy makers are wary of greater transparency at that level, they may want to enlist the help of citizens to promote local accountability to improve service delivery. Local institutions of political engagement, supported by local-level information and communication, can enable citizens to hold local leaders accountable. Furthermore, one way for national leaders to constructively channel demands from citizens for political engagement may be by applying the lessons of this report at the local level. These two objectives have significant complementarities. The available research highlights the importance of local electoral institutions in enabling local communities to hold officials accountable, with correspondingly little evidence that transparency can galvanize other forms of local participation to improve accountability.[12]

Civil society organizations

Civil society organizations might be hesitant to address the political impediments to achieving development goals because doing so might affect their ability to function in a country and receive support from external funders. The bulk of their effort therefore may go toward social accountability and citizen participation efforts so that citizens can directly solve local problems. However, if these efforts bypass the problems of malfeasance and mismanagement in government, the public sector would continue to fail in using its powers and resources to achieve the goals of development.

Although international donors and development partners have been providing significant financial support to growing numbers of civil society organizations, there is little evidence on and understanding of the impact of these organizations in contexts in which elections are marred by unhealthy practices such as vote buying, allowing power to be sustained without delivering public goods. Although bypassing elections and providing funding to civil society organizations may be a convenient and feasible way for international organizations to support citizens' roles in improving governance, there is little understanding and evidence on how citizens can play these roles in the shadow of flawed electoral institutions without altering or interacting with those institutions.

Whether civil society action has an impact depends upon the institutional environment. It is more likely to work in places with strong internal checks and balances and the rule of law, but less likely to work in weak institutional contexts in which the law can be bent at the will of powerful leaders. In places with strong institutions and the rule of law, internal checks and balances within government are of primary importance in checking malfeasance. Civil society organizations may use transparency regimes to serve as watchdogs to complement formal government institutions, and sniff out the stray transgressions that formal institutions might miss. Civil society organizations would be effective in this role because once they bring the transgressions to light, the formal checks and balances and laws would kick in. Political engagement in such cases would support the functioning of internal checks and balances by making corruption prohibitively costly—leaders would face a high likelihood of losing office if they tried to interfere and protect the perpetrators.

However, in institutional contexts such as those in large parts of the world where a majority of poor people live, leaders of and agents within government bureaucracies might not fear public pressure, even when it is applied. The political processes, such as elections, that get them to their positions of power are tolerant of corruption, revolving as they do around the use of vote buying, violence, and ethnic favoritism.

If the political incentives that support corruption are unchanged, even a successful example of diminished corruption might mask the displacement of corruption to another time and place, when it is out of the limelight. Relying on civil society organizations to prevent such displacement and shine a light everywhere, across vast numbers of complex bureaucratic transactions, is asking for them to take on the burden of internal checks and balances that should emanate from within government. This process comes full circle to beg the question of how civil society organizations will provide these institutions and overcome the problems that plague the formal institutions in the first place, without some form of political engagement. Civil society may need to rely on healthy political engagement that would give leaders the incentives to fear and respond to public protests against corruption.

Because of the lack of research evidence on how civil society organizations form, and with what incentives,[13] the report is not able to make any specific policy recommendations in the area of generalized support to civil society organizations. Instead, it highlights specific activities that civil society organizations could undertake to improve governance, such as generating the data or providing the persuasive media programming that nurtures political engagement by individual citizens. As noted in the recommendations above, to be effective, these organizations would need to build credibility on the basis of political and ideological independence, relying on technical capacity to use data-based evidence.

International development partners

External agents, such as international development partners, can play an important role in overcoming political impediments to development when their incentives are aligned with development goals. Yet external agents are constrained by their limited powers to bring about change from the outside. International development partners, such as bilateral agencies that directly engage in supporting political institutions, sometimes seek to advocate for democracy and for elections as its key institution. The report shows that elections alone will not solve governance problems—platforms of competition, whether on the basis of public good programs or not, or the characteristics of political engagement, matter. Although this is not likely to be news, the report serves these organizations by bringing current research to bear upon their endeavors and highlighting the design issues that surround the use of transparency to improve political engagement to serve the goals of economic development. For partners such as the World Bank that are prohibited from engaging in political affairs, the research covered in this report provides evidence that can support non-partisan and non-ideological transparency initiatives to improve economic outcomes (box 7.3).

The recommendations of the report are particularly relevant to operations and technical policy dialogue on decentralization to locally elected governments and community-based groups. Sovereign national governments invite international experts, including those at the World Bank, to give technical policy advice on the design of these subnational, local institutions of governance. Research on citizens' political behavior, as voters and contenders for leadership positions at local levels, has implications for this advice. Targeting information to improve local political behavior in elections can strengthen local institutions so that they can effectively deliver public policies for development.

Some of the findings of the report may be particularly applicable at the local level in contexts in which the legitimacy of national political

Box 7.3   Implications for the World Bank

The World Bank (henceforth "the Bank") is founded on Articles of Agreement that prohibit interference in the political affairs of its member states:

> The Bank and its officers shall not interfere in the political affairs of any member; nor shall they be influenced in their decisions by the political character of the member or members concerned. Only economic considerations shall be relevant to their decisions, and these considerations shall be weighed impartially in order to achieve the purposes stated in Article I.[a]

This political prohibition has been analyzed and interpreted extensively over the years. The most current thinking on the meaning of the political prohibition is set out in the 2012 Legal Note on Bank Engagement in the Criminal Justice Sector.[b] Acknowledging that politics and economics are often two sides of the same coin, the Note takes the view that it is appropriate for the Bank to consider political issues that have implications for economic development, so long as this is done in a nonpartisan, neutral manner. In addition, recommendations or activities that have a political aspect must satisfy two criteria: *first*, they must be grounded in an appropriate and objective economic rationale; and *second*, they must be examined closely to ensure that they do not involve the Bank in political affairs of a member or appear to endorse a political party, ideology, or particular form of government.

While constraining the Bank's mandate in some respects, this prohibition also provides the Bank with an important comparative advantage. The Bank's nonpartisan, nonideological business model, together with its technical capacity to manage and analyze vast amounts of data, lends it a special credibility with stakeholders. The analysis of the report, showing mounting research evidence on how citizens' political engagement matters for governance and development outcomes, suggests opportunities for creating a policy space to leverage this comparative advantage of the Bank.[c]

The economic rationale for the recommendations in this report rests on the research evidence that political engagement by citizens significantly influences economic development outcomes. Research also shows the specific channels through which political engagement affects economic outcomes—by shaping the quality and incentives of leaders to pursue public policies on the basis of technical merit. And finally, research shows that transparency's impact in overcoming governance impediments depends upon political engagement. The evidence specifically points to the role of information to improve the quality of political engagement within existing institutions, for greater accountability for better development results. Thus, the analysis in this report can constructively inform the Bank's work in pursuit of its core mandate to provide financing for economic development, by enhancing the effectiveness with which this financing is used to deliver results.

As for avoiding involvement in the political affairs of a member or endorsing a particular political party, the report has argued that information about government performance in delivering public goods should be based strictly on technical data and analysis, produced by credible, nonpartisan sources. The implications of such technical data and information for the electoral fortunes of different political parties, or the policies they choose, is a matter of how citizens and leaders themselves choose to respond to this information. The report's recommendations to provide such information

(continued)

Box 7.3   Continued

widely, and to focus its content on the technical performance of both incumbents and challengers in delivering economic development, apply across a wide range of institutional settings.

Specific practical applications of the general lessons in the report are expected to vary considerably across countries and projects. Teams within the Bank should use this research report as they deem appropriate for their context within the parameters of the Bank's mandate, recognizing that there are some activities that would present a risk of political interference in one context but not another.

a. See IBRD Articles of Agreement, Article IV, Section 10 and IDA Articles of Agreement, Article V, Section 6.

b. See http://siteresources.worldbank.org/INTLAW-JUSTINST/Resources/CriminalJusticeLegalNote.pdf.

c. For a similar model, see World Bank (2009) "Guidance Note on Bank Multi-Stakeholder Engagement." Footnote 22 of this document provides an example of how certain activities that would be typically included in a list of political activities would nevertheless be consistent with the mandate prescribed under the Articles: "With respect to participation and consultation requirements in the preparation of environmental assessments, former General Counsel Ibrahim Shihata previously noted the following: 'Such participation and consultation, to be useful at all, require a reasonable measure of free expression and assembly. The Bank would, in my view, be acting within proper limits if it asked that this freedom be insured when needed for the above purposes. Its denial of lending for a given project in the absence of this requirement where it applies cannot be reasonably described as an illegitimate interference in the political affairs of the country concerned, just because the rights to free expression and assembly in general are normally listed among political rights.' I. Shihata, *Prohibition of Political Activities in the Bank's Work* (July 12, 1995) at 12-3."

leaders may be eroded or unsustainable. For example, public financial management reforms advocated by national reform leaders may not be implemented in practice by local leaders. Complementing such reforms with transparency targeted at improving the functioning of local electoral institutions may make it more likely that local leaders have the incentives and motivation to comply with the reforms.

The recommendations of this report on the topic of transparency apply to participatory local development programs and to initiatives for social accountability. For starters, an audit of media markets could be a useful routine part of these interventions. It is important to know how the population that is the focus of participatory interventions receives information, what media they have access to, what media they consume, what media they find credible, and so on. Surprises may abound in this area once such analysis is conducted. For instance, the villager in India or Malawi or rural Algeria actually lives in an information-rich environment that needs to be understood.

Improving the functioning of local electoral institutions can be an important area of work to which this report applies across a variety of national political systems. Not only are local governments at the last mile of service delivery, which national leaders across the spectrum may want to improve, but they are also at the "first mile" at which citizens determine the platforms on which leaders are selected and sanctioned. These platforms, whether they are the healthy ones of good public performance or the unhealthy ones of vote buying and ethnic favoritism, for example, not only determine the incentives and quality of selected local leaders but can also shape the behavioral norms in the public sector as a whole. This first mile can matter for building legitimacy and capacity of state institutions in fragile contexts. It can matter for building capable and accountable local governments in rapidly urbanizing environments that plan well for urban development and mobilize the domestic resources needed for sustainable development. The local level can matter for improving political attitudes and behavior of citizens in rich country contexts as well, where the national stage appears to be hopelessly mired by political polarization among citizens. Targeting transparency to improve the functioning of local institutions of political engagement along the lines recommended in this report can therefore address some of the growing areas of economic concern throughout the world.

Technocratic reforms alone are not enough

Building effective state capacity for development requires changes in political behavior—investments in formal capacity and innovative technologies are not enough. Transparency can be targeted to bring about the needed changes in political behavior. International development partners' data and analytical capacity yields rich information about the performance of public policies and of governments. This data and evidence can be shaped to be more timely and relevant to the processes through which citizens hold leaders accountable.

For example, country diagnostics could invest more in generating data and evidence at disaggregated levels on what different government jurisdictions deliver in implementing public policies. This process entails an expansion of the analysis that focuses on using household surveys to describe characteristics of poverty as the main "diagnostic" to inform country strategies. It involves investing in more data to examine the performance of existing public policies and public spending programs at disaggregated jurisdictions within a country. That is, country diagnostic products could not only analyze countries' poverty profiles and describe the characteristics of the poor and of drivers of growth, but could also invest similarly in hard data and empirical evidence to assess what the government has been doing, with international support, through the policy levers and spending programs at its disposal, and shape that data to the level of existing geographic and administrative units at which citizens are politically engaged.

If governance problems are identified, the diagnostic would serve the purpose of providing a better understanding of these problems by extending to examine existing institutions of political engagement in the country and assessing the media environment. The diagnostic would answer the following questions: Given existing institutions or jurisdictions of political engagement in the country, what information on public goods performance of those jurisdictions is available? What new data are needed? What is the state of media markets—what forms of communication do citizens use for public debate?

This recommendation follows from the research evidence provided in the report that moving out of a situation of systemic and persistent governance problems is likely to require the disciplining effects of political engagement and the use of transparency policies to make engagement healthy. This approach would be a departure from practices that might have focused exclusively on high-level policy dialogue to persuade leaders to adopt changes, with no role for political engagement by citizens.

Analysis of media markets can go beyond supporting a particular donor project. Once the sector analysis is complete, different partners can pick up aspects of the work that their circumstances make them particularly suited to address. Bilateral donors are freer to engage more directly with these issues. Multilateral donors can support research and provide technical evidence on the consequences of different characteristics of media markets for economic development. In any event, the heavy lifting in securing media sector reform in any particular context is the work of coalitions of local players: the existing media, civil society organizations, reformers in government and the legislature, and so on. The task of international actors is to support and empower those whose country it is. Despite the oft-repeated objection that intervening in the media sector is too political, the "Guidance Note on Bank Multi-Stakeholder Engagement" (World Bank 2009) has provided clear guidance on how the Bank can work in the media sector and still keep within its non-political mandate under the Articles. In addition to the general considerations relating to political interference outlined above, it states,

In this context, good practice in dealing with media can be broken into two stages. The first involves diagnostic work to assess country conditions and, in particular, to determine whether in light of the country context and country relationship it would be productive to engage in supporting development of the media sector. This assessment in turn will have a bearing on the second stage, which involves managing potential political and reputational risks of media work and promoting good practice in media development, through specific types of activities the Bank may choose to support or undertake in a given country context. (World Bank 2009, 12)

The report suggests that policies to support independent and plural mass media can be a central plank of work in transparency. In contrast to a focus on media strengthening, exclusive support to generalized transparency policies, such as enacting freedom of information (FOI) or disclosure laws, although useful and probably necessary, may be insufficient and lacking the potential of other steps policy actors could take. General transparency legislation can have intrinsic value as a practice of good governance, as well as being necessary for creating an enabling environment for accountability. However, it is unlikely to be sufficient to solve governance problems. The evidence covered in this report on how political incentives matter for governance suggests that in places with weak institutions and perverse political incentives, general policies toward legislating transparency are subject to the same governance problems they seek to fix. Leaders within the political institutions that sustain governance problems might not want to improve governance so that they can preserve their political rents. Transparency for transparency's sake can help them implement cosmetic changes that have no real impact on governance, but still win them accolades.

Evidence on the role of mass media indirectly suggests that incremental changes toward an independent and plural media environment, including through technological and market forces that are difficult for policy makers to control, might have a larger impact on governance than FOI legislation alone. For example, research has shown that some authoritarian regimes allow greater media freedoms as a way to monitor and manage local public officials (Egorov, Guriev, and Sonin 2009). Authoritarian leaders may have incentives to adopt those transparency policies (independent media) that generate new and credible information that the leaders lack—on the local performance of their public officials—rather than to disclose the information that they already possess.

Technical governance work, such as public sector and financial management reforms, could be complemented by transparency targeted at improving political incentives, rather than bypassing or ignoring politics. For example, some research suggests that instituting anticorruption agencies and building capacity may not make a dent in corruption in the absence of political incentives to use these agencies and the built capacity to reduce corruption. These agencies can even be deliberately designed to be ineffective, or can face political resistance when trying to fulfill their mandate. Although evidence to test this hypothesis, or indeed the effectiveness of such anticorruption policies, is unavailable, the evidence across countries that does exist finds little correlation between the existence of anticorruption agencies and the control of corruption. Some case studies suggest that anticorruption agencies do not address systemic corruption and, in badly governed contexts, can be ineffective and in some cases harmful.

Since 2000, donor support for public financial management increased more than aid for any other subsector. This greater focus on public financial management, particularly support to supreme audit institutions, has led to stronger public financial management results. The World Bank Independent Evaluation Group's report on public sector reform states that about two-thirds of all countries that borrowed for financial management showed improvement, and it was the most consistent area of improvement in the case studies (World Bank 2008). This finding should not be taken at face value, however, given that the Independent Evaluation Group's report on the Bank's Governance and Anticorruption Strategy (World Bank 2011) states that although standardization of assessments and operational support for public financial management systems improved, the implications for frontline service delivery are unclear. Does strengthening public financial management systems, or the building of institutional capacity, lead to improved results in contexts in which political incentives are weak? The examples presented in this report suggest that institutional capacity building on its own, without complementary investments in strengthening incentives and behavioral norms, can be undermined by politics.

This report provides evidence that policy actors can use their instruments to align political incentives with development objectives. One such instrument is transparency, which can be targeted to improve political engagement. Another is citizen engagement through which leaders can hold a number of lower level public officials in government agencies more accountable. An overarching recommendation is that practitioners shift their approach from seeking to bypass politics, or lowering expectations when it is a problem, to confronting it and incorporating it into the technical solutions to development problems. This does *not* mean prioritizing attention to political incentives or "waiting" until political problems are solved. Instead, the suggested approach opens up avenues for development practitioners to do what they do a little bit differently to take advantage of the growing forces of political engagement and transparency.

The scope of the report does not allow for a detailed examination of how technical governance arrangements should be designed within specific sectors or agencies. It focuses on examining governance as a cross-cutting issue. Many of its implications are therefore pertinent to those who are engaged in cross-cutting governance work rather than in specific sectors. We invite development practitioners within sectors, in addition to in governance, to test whether the paradigm offered by the report yields new ideas for how to do their work differently. This includes not just getting governments to adopt good policies, but designing implementation arrangements that are more likely to succeed because they are based on a better understanding of political incentives and behavioral norms in the public sector. Our hope is that such future work, combining political economy with sector-specific technical expertise, will yield better ideas to make politics work for rather than against development, such that public sector institutions around the world will be capable of tackling global problems of public goods.

Notes

1. After studying actual practice within the United Kingdom's Department for International Development and the World Bank, Yanguas and Hume (2015) come to the following conclusion: "An emerging community of aid practitioners and scholars is promoting the use of political or political-economy analysis (PEA) as a new tool for improving aid effectiveness. Its institutionalization into actual aid practice, however, is likely to encounter entrenched organizational procedures, incentives and sub-cultures." Carothers and de Gramont (2013) describe the situation thus: "Major donors have made significant progress in adopting politically smart methods. The growing use of tools such as political analysis has helped aid practitioners navigate complex local realities. Yet these methods struggle against inflexible aid delivery mechanisms and entrenched technocratic preferences within aid organizations."

2. One of the authors of the WDR 2004 subsequently clarified his thinking that the short route pertains to market-based transactions and the long route applies every time there is a government intervention to solve a market failure (Devarajan 2014; Devarajan, Khemani, and Walton 2014).

3. The conceptual framework in chapter 4 discusses these three principal-agent relationships, and how political engagement influences all of them.

4. Stokes (2005) has examined such perverse accountability.

5. Chapter 4 provides support from the theory on the channels of transparency's impact and risks of unintended consequences when information on the consequences of policy actions is not available. Chapter 6 on the empirical evidence of transparency's impact also shows that performance information is crucial. For example, Kendall, Nannicini, and Trebbi (2015) provide detailed evidence about how voters update their beliefs in response to greater availability of information. They find that information on "valence issues," which most voters find desirable, such as the competence and effort of politicians and their performance in service delivery, has greater impact than information about ideological policy positions that divide voters. In contrast, studies of interventions that provide information about politicians' specific actions, such as in legislative debate, find little impact and suggest the leaders can obfuscate the information (Humphreys and Weinstein 2012).

6. Alt, Lassen, and Marshall (2014) find that the effects of information vary with the source of information within the same strong institutional context (Denmark): an unemployment projection from the Danish Central Bank, which is highly credible among citizens, caused voters to update their beliefs more than did information received from government or opposition political parties. Results from Brazil, Mexico, and Puerto Rico on how official audit disclosure contributes to reducing corruption contrasts with an information experiment in Mexico in which corruption information was provided by a nongovernmental organization (reviews in chapter 6).

7. Several recommendations here are consistent with previous work in the *World Development Report 2002: Building Institutions for Markets* (WDR 2002). The strengthening of mass media for economic development was highlighted in the WDR 2002 in a chapter devoted to the topic. A companion volume expanded the analysis of the role of media (World Bank 2002). This report builds on the previous work by reviewing new research since 2002 in chapter 6 and the implication for policy of the interaction between media and political markets uncovered in recent research.

8. Chapter 6 discusses how media markets matter not just for accountability and corruption, but also for ideological polarization and shaping citizens' political beliefs.

9. Several papers show that in the absence of concerted information campaigns, citizens can be unaware of information they could use or of the institutions through which they might exact accountability. For example, Banerjee et al. (2010) find at baseline that citizens were unaware of the existence of a village education committee that could provide powers to citizens, even when they are supposed to be members of it. Humphreys and Weinstein's (2012) and Malesky, Schuler, and Tran's (2012) research designs are predicated on problems of information flows from the national to local levels.

10. For example, Ferraz and Finan (2008) in Brazil; Bobonis, Cámara Fuertes, and Schwabe (forthcoming) in Puerto Rico; and Larreguy, Marshall, and Snyder (2014) in Mexico, where the disclosure of audit information has a bearing, particularly when it happens close to elections.

11. Chapter 5 links different strands of literature on the persistence of historical institutions to make such an argument.

12. Various meta-evaluations of social accountability and the Bank's reports on this topic (Grandvoinnet, Aslam, and Raha 2015; Mansuri and Rao, 2013), have concluded that simply setting up local institutions for collective action by citizens outside of elections (such as village-level education and health committees) does not guarantee that citizens will, in fact, take actions through these institutions. The evidence shows that transparency plays little role in activating these committees when they are in reality defunct (Banerjee et al. 2010). Keefer and Khemani (2015) provide another example from Benin where greater information among citizens about the value of antimalaria bednets that were supposed to be distributed free of charge by the government, enabled local health workers to charge a price for these nets. Although the welfare consequences of this are uncertain and depend upon the incentives of health workers to use the fees charged to improve health services, the result shows that transparency can have the opposite effect, resulting in "leakage" from free to paid bednets. If the goal of national policy makers is to have local officials adhere to nationally set policy guidelines, then this study shows that transparency alone will not guarantee it and could, in some contexts, have the opposite effect.

13. Although there is plenty of case study evidence on civil society organizations, and even some cross-country correlations that use data on numbers of organizations, the evidence on the causal effect of civil society organizations is not of comparable quality to that available on political engagement through electoral institutions.

Bibliography

Acemoglu, Daron, Tristan Reed, and James A. Robinson. 2014. "Chiefs: Economic Development and Elite Control of Civil Society in Sierra Leone." *Journal of Political Economy* 122 (2): 319–68.

Alt, James E., David D. Lassen, and John Marshall. 2014. "Information Sources, Belief Updating, and the Politics of Economic Expectations: Evidence from a Danish Survey Experiment." Unpublished.

Ananthpur, K., K. Malik, and V. Rao. 2014. "The Anatomy of Failure: An Ethnography of a Randomized Trial to Deepen Democracy in Rural India." Policy Research Working Paper 6958, World Bank, Washington, DC.

Anderson, Siwan, Patrick Francois, and Ashok Kotwal. 2015. "Clientelism in Indian Villages." *American Economic Review* 105 (6): 1780–816.

Andrews, M., L. Pritchett, and M. Woolcock. 2013. "Escaping Capability Traps through Problem Driven Iterative Adaptation (PDIA)." *World Development* 51: 234–44.

Banerjee, Abhijit. 1997. "A Theory of Misgovernance." *Quarterly Journal of Economics* 112 (4): 1289–332.

Banerjee, Abhijit, Rukmini Banerji, Esther Duflo, Rachel Glennerster, and Stuti Khemani. 2010. "Pitfalls of Participatory Programs: Evidence from a Randomized Evaluation in Education in India." *American Economic Journal: Economic Policy* 2 (1): 1–30.

Banerjee, Abhijit, Rema Hanna, Jordan C. Kyle, Benjamin A. Olken, and Sudarno Sumarto. 2015. "The Power of Transparency: Information, Identification Cards and Food Subsidy Programs in Indonesia." NBER Working Paper 20923, National Bureau of Economic Research, Cambridge, MA.

Banerjee, Abhijit, and Lakshmi Iyer, and Rohini Somanathan. 2007. "Public Action for Public Goods." In *Handbook of Development Economics*, volume 4, edited by T. Paul Schultz and John Strauss, 3117–54. Amsterdam: Elsevier.

Banerjee, Abhijit, Sendhil Mullainathan, and Rema Hanna. 2012. "Corruption." NBER Working Paper 17968, National Bureau of Economic Research, Cambridge, MA.

Bobonis, Gustavo J., Luis R. Cámara Fuertes, and Rainer Schwabe. Forthcoming. "Monitoring Corruptible Politicians." *American Economic Review.*

Brixi, Hana Polackoval, Ellen Marie Lust, and Michael Woolcock. 2015. *Trust, Voice, and Incentives: Learning from Local Success Stories in Service Delivery in the Middle East and North Africa.* Washington, DC: World Bank Group. http://documents.worldbank.org/curated/en/2015/04/24367276/trust-voice-incentives-learning-local-success-stories-service-delivery-middle-east-north-africa.

Campante, Filipe, and Quoc-Anh Do. 2014. "Isolated Capital Cities, Accountability and Corruption: Evidence from US States." *American Economic Review* 104 (8): 2456–81.

Campante, Filipe, and Daniel Hojman. 2013. "Media and Polarization: Evidence from the Introduction of Broadcast TV in the US." *Journal of Public Economics* 100: 79–92.

Carothers, Thomas, and Diane de Gramont. 2013. *Development Aid Confronts Politics: The Almost Revolution.* Washington, DC: Carnegie Endowment for International Peace.

Casey, Katherine, Rachel Glennerster, and Edward Miguel. 2012. "Reshaping Institutions: Evidence on Aid Impacts Using a Pre-Analysis Plan." *Quarterly Journal of Economics* 127 (4): 1755–812.

Devarajan, Shantayanan. 2014. "What the 2004 WDR Got Wrong," blog post. http://blogs.worldbank.org/futuredevelopment/what-2004-wdr-got-wrong.

Devarajan, Shantayanan, Stuti Khemani, and Michael Walton. 2014. "Can Civil Society Overcome Government Failure in Africa?" *World Bank Research Observer* 29 (1): 20–47.

Egorov, Georgy, Sergei Guriev, and Konstantin Sonin. 2009. "Why Resource-Poor Dictators Allow Freer Media: A Theory and Evidence from Panel Data." *American Political Science Review* 103 (4): 645–68.

Ferraz, Claudio, and Frederico Finan. 2008. "Exposing Corrupt Politicians: The Effect of Brazil's Publicly Released Audits on Electoral Outcomes." *Quarterly Journal of Economics* 123 (2): 703–45.

———. 2011. "Electoral Accountability and Corruption: Evidence from the Audits of Local Governments." *American Economic Review* 101 (4): 1274–311.

Ferraz, Claudio, Frederico Finan, and Diana Moreira. 2012. "Corrupting Learning." *Journal of Public Economics* 96 (9–10): 712–26.

Fox, Louise, and Thomas P. Sohnesen. 2012. "Household Enterprises in Sub-Saharan Africa: Why They Matter for Growth, Jobs, and Livelihoods." World Bank Policy Research Working Paper 6184, World Bank, Washington, DC.

Fujiwara, Thomas, and Leonard Wantchekon. 2013. "Can Informed Public Deliberation Overcome Clientelism? Experimental Evidence from Benin." *American Economic Journal: Applied Economics* 5 (4): 241–55.

Grandvoinnet, Helene, Ghazia Aslam, and Shomikho Raha. 2015. *Opening the Black Box: The Contextual Drivers of Social Accountability.* Washington, DC: World Bank.

Humphreys, Macartan, and Jeremy Weinstein. 2012. "Policing Politicians: Citizen Empowerment and Political Accountability in Uganda—Preliminary Analysis." Working Paper, International Growth Center, London.

Keefer, Philip, and Stuti Khemani. 2014. "Radio's Impact on Preferences for Patronage Benefits." Policy Research Working Paper 6932, World Bank, Washington, DC.

———. 2015. "The Government Response to Informed Citizens: New Evidence on Media Access and the Distribution of Public Health Benefits in Africa." *The World Bank Economic Review*, Advance Access published August 6, 2015.

Kendall, Chad, Tommaso Nannicini, and Francesco Trebbi. 2015. "How Do Voters Respond to Information? Evidence from a Randomized Campaign." *American Economic Review* 105 (1): 322–53.

Larreguy, Horacio, John Marshall, and James Snyder, Jr. 2014. "Revealing Malfeasance: How Local Media Facilitates Electoral Sanctioning of Mayors in Mexico." NBER Working Paper 20697, National Bureau of Economic Research, Cambridge, MA.

Malesky, Edmund, Paul Schuler, and Anh Tran. 2012. "The Adverse Effects of Sunshine: Evidence from a Field Experiment on Legislative Transparency in an Authoritarian Assembly." *American Political Science Review* 106 (4): 762–86.

Mansuri, Ghazala, and Vijayendra Rao. 2013. *Localizing Development: Does Participation Work?* World Bank Policy Research Report. Washington, DC: World Bank. https://openknowledge.worldbank.org/handle/10986/11859.

Muralidharan, Karthik, Paul Niehaus, and Sandip Sukhtankar. 2014. "Building State Capacity: Evidence from Biometric Smartcards in India." NBER Working Paper 19999, National Bureau of Economic Research, Cambridge, MA.

Olken, Benjamin. 2007. "Monitoring Corruption: Evidence from a Field Experiment in Indonesia." *Journal of Political Economy* 115: 200–49.

Peisakhin, Leonid. 2012. "Transparency and Corruption: Evidence from India." *Journal of Law and Economics* 55 (1): 129–49.

Prat, Andrea, and David Strömberg. 2011. "The Political Economy of Mass Media." CEPR Discussion Paper 8246, Centre for Economic Policy Research, London.

Roberts, Alasdair. 2010. "A Great and Revolutionary Law? The First Four Years of India's Right to Information Act." *Public Administration Review* 70 (6): 925–33.

Sacks, Audrey, Jean Ensminger, and Sam Clark. 2014. "Scoping Mission—Anti-Corruption Mitigation in the Village Law Implementation, Jakarta March 23–26." Unpublished, World Bank, Washington, DC.

Snyder, James M., and David Strömberg. 2010. "Press Coverage and Political Accountability." *Journal of Political Economy* 118 (2): 355–408.

Stokes, S. 2005. "Perverse Accountability: A Formal Model of Machine Politics with Evidence from Argentina." *American Political Science Review* 99 (3): 315–25.

Strömberg, David. 2015. "Media and Politics." *Annual Review of Economics* 7: 173–205.

World Bank. 2002. *The Right to Tell: The Role of Mass Media in Economic Development.* Washington, DC: World Bank.

———. 2004. *World Development Report 2004: Making Services Work for Poor People.* Washington, DC: World Bank. https://openknowledge.worldbank.org/handle/10986/5986.

———. 2008. *Public Sector Reform. What Works and Why? An IEG Evaluation of World Bank Support.* Washington, DC: Independent Evaluation Group, World Bank.

———. 2009. "Guidance Note on Bank Multi-Stakeholder Engagement." World Bank, Washington, DC.

———. 2011. *An Evaluation of the 2007 Strategy and Implementation Plan: World Bank Country-Level Engagement on Governance and Anticorruption.* Washington, DC: Independent Evaluation Group, World Bank.

———. 2016. *World Development Report 2016: Internet for Development.* Washington, DC: World Bank.

Wu, Tim. 2010. *The Master Switch: The Rise and Fall of Information Empires.* New York: Vintage Books.

Yanguas, Pablo, and David Hulme. 2015. "Barriers to Political Analysis in Aid Bureaucracies: From Principle to Practice in DFID and the World Bank." *World Development* 74 (October): 209–19.

Index

Figures, notes, and tables are indicated by *f*, *n*, and *t*, respectively.

F

www.ingramcontent.com/pod-product-compliance
Lightning Source LLC
Chambersburg PA
CBHW080521220326
41599CB00032B/6157